# The Psychology of Terrorism

MW01040674

This edited book explores how psychology can be used to improve our understanding of terrorism and counter-terrorism.

This work firstly aims to provide balanced and objective insight into the psychology of terrorists; what their motivations are, what keeps them involved in terrorist groups, and what eventually forces most to end their active involvement in terrorism. Secondly, the contributors focus on the challenging issue of how to respond to terrorism. These chapters provide information for those concerned with short-term tactical problems (e.g. interviewing), as well as those looking towards the more long-term strategic questions of bringing an entire terrorist campaign to an end. Ultimately, the individuals involved in terrorism require a more complex response from society than simply a quest for their apprehension. Believing inaccurate and misleading characterizations leads inevitably to damaging policies and deficient outcomes, with campaigns of violence being needlessly prolonged. It is from this perspective that the concern arises with how researchers – and the policy makers guided by them – perceive the psychology of terrorists and of terrorism.

This innovative book will be of great interest to students of terrorism and counter-terrorism, security studies, psychology and politics, as well as security professionals and military colleges.

**Andrew Silke** is the Field Leader for Criminology and the Director of Terrorism Studies at the University of East London. He is author of several books and over 100 articles on terrorism.

## Cass series on political violence
Series Editors: Paul Wilkinson and David Rapoport

This book series contains sober, thoughtful and authoritative academic accounts of terrorism and political violence. Its aim is to produce a useful taxonomy of terror and violence through comparative and historical analysis in both national and international spheres. Each book discusses origins, organisational dynamics and outcomes of particular forms and expressions of political violence.

**Aviation Terrorism and Security**
*Edited by Paul Wilkinson and Brian M. Jenkins*

**Counter-Terrorist Law and Emergency Powers in the United Kingdom, 1922–2000**
*Laura K. Donohue*

**The Democratic Experience and Political Violence**
*Edited by David C. Rapoport and Leonard Weinberg*

**Inside Terrorist Organizations**
*Edited by David C. Rapoport*

**The Future of Terrorism**
*Edited by Max Taylor and John Horgan*

**The IRA, 1968–2000**
An analysis of a secret army
*J. Bowyer Bell*

**Millennial Violence**
Past, present and future
*Edited by Jeffrey Kaplan*

**Right-Wing Extremism in the Twenty-First Century**
*Edited by Peter H. Merkl and Leonard Weinberg*

**Terrorism Today**
*Christopher C. Harmon*

**The Psychology of Terrorism**
*John Horgan*

**Research on Terrorism**
Trends, achievements and failures
*Edited by Andrew Silke*

**A War of Words**
Political violence and public debate in Israel
*Gerald Cromer*

**Root Causes of Suicide Terrorism**
Globalization of martyrdom
*Edited by Ami Pedahzur*

**Terrorism versus Democracy**
The liberal state response, 2nd Edition
*Paul Wilkinson*

**Countering Terrorism and WMD**
Creating a global counter-terrorism network
*Edited by Peter Katona, Michael Intriligator and John Sullivan*

**Mapping Terrorism Research**
State of the art, gaps and future direction
*Edited by Magnus Ranstorp*

**The Ideological War on Terror**
World-wide strategies for counter-terrorism
*Edited by Anne Aldis and Graeme P. Herd*

**The IRA and Armed Struggle**
*Rogelio Alonso*

**Homeland Security in the UK**
Future preparedness for terrorist attack since 9/11
*Edited by Paul Wilkinson et al.*

**Terrorism Today 2nd Edition**
*Christopher C. Harmon*

**Understanding Terrorism and Political Violence**
The life cycle of birth, growth, transformation, and demise
*Dipak K. Gupta*

**Global Jihadism**
Theory and practice
*Jarret M. Brachman*

**Combating Terrorism in Northern Ireland**
*Edited by James Dingley*

**Leaving Terrorism Behind**
Individual and collective disengagement
*Edited by Tore Bjørgo and John Horgan*

**Unconventional Weapons and International Terrorism**
Challenges and new approaches
*Edited by Magnus Ranstorp and Magnus Normark*

**International Aviation and Terrorism**
Evolving threats, evolving security
*John Harrison*

**Walking Away from Terrorism**
*John Horgan*

**Understanding Violent Radicalisation**
Terrorist and jihadist movements in Europe
*Edited by Magnus Ranstorp*

**Terrorist Groups and the New Tribalism**
Terrorism's fifth wave
*Jeffrey Kaplan*

**Negotiating With Terrorists**
Strategy, tactics and politics
*Edited by I. William Zartman and Guy Olivier Faure*

**Explaining Terrorism**
Causes, processes and consequences
*Martha Crenshaw*

**The Psychology of Counter-Terrorism**
*Edited by Andrew Silke*

# The Psychology of Counter-Terrorism

Edited by
**Andrew Silke**

Routledge
Taylor & Francis Group

LONDON AND NEW YORK

First published 2011
by Routledge
2 Park Square, Milton Park, Abingdon, Oxon, OX14 4RN

Simultaneously published in the USA and Canada
by Routledge
711 Third Avenue, New York, NY 10017

*Routledge is an imprint of the Taylor & Francis Group, an informa business*

Typeset in Times New Roman by Swales & Willis Ltd, Exeter, Devon

*British Library Cataloguing in Publication Data*
A catalogue record for this book is available
from the British Library

*Library of Congress Cataloging-in-Publication Data*
The psychology of counter-terrorism / edited by Andrew Silke.
    p. cm.
    1. Terrorism—Prevention. 2. Terrorism—Psychological aspects.
3. Terrorism—Government policy. I. Silke, Andrew.
    HV6431.P7967 2010
    363.325'16019—dc22
    2010018498

ISBN13: 978–0–415–55839–6 (hbk)
ISBN13: 978–0–415–55840–2 (pbk)
ISBN13: 978–0–203–84026–9 (ebk)

# Contents

# About the Editor

**Professor Andrew Silke** (BSc Hons, AFBPsS, CSci, CPsych, PhD) is internationally recognised as a leading expert on terrorism in general and terrorist psychology in particular. He has a background in forensic psychology and criminology and has worked both in academia and for government. He has written over 100 articles and reports dealing with the subject of terrorism and counter-terrorism and these have been published in academic books and journals, practitioner magazines and in the popular media. He is frequently invited to give talks at international conferences and universities throughout the world.

He has worked with a variety of government departments and law enforcement and security agencies. In the United Kingdom these include, the Home Office, the Ministry of Justice, the Ministry of Defence, the UK prison service, the London Metropolitan Police as well as several other UK police forces. Overseas he has worked with the United Nations, the United States Department of Justice, the United States Department of Homeland Security, NATO, the European Defence Agency, the European Commission, and the Federal Bureau of Investigation.

Professor Silke has provided expert advice and testimony in many terrorism-related cases, both in the UK and in the US, working at different times for prosecution and for defence. He sits on the British Psychological Society's working group on the Psychological Risk Assessment of those Convicted or Detained under Terrorist Related Offences

Professor Silke serves by invitation on the United Nations Roster of Terrorism Experts and the European Commission's European Network of Experts on Radicalisation and formerly on the European Commission's Expert Group on Violent Radicalisation. He has provided research advice to both the Royal Society in the UK and the National Academy of Sciences in the US. He has provided invited briefings on terrorism-related issues to Select Committees of the House of Commons and was appointed in 2009 as a Specialist Advisor to the House of Commons Communities and Local Government Committee for its inquiry into the Government's programme for preventing violent extremism. He is a member of the International Association for Counter-terrorism and Security Professionals. He is an Honorary Senior Research Associate of the renowned Centre for the Study of Terrorism and Political Violence at the University of St Andrews and is a Fellow of the University of Leicester. His work has taken him to Northern Ireland, the Middle East and Latin America. He currently holds a Chair in Criminology at the University of East London where he is the Field Leader for Criminology, and the Programme Director for Terrorism Studies.

**E-mail:** andrew_silke@yahoo.co.uk
a.silke@uel.ac.uk

# About the Contributors

**Randy Borum** is a Professor in the Department of Mental Health Law and Policy at the University of South Florida. He also holds faculty appointments in the Department of Criminology and the College of Public Health. He has taught courses on Terrorism, Custodial Interrogation, Intelligence Analysis, and Criminal Psychology and is author/ co-author of more than 100 publications. In addition to having served as a sworn police officer for municipal departments in Maryland and Florida, he has been an instructor since 1999 with the BJA State & Local Anti-Terrorism Training (SLATT) Program. Dr Borum is a Board-Certified and fellowship-trained Forensic Psychologist who worked as a Senior Consultant to the U.S. Secret Service for more than a decade helping to develop, refine and study behaviour-based protocols for threat assessment and protective intelligence, and he also serves on the Forensic Psychology Advisory Board for the FBI's Behavioral Science Unit. He served as the Principal Investigator on the Psychology of Terrorism initiative for an agency in the US Intelligence Community, and now serves on the United Nations' Roster of Experts in Terrorism. Dr Borum is Past-President of the American Academy of Forensic Psychology.
**E-mail:** borum@fmhi.usf.edu

**Lorraine Bowman-Grieve** currently works as a lecturer in Forensic Psychology at Leeds Trinity and All Saints. She holds an MSc in Forensic Psychology from University of Kent at Canterbury, and is also a PhD graduate in Applied Psychology from University College Cork in Ireland. Lorraine's doctoral research, which was awarded an IRCHSS scholarship, focused on the use of the internet by terrorist movements and their supporters. Ranging from websites to virtual communities Lorraine's research investigated the exchange, sustenance and dissemination of discourses supportive of extremist ideologies and the use of terrorism. She continues to carry out research on the terrorist use of the internet, and is also involved in conducting prison-based research in Leeds.
**E-mail:** lorraine.grieve@gmail.com

**Deborah Browne** (B.A., Ph.D.) comes from a background in psychology, and has worked in academia and for both the Home Office and the Ministry of Justice. Dr Browne has published papers in various academic journals and books and has presented at a wide range of national and international conferences. Over the years, her key areas of interest have included: drug markets and trafficking, prisons, probation and offender management, radicalisation and consequences of terrorism, the development of anti-social behaviour in children and young people, the consequences of child abuse, and psychological issues affecting foster children. Among other roles she is currently a visiting senior research fellow at the University of East London.

**E-mail**: debcbrowne@yahoo.co.uk

**Neil Ferguson** (D.Phil., University of Ulster, 1998) is the Director of the Desmond Tutu Centre for War and Peace and Associate Professor of Political Psychology at Liverpool Hope University. He has been a visiting lecturer to Lock Haven University of Pennsylvania and the University of York, a Research Fellow at University of St Andrews, the Sr. Mary Linscott Research Fellow at Liverpool Hope University, is an Honorary Research Supervisor at the University of Liverpool and previously lectured at the University of Ulster prior to joining Liverpool Hope University in 1996. His research and writings deal with moral development and a number of topics located within political psychology. His research mainly focuses on the conflict, division and the peace process in Northern Ireland and he has recently published in the *International Journal of Conflict and Violence, Journal of Social Psychology, Peace & Conflict: Journal of Peace Psychology* and *Political Psychology* while also contributing to a number of books. Dr. Ferguson is currently the chair of the *Moral and Social Action Interdisciplinary Colloquium*, serves on the Governing Council of the *International Society of Political Psychology*, is a member of the Editorial Board for the *Journal of Moral Education* and the *Irish Journal of Psychology*.

**E-mail**: Fergusn@hope.ac.uk

**Peter Fussey** is a Senior Lecturer at the University of Essex where he is heavily involved in a number of research projects on terrorism and counter-terrorism. These include a major EPSRC project on detecting terrorist activity and a separate ESRC/EPSRC funded project examining resilience and sustainability of national infrastructure. Prior to joining the University of Essex in 2010 he was the Programme Leader for the BA (Hons) Criminology and Criminal Justice degree at the University of East London, and was also heavily involved in developing and delivering UEL's MSc in Terrorism Studies. Dr Fussey's main area of expertise concerns the application of surveillance to tackle crime and terrorism. He has given conference presentations in the UK and overseas, been invited to comment on it on national television and in the print media, has published numerous academic articles and written a doctoral thesis on the subject.

**E-mail**: p.fussey@uel.ac.uk

**Reena Kumari** (B.Sc., P.G.Dip) is currently undergoing doctoral training in Counselling Psychology. Reena has previous experience in prison services and youth offending teams and extensive experience in various CAMHS settings. She has worked with children who have experienced sexual abuse, substance misuse and attachment difficulties in looked after children. Her areas of research have included moral development and juvenile delinquency and attitudes towards terrorism. Her particular area of interest is offending behaviours in people with learning disabilities and she is planning to carry out doctoral level research in this area.

**E-mail**: reena_libra50@hotmail.com

**Rick O'Gorman** (B.Sc., M.A., Ph.D.) is currently a Lecturer in Psychology at University of Essex. He has extensive experience with the field of evolutionary psychology, having 15 peer-reviewed publications in the area. He has a long-standing interest in human conflict and cooperation, and has published empirical and theoretical papers on social norms, policing, and cooperation from an evolutionary perspective. His approach draws on the standard inclusive fitness and reciprocity models for understanding human cooperative behaviour and also utilises multilevel selection theory to understand human behaviour as individuals and within groups.

**E-mail**: rogorman@essex.ac.uk

**John Pearse** (BSc (Hons), PhD, CPsych, AFBPsS, FRSM) is a chartered psychologist, and managing director of Forensic Navigation Services Ltd, an independent company that combines forensic consultancy and investigation with psychological training and empirical research. For example, John has recently undertaken a confidential national review of police interviewing with terrorist suspects in the United Kingdom and has designed and delivered a specialist national interview course combining essential interpersonal and cultural awareness with effective contingency planning and related security measures. John was also responsible for the el selection theory to understand human behaviour as individuals and within groups

For more than three decades John served as a detective in London and was engaged in the fight against organised crime at a senior level. His work in specialist roles included armed robbery, criminal intelligence, hostage and kidnap negotiation, and he concluded his service as a senior officer in the terrorist arena with a number of high profile and innovative terrorist prosecutions. He has provided counter-terrorist advice and training around the world on behalf of the Foreign Office and New Scotland Yard and he has been responsible for the design and delivery of a number of acclaimed international multi-agency counter-terrorism seminars.

As a psychologist he has been conducting and publishing research in the area of interviewing and related issues since 1991. His most recent publication examined the 'banality of torture' in Williamson (2006) *Investigative Interviewing: rights, research regulation*, Willan Publishing. A number of other articles are in press.

**E-mail**: FNSLtd@aol.com

**Anthony Richards** is a Senior Lecturer in Terrorism Studies at the University of East London, where he teaches on the Critical Perspectives on Terrorism, Critical Perspectives on Counter-Terrorism and Transnational Organised Crime modules. Prior to this he was a Senior Research Associate at the Centre for the Study of Terrorism and Political Violence, University of St Andrews, where he taught on the terrorism studies distance learning programme, for which he designed two modules: Terrorist Ideologies, Aims and Motivations; and Terrorist Modus Operandi. He also worked on the UK Economic and Social Research Council project 'The Domestic Management of Terrorist Attacks in the UK', which was an assessment of both the UK's ability to preempt a major terrorist attack and of her capacity to deal with the consequences of one (three of his chapters have been published in the book version of the report: *Homeland Security in the UK: Future Preparedness for Terrorist Attack Since 9/11*, Routledge, 2007). He is currently working on a terrorism textbook (co-authored with Dr Peter Lehr, University of St Andrews), an edited volume on *Terrorism and the Olympics* (co-edited with Dr Peter Fussey and Professor Andrew Silke, both University of East London) and various articles within the field of terrorism studies. He was Assistant Editor of the academic journal *Terrorism and Political Violence* from 2002-2005.
**E-mail**: a.richards@uel.ac.uk

**Brooke Rogers** is a Lecturer in Risk and Terror in the Department of War Studies at King's College London. She is a social psychologist by training and holds a number of grants targeted at generating a better understanding of the role of resilience in responding to terrorist incidents and the psychology of terrorism and martyrdom. Dr Rogers is a director of the MA programme in Terrorism, Security and Society, advises a number of government and private organisations on CBRN terrorism and violent radicalisation, and holds a number of honorary associations, including a research fellowship with the Health Protection Agency (HPA) Centre for Emergency Preparedness and Response.
**E-mail**: brooke.rogers@kcl.ac.uk

**Graeme Steven** (MA Hons, M Litt, MSyI) is an international security consultant. He has worked for both the private and public sector. He has undertaken work and research in the Middle-East, the Philippines, the Balkans, Latin America and Europe. His research interests include security and resilience, counter-terrorism, terrorist tactics, recruitment, entry and exit to/from terrorist groups, suicide-terrorism, and the operational and support networks of terrorist organizations. He has written on these subjects and published in academic journals and practitioner magazines. He is also the author of a book on *Counter-Terrorism*, and is still deliberating over whether he should undertake a PhD!
**E-mail**: graemesteven@hotmail.com

# 1 The psychology of counter-terrorism

## Critical issues and challenges

*Andrew Silke*

> Terrorism wins only if you respond to it in the way the terrorists want you to; which means that its fate is in your hands and not in theirs.
>
> Fromkin (1975)

Wars are won when one side breaks the will of the other to fight on. When they capitulate, the defeated almost always still have armies in the field and still have some resources to draw upon. True, these may be greatly diminished compared to what existed at earlier stages of the conflict but it is extraordinarily rare for every soldier to have been slain or imprisoned and every town and city captured before the white flags of surrender are raised. What the vanquished have lost however is the belief that victory is possible or that the cost of the struggle can be borne any further. Victory or defeat then, ultimately boils down to a question of psychology, and terrorist conflicts are no different from other conflicts in this respect.

Indeed, most people understand – even if only instinctively – that there is a special psychological dimension to terrorism that is not always found in other types of violence. *Terrorist* violence is not simply about physical suffering, it is about making a psychological impact, partly about the creation of a wider sense of terror and partly about winning a psychological battle for hearts and minds. Inevitably, countering terrorism must also grapple with this psychological dimension if it is to be effective. Ignoring the psychology of counter-terrorism is to miss the crux of the problem.

At its core, there is a general acceptance that an act of terrorism is not aimed just at its direct victims but at wider audiences where the perpetrators are expecting and hoping for a diverse range of impacts. Beyond this, there is often fierce controversy over what is and is not an act of terrorism. The word itself was certainly first used to describe the violent repression carried out by a government against its own citizens: the 'reign of terror' waged by the government of revolutionary France saw up to 40,000 French citizens butchered in the space of barely a year. The chief architect of the Terror, Maximilien Robespierre, summed up its purpose succinctly:

> We must smother the internal and external enemies of the Republic or perish with it; now in this situation, the first maxim of your policy ought to be to lead the people by reason and the people's enemies by terror.

In the decades that followed, however, the term drifted away from the state violence of its origins and was increasingly applied to violence carried out by smaller movements and organisations. As early as 1868, for example, many American newspapers routinely described the violence carried out by the newly emerged Ku Klux Klan as 'terrorism' (Hurst, 1993). This shift in seeing terrorism as something non-state groups did gathered pace, and by the end of the twentieth century among the wider public the word was used almost exclusively within the context of non-state groups.

The question as to what constitutes terrorism, and who is a terrorist, however is still deeply problematic. There is no widely agreed definition of terrorism, and some writers have concluded that 'it is unlikely that any definition will ever be generally agreed upon' (Shafritz et al., 1991). The failure to find a widely acceptable definition of terrorism is tied to the political use of the word. Fundamentally, 'terrorism' is a pejorative term with a range of negative meanings. For this reason, many media organisations such as the BBC and Reuters are extremely reluctant to describe any individual or group in their reports as 'terrorists', preferring instead to use terms such as 'militants', 'insurgents' or 'guerrillas'. These concerns tie into the long-standing truism that 'one man's terrorist is another man's freedom fighter'. Individuals such as Nelson Mandela, for example, were labelled as terrorists for many years, and yet Mandela went on to become an internationally respected statesman. Indeed, on this point it is worth bearing in mind Audrey Kurth Cronin's (2009) finding from a review of 450 terrorist groups that the terrorists actually *win* the conflict against the state in 6 per cent of cases.

Gearty (1991, p. 6) sums up well the major challenge with the definition problem when he notes:

> The label itself is inevitably value-laden. Its meaning is moulded by government, the media and in popular usage, not by academic departments. The word resonates with moral opprobrium and as such is, as far as the authorities and others are concerned, far too useful an insult to be pinned down and controlled.

We will not continue further with the definition debate here – though a few of the subsequent chapters will touch on this point again – but in order to give some boundaries to the focus of this volume, we will follow the concise definition provided by Crenshaw (1992) who described terrorism as 'a particular style of political violence, involving attacks on a small number of victims in order to influence a wider audience'. The claims as to what behaviours fit this definition still vary considerably but the focus here is very much on what could be termed 'insurgent' terrorism, which is essentially a strategy of the weak, adopted 'by groups with little numerical, physical or direct political power in order to effect political or social change' (Friedland, 1992).

In practical terms, 'insurgent' terrorists are members of small covert groups engaged in an organised campaign of violence. This violence that they commit is often extreme and frequently indiscriminate. The terrorists themselves tend to live isolated and stressful lives and enjoy varying levels of wider support. Groups that fit within this framework have included movements such as the IRA, ETA, the Red Army Faction, the Italian Red Brigades and al-Qaeda.

## What is *counter-terrorism*?

By and large, terrorist conflicts are not won by terrorist groups. Sometimes, however, they are *lost* by the states opposing them. The policies, strategies and tactics that states use to combat terrorism and deal with its consequences are referred to as counter-terrorism. Counter-terrorism is not specific to any one agency or department. It can be carried out by government departments, the military, law enforcement agencies, intelligence agencies, emergency responders and many other groups in society.

States can respond to terrorism with a range of approaches. Traditionally, states will initially attempt to deal with the conflict using existing measures to exert order and control. In Western democratic states, for example, such measures will usually be found within the criminal justice system. Frequently these prove adequate to the situation and the problem is dealt with. The threat is eliminated or else reduced to a broadly acceptable level. When the threat is more prolonged or there has been an especially provocative attack, however, the state faces considerable challenges in determining how best to tackle terrorism.

Counter-terrorism can take a variety of forms. Some of the most common approaches are listed below and it is normal for a state to use a combination of different approaches rather than to rely on just one exclusively:

- Introduction of special counter-terrorism legislation.
- Creation of specialist counter-terrorism units in state services (including police and military).
- Use of repression.
- Use of military intervention and reprisals.
- Introduce Special Incarceration and Detention policies.
- Media management.
- Negotiated settlement.

While the above list outlines some broad ways of reacting to terrorism, one common problem is that the specific aims for these different interventions can vary considerably. For example, in reacting to a terrorist group, veteran terrorism analyst Paul Wilkinson (2001) highlights that the state might be trying to:

- Tackle underlying grievances and problems (the root causes of the violence).
- Deter terrorists by introducing severe penalties and punishments.

- Increase powers to the state (e.g. to allow search, seizure, detention, international co-operation, etc).
- Address symbolic needs (e.g. being seen to share public revulsion/outrage to an event).
- Enhance public security.
- Suppress terrorist organisations.

These aims are not always easily compatible with each other, and as a result some counter-terrorism policies which do a very good job with regard to one aim might be deeply counter-productive for another. This can give rise to counter-terrorism policy and practice overall being viewed as disjointed and flawed.

Which counter-terrorism policies are the most effective? This is not a straightforward question to answer. To begin with, as we have already touched upon the different policies do not all have the same aim and they are all trying to tackle different issues. In considering the overall impact, it is useful to start by first considering how terrorism itself is actually intended to work. Successful terrorist campaigns – from the perpetrators' perspective – can be broken down into four general elements:

- **Provocation** – The terrorists carry out acts of violence, which are intended to provoke a strong reaction from the state and its forces. Normally one of the first reactions is to suspend or sideline the normal methods and operation of law and order. As the violence continues there is an increasing role for the military and special rules and regulations (often classed as 'emergency powers') are brought into the play. The terrorists are still referred to as criminals but they are no longer targeted or treated as criminals normally are.
- **Escalation** – having already convinced the state to abandon the old (and accepted) rule book, the terrorists attempt to increase the severity of attacks. This results in a demand for even greater security and protection. In response, the state takes increasingly severe and exceptional measures – sometimes including blatantly illegal tactics – in the search for victory.
- **Blame** – In the face of increased atrocities and rule-breaking on both sides, the conflict enters a blame phase where all parties attempt to place the responsibility for *all* atrocities at the feet of the other. This is the classic battle for hearts and minds.
- **Endurance** – The final phase. The terrorists aim to break the will and morale of the state to sustain the conflict. Amid the carnage of the escalation and the battle for hearts, the terrorists seek to convince the state and its supporters that the terrorists' commitment to the conflict and ability to stay in the fight is greater than the state's ability to continue to pay the mounting costs for the struggle. As belief in final victory fades, the search for ways out and alternative solutions increases.

In order for counter-terrorism to be effective then it somehow has to prevent the terrorists from realising this chain. As we consider different approaches both in this chapter and throughout the whole book is worth returning to this model and considering how does each counter-terrorism policy, strategy or tactic fit into the terrorist's strategy. How does it hinder the process? Or is it actually facilitating the terrorists' needs and requirements?

## What works in counter-terrorism?

In confronting terrorism, the first question to ask is 'what works?' Because terrorist groups are so often relatively weak, the truth is that many things can work in defeating them, but they do not all work equally well. Indeed, it is crucial to recognise the fundamental weakness and frailty of most terrorist groups. They are vastly outmatched by the states that oppose them especially in the opening phases of any conflict. The Provisional IRA is a good example to use here. Widely regarded as one of the larger, more dangerous and more skilled terrorist groups of the 1980s and 1990s, it was still very weak when compared with the state it was fighting against. The average annual budget of the PIRA in the early 1990s had risen to around £11 million – a large sum compared to what most terrorist groups can raise (Horgan and Taylor, 1999). In contrast, the annual budget of the UK government in 1990 was roughly £200.9 billion.[1] Thus in crude economic terms, for every £1 the PIRA managed to raise and spend that year, the government fighting it raised and spent £18,263.

This massive disparity in economic strength was not surprisingly also seen in manpower. In 1990, the PIRA had about 600 active members. Most of these people were part-timers who fitted in their involvement with the PIRA around other commitments and jobs. Only a relatively small proportion were full-time 'volunteers' (Horgan and Taylor, 1997). There were also roughly another 250 PIRA members serving prison sentences.

Opposing this organisation of some 850 members, the state had over 487,000 personnel in the armed services,[2] 162,533 personnel in the police forces,[3] 20,000 prison staff,[4] and at least a further 7,000 people in the intelligence services. Not only were the PIRA members thus outnumbered almost 800 to 1,[5] almost all of these 676,533 individuals were better paid, better trained and better equipped than the terrorists.

The reason for highlighting these massive differences in strength is to drive home the point that usually in any conflict between a state and a terrorist group, the state will eventually win. State victories are the rule, not the exception (Cronin, 2009). Most terrorist groups are eventually defeated and indeed most are usually defeated relatively quickly. One survey found that 90 per cent of terrorist groups were defeated within one year of their first attack (Rapaport, 1992). Of those few who managed to survive the first year, nearly half were finished off within ten years. This should not surprise us. If two business companies are competing in the same market, but one has 18,000 times more resources than the other, we would not be surprised to hear that the smaller company is driven out of business. Indeed, the larger company could be very clumsy and wasteful in many of its decisions and yet still eventually overwhelm its small rival.

Any effort to try to highlight what works in terms of defeating terrorism has to remember this massive discrepancy in strength. A state could use one mediocre policy after another and still crush a terrorist group simply because it is so much stronger. Just because it wins does not mean that the policies used have been extremely effective. On the contrary, even deeply flawed policies can work when they are backed by such overwhelming advantages in resources.

Not surprisingly, there is a tremendous hunger among those working in the security forces for tools and techniques that can help them to counter terrorism effectively. One unfortunate consequence of this hunger, however, is the profusion of fraudulent systems that have been offered up as effective tools for countering terrorist activity. The UK government for example recently banned the export of a device, the ADE-651, which the makers had been claiming could detect explosives. Equipment that can detect the presence of explosives is not new, but the ADE-651 had the formidable selling advantages of being a handheld device that was very quick to use and could be easily carried and operated by one person. The device became popular in many countries with the Iraqi government for example spending US$85m on the devices (at a rough cost of US$40,000 each) where at the time of writing they are still widely used at most checkpoints in Baghdad.

Scandal erupted however when investigations in the UK revealed that the science behind the devices was bogus. The ADE-651 did not use any of the well-established techniques for detecting explosives and indeed the computer cards in the devices appear not to have any relevance whatsoever for such a task. As a consequence, the government stepped in to ban the export of the device and the director of the company making them was arrested for fraud.[6]

Yet the enormous sales success the ADE-651 enjoyed in some markets before the ban is a telling lesson in the demand that exists for simple and straightforward solutions to terrorist threats. Some similar issues exist with regard to the use of behavioural science to efforts to detect terrorist activity and it is this particular issue that attracts the focus of this chapter.

Efforts to create systems that can detect terrorists by observation alone have accelerated dramatically since 9/11, and this is an area where psychology in theory should play a clear role. At any event or location the ability to spot terrorists before violence has been committed is highly prized. Nowhere has this been more keenly illustrated than at airports and transportation hubs, which have been repeatedly targeted for attack. The attempt by Umar Farouk Abdulmutallab in December 2009 to destroy a passenger jet in flight raised concerns about the ability of the authorities to effectively screen passengers. Abdulmutallab was apparently able to carry explosive material through the screening systems of two airports – including Schiphol, one of the world's largest and most modern airport hubs. In response to this threat, screening efforts in the UK have been stepped up. In the UK, these measures have included increased restrictions for passengers but have also seen more effort and resources invested in screening activity. The phased introduction of full body scanners – capable of providing detailed images of the body and items hidden under clothes – has been accelerated at UK airports, and the use of sniffer dogs in passenger areas to detect explosives has also been increased.

Some new approaches have also been adopted. In particular, a further layer of security has been added with the introduction of behavioural screening at Heathrow Airport (and a strong likelihood that this new layer will be rolled out at the UK's other major airports in due course). Heathrow adopted a behavioural screening approach just weeks after the failed Detroit attack. The system is also being introduced on London's underground train network. While the Detroit attack itself ultimately was a failure, the bomber did succeed in smuggling explosives on board a passenger jet and was himself able to get on board despite, apparently, possessing a background that should have flagged him as a serious security concern. Behavioural screening – in theory – could have helped in this case as it works on the premise that terrorists on missions act in certain ways and that their behaviour while engaged in illegal activity will unintentionally betray their presence. This type of approach to security has been in operation – in one form or another – for many years in some airports overseas. At Heathrow, the police announced that a specialist unit of airport staff were to be trained in a new screening system referred to as the Behavioural Analysis Screening System (BASS). This new system apparently draws on an existing Israeli model and aims 'to recognise the body language of potential suicide bombers'.[7] Among the features staff will look for will include individuals avoiding eye-contact, individuals who appear drugged; the wearing of excessively heavy or bulky clothing and the way someone handles their bag or backpack.

The evidence base for some parts of this new system is questionable – particularly with regard to claims about the specific behaviours of suicide terrorists – but in many other respects BASS bears comparison to similar systems that have been in use in the United States since 2003. In particular, US airports have been using the SPOT (Screening Passengers by Observation Technique) system for several years. This system is now used in 161 airports across the USA, and more than 3,000 Behaviour Detection Officers (BDOs) trained in the system now work in these airports.[8] Like BASS, the SPOT approach is primarily designed to detect terrorists. One difference however is that SPOT rests its foundation primarily on detecting anxious behaviour and does not make more esoteric claims with regard to suicide terrorists.

The key question with systems like BASS and SPOT is: do they actually work? The answer is mixed. These systems both assume that terrorists will act in a specific and detectable manner. BASS goes further and says that suicide terrorists will have even more specific behaviours. There is no compelling evidence, however, that terrorists have unique personality traits or genuinely distinctive behaviour profiles (e.g. Taylor, 1988; Borum, 2004; Victoroff and Kruglanski, 2009). Systems that claim that terrorists have specific behavioural signatures primarily rely on anecdotal evidence. Anecdotal cases can be useful and interesting but they are no substitute for more rigorous evidence.

SPOT does not argue that terrorists will have unique behavioural signatures but rather argues that they will display anxious behaviour and this behaviour can be spotted. Put another way, this approach is working on the assumption that terrorists experience stress when they are engaged in operations and that they will display signs of this, signs that can be detected. Despite the indiscriminate and extreme violence of many terrorist attacks, the vast majority of research on terrorist psychology has concluded that they are not mentally or psychology abnormal. On the contrary, many studies have found that terrorists are actually psychologically much healthier and far more stable than other violent criminals. Psychologists have gradually been forced to accept that the outstanding characteristic of the terrorists is their normality. Thus, in short, there is no obvious barrier to their experiencing and displaying emotions and states that are experienced by members of the general population. As a result, they are as capable of experiencing stress, fear and anxiety as everyone else (Silke, 2004).

It is possible of course to reduce the level of stress experienced in any given situation. The main approaches to overcoming stress effects in cognitive processes is to change either how the stressful situation/event is perceived, or, secondly, to engage in training to develop appropriate patterns of behaviour. Experience of similar situations has been found to be very beneficial in reducing the negative impact of stressful/dangerous situations. A major tenet of most organisations that must deal with critical incidents is that staff need to be appropriately trained in order to cope effectively with the stress and anxiety impacts of critical incidents.

The more experience of a stressful situation an individual has the better able they are to cope and the less anxiety they experience. Training plays a pivotal role in managing stress reactions. A range of techniques has been tested for 'stress-proofing' individuals, with controlled exposure (especially in the form of simulation training) playing a key-role. Well designed simulation training has generally been found to be an effective rehearsal for real events. Ultimately, learning and training are the cornerstones of the prevention of negative reactions to stress in dangerous situations.

Terrorist organisations however are rarely able to provide their members with extensive training to help them prepare for the stress of carrying out an attack. As a general rule terrorists will often be more vulnerable to acute stress than personnel in the military or police (where resources and opportunities for training are far greater). The issue of relatively limited training can certainly also apply to terrorists who are planning suicide attacks. While the terrorist teams who carried out the 9/11 attacks appear to have had extensive training and preparation in the build-up to the event, most suicide terrorists receive far more limited preparation. For most of the plots in the UK over the past decade, normally only one or two members of each terrorist team had received specialised training overseas and even this was usually restricted to just a few weeks or at most a few months in a camp somewhere like Pakistan or Afghanistan.

In real terms such training is quite limited and would not, for example, meet the basic training requirements for most modern Western militaries. Further, most members of the plots do not even receive this limited preparation.

Limited training is also a common feature of suicide terrorism elsewhere. Speaking before US Congress, Ariel Merari (2000) an Israeli expert on terrorist psychology noted that in the case of Palestinian suicide terrorism:

Once the . . . people responsible in the organisation are convinced that the person is serious they put them usually in a training process that may last in most cases from weeks to months.

Indeed, it has been noted by a number of sources that the level of training Palestinian suicide terrorists received in the second *intifadeh* declined even further compared to what their predecessors received in previous years (e.g. Bloom, 2005). Many bombers appeared to have had only a few days' preparation and training. In such circumstances, suicide bombers can be expected to be especially vulnerable to stress effects. In the Palestinian case, the terrorist organisation tries to minimise this by having a relatively large support group who guide and direct the bomber and only leave his or her company when they are very close to the intended target.

Such support groups are not generally a feature of al-Qaeda suicide attacks in the West, however, and potential bombers here are much more dependent on their own decision-making, reactions and preparation in carrying out attacks. In such circumstances, it is quite reasonable to argue that terrorists – including suicide terrorists – will generally feel high levels of stress indeed and will show signs of anxiety. Approaches that work on this basis then are on much more solid ground than those that are based on untested anecdotal theories of how suicide terrorists act.

However, even with the anxiety approach, problems remain. The most fundamental one is that while one can spot anxious behaviour, one cannot tell from observation alone why the individual is anxious. Major airports are stressful environments at the best of times. Missed connections, flight delays and cancellations, missing luggage, tiredness, sleep deprivation, crowded environments, long queues and so on all have impacts. Indeed, for many (if not most) being stressed and anxious is an entirely routine experience at a busy airport.

As a result, a system that relies on detecting anxious behaviour is in real danger of being swamped. It is perhaps not terribly surprising then to learn that even though SPOT has been in use in the United States since 2003, the system has not been credited yet with even one clear terrorist detection. This is not for a want of effort. Since 2006, officers using SPOT have identified on average 70,000 passengers each year who are marked for further screening. In 2006 and 2007 this led to between 400 to 600 arrests each year. These numbers rose in 2008, when SPOT identified 98,805 passengers for additional screenings, leading to 813 arrests.[9] To date, SPOT has flagged over 250,000 passengers for further attention and has led to some 2,000 arrests. It has not, however, clearly yet led to even one terrorist conviction. Nevertheless, the system is still primarily seen and sold as a counter-terrorism measure.

Given the relative failure of SPOT to catch actual terrorists, is there really a point in these types of systems and should their introduction in new locations and countries be encouraged? The answer depends on a number of factors. In both the USA and the UK, the authorities have been keen to stress that behavioural detection systems at airports are simply one layer – and by no means the most important – in a multi-layered screening system. Other screening measures – metal detectors, pat-downs, sniffer dogs, body scanners, explosives detectors, etc – all continue to be used. Behavioural detection systems are seen as an adjunct to these other systems and not as a replacement. This is unquestionably sensible.

One value of SPOT and its kin is that it adds an extra level of security for terrorists to contend with. Al-Qaeda, for example, has shown a great interest and ability in developing methods to penetrate traditional screening measures. A system like SPOT or BASS adds an extra layer that the group must contend with. Even if the likelihood of an actual terrorist being detected is extremely low, it is one additional factor that the terrorists must consider in their planning and preparation processes (Clarke and Newman, 2006). How much attention al-Qaeda devotes to this particular issue is debateable but the authorities are certainly hoping that it makes the terrorists' task at least slightly more difficult.

The fact that these systems have led to the arrest and conviction of other offenders should not be disregarded either. After all, SPOT has helped to catch individuals on charges of murder, kidnapping, drug smuggling, weapons violations, identity fraud, illegal immigration, outstanding warrants and other offences.

Perhaps crucially, these benefits have been achieved at a very low cost. Running the SPOT system cost the USA a very modest $3.1 million in 2008 (though this does not include potential costs caused by the disruptions to the 9,000 passengers who were sent for police questioning but released without charge). It is likely that the system being rolled out at Heathrow and London's underground systems will also be fairly cheap to introduce and run. Behavioural Detection Officers in the US receive only four days' classroom training in the system, followed by 24 hours of on-the-job training.[10] Certainly, in comparison with the vastly higher amounts needed to acquire and run other screening systems such as metal detectors and full body scanners, the outlay for behavioural systems is so low that doubts and concerns over its effectiveness are not as critical.

Given the relatively modest costs involved in introducing systems like SPOT and BASS at airports and other transportation hubs, it is likely that we will see the continued spread and expansion of this approach. It allows the authorities to be seen to be taking action with regard to serious threats but does not entail heavy costs and crucially does not significantly impact on passenger experiences or travel times. There are also likely benefits for the morale of staff, who may feel they have a better understanding of the potential threats and now possess more confidence and knowledge about meeting the challenges involved. Whether such systems actually result in terrorist convictions or act as a serious deterrent to terrorist attacks is much less certain, and expecting great results in those terms is not justified. Nevertheless, so long as the relevant authorities have modest expectations and a realistic understanding of the limits of this approach, then there should be no serious problems. Used as a low-cost supporting element in a multi-layered screening effort, behavioural detection can have value. Placing a very heavy reliance on them, however, is simply asking for trouble.

# Counter-terrorism 'policies', not 'policy'

The second critical issue is that states use a range of policies and tactics to defeat terrorism, at least several of which are usually in operation at any one time. If the terrorist group is defeated while a wide series of different policies are in play, it can be impossible to tell for certain what impact any one policy has had on the conflict.

To take an analogy, imagine a doctor administers ten different drugs in the same week to a patient with a troublesome disease. The patient comes back a month later, cured of the illness. How can you tell which drug helped? In hindsight, you simply cannot. However, the drug companies that manufacture the ten drugs will all try and claim that it was their particular drug that had the most positive impact!

Reviews that try to identify 'what works' in combating terrorism face this same problem. In reality, most of these reviews say essentially not what works, but rather they simply list what states have tried. Cronin (2009) has provided a variation on this theme by highlighting how terrorist campaigns are ended. She examined the life cycles of 450 terrorist groups and identified six scenarios in which the campaigns were finally halted:

- The terrorists leaders are captured or killed.
- The terrorists are crushed by state repression.
- The terrorists win (which happened in 6 per cent of cases).
- The terrorist group moves away from politics and into criminality.
- The terrorists negotiate and accept a compromise settlement.
- The terrorists lose popular support.

Cronin argues that the state should try to facilitate one of these scenarios in order to bring about the demise of a current group. Let us assume that no state will be particularly keen on option 3 (the terrorists winning the conflict) and focus on the rest. One immediate challenge is which option do you go for? Which works best? Cronin does not say. Indeed she cannot. The evidence does not exist to provide that type of answer. This was simply an assessment of what happened in the run-up to the terrorist groups finally laying down arms.

Another problem is that some of the scenarios are incompatible with each other. Repression and killing the terrorist group leader would probably be very compatible, but a mix of repression and negotiation seems unlikely to work. Thus, if a government favours one scenario it can weaken the ability to also try to incorporate elements of some of the other approaches.

The current UK policy aimed at jihadi extremism – of which there is much more below – is probably primarily focused on a scenario of terrorists losing popular support combined with weaker elements of terrorists being crushed by state repression. There is currently no role for negotiation and no sense of terrorists being encouraged to move into criminality either.

## Case Study: Counter-terrorism in the UK

The UK has certainly had a long history of facing threats from terrorism and politically-motivated extremism. The gunpowder plot in 1605 would clearly – and reasonably – be seen as an act of terrorism if it were attempted today (Bowden and Davis, 2008). The measures taken by the state to counter terrorism threats have evolved steadily over the course of the past two centuries in particular.

In the modern era, though, counter-terrorism in the UK is guided by what is called the *CONTEST strategy*.[11] CONTEST (COuNter TErrorism STrategy) aims to tackle terrorism in a holistic way. The strategy was first introduced in 2003 and an updated version (CONTEST 2) was added in 2009, though the main principles of both versions are the same. CONTEST focuses not only on identifying and apprehending active terrorists but also on tackling the root causes of extremism in order to deprive terrorist groups of recruits and support from communities. Added to this, CONTEST also acknowledges that terrorist attacks may still occur despite the best efforts of law enforcement and the intelligence agencies, and as a result the strategy incorporates an important resilience strand. This is aimed at ensuring that there will be a capable emergency response if a terrorist attack occurs and that society will be able continue to work effectively in the aftermath.

Four key elements provide the foundation for CONTEST.[12] These are commonly known as the four pillars or four Ps:

- **Prevent** is aimed at stopping radicalisation and is also the strand most keenly aimed at winning the battle for hearts and minds. The prevent strand aims at deterring people who encourage support for terrorism, and tackling the root causes of extremism.
- **Pursue** is aimed at identifying and disrupting existing terrorist networks and operations. Intelligence work plays a major role here in efforts to identify and monitor potential threats. This strand is also concerned with the collection of evidence to secure the conviction of terrorists.
- **Protect** is concerned with reducing the UK's vulnerability to terrorist attacks. Elements in this strand aim to make it more difficult for terrorists to move in and out of the UK through enhanced border security. This strand is also focused on the protection of the nation's critical infrastructure, sites and facilities which if attacked could cause massive disruption. Target hardening of such sites against attack is an important aspect of this strand.
- **Prepare** is the final strand. This recognises that it may not be possible to prevent every single terrorist attack and planning is needed for improving the nation's ability to respond to an attack if it occurs. Efforts are made to identify potential risks and scenarios and to build up training and capabilities to respond to these as effectively as possible.

Figure 1.1 below provides an overview of how the aims of the Contest process fit together in terms of tackling terrorism.

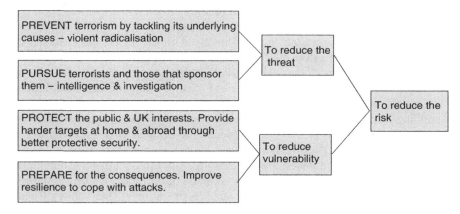

*Figure 1.1*  The aims of the UK CONTEST strategy

Adapted from Weston (2005).

In many respects, insights from psychology are perhaps most obvious when exploring the PREVENT strand. PREVENT is aimed at stopping radicalisation and is also the strand most keenly aimed at winning the battle for hearts and minds. This has been developed with a clear focus on jihadi extremism in the UK, though in theory the principles should apply to any violent extremist movement.

Al-Qaeda has enjoyed little apparent success in the UK in recent years. There have been no successful attacks whatsoever since the bombings in July 2005; the number of plots appears to be declining; and, if court cases and prisoner numbers are reliable indicators, the number of fresh recruits to the cause in the UK are falling as well. Does this then mean that the battle is almost over on these shores and that al-Qaeda is a largely spent force in the UK? Have we entered the beginning of the end?

Victory in any terrorist conflict ultimately depends on two critical factors. One is the intelligence war. Each side must protect its own secrets and plans while uncovering those of the enemy. The second, and arguably the more important, is what has come to be called the battle for hearts and minds. This is a psychological struggle to win and hold support. So long as a terrorist cause enjoys a significant amount of popular support, then a conflict can continue. If that support ebbs away, however, then the terrorists and their cause become fish out of water and their days are numbered.

How then is the battle for hearts and minds going in the UK? PREVENT was for a long time the poor relation in the UK government's counter-terrorism portfolio. The vast majority of work and funding was applied in other areas. The relatively peripheral nature of PREVENT can be illustrated in looking at the resources invested here. In 2006 the police Anti-Terrorism Branch was merged with the Metropolitan Police Service's Special Branch to create a new organisation: special operations 15 (SO15) counter-terrorism command (CTC). By 2007, some 2000 police and support staff were involved in running the CTC and its three regional units.

While the CTC is certainly heavily involved in the PURSUE element of CONTEST, very little effort seems to be focused on PREVENT. One notable exception, the Muslim Contact Unit (MCU), has played an important role in building positive links between the police and Muslim communities.[13] Established in 2002, the Muslim Contact Unit aimed to create partnerships with Muslim community leaders who could help tackle the spread of extremist propaganda in London. This helped to facilitate some pioneering counter-terrorism community engagement projects. The Muslim Contact Unit's remit was then expanded to cover all of England and Wales however resources for this activity have remained extraordinarily limited with in theory a maximum of only eight officers assigned to the work of the Unit (and in practice often less than this) (Thiel, 2009). Eight officers out of a staff of 2,000 does not suggest a high priority area for work.

The overall government budget for counter-terrorism work also drives home the relatively peripheral nature of support for PREVENT activity. Investment in counter-terrorism overall has increased enormously since 2001 when roughly £1 billion was spent on UK security costs. By 2009, annual spending on counter-terrorism had reached £2.5 billion and this is expected to rise to £3.5 billion by 2011.[14] Exactly how much was being spent on PREVENT-related work was unclear until the report of the Communities and Local Government Select Committee (2010), which highlighted that for 2008–2009, the government had allocated some £140 million on meeting the key deliverables in this area. Bearing in mind that the total CT budget for 2009 was £2,500 million this tells us something about the relative importance of PREVENT in the government strategy in real terms. Even more ominously, the Home Office has already warned that funding for PREVENT projects is set for a sharp fall in the coming years given the harsh current economic climate.

One reason for the relatively peripheral nature of PREVENT is not necessarily a widespread belief that the hearts and minds battle is unimportant, but rather widespread uncertainty as to what actually works in this arena. The government has deliberately avoided using any objective measures for assessing its counter-radicalisation efforts. The current government yardstick, *National Indicator 35: Building Resilience to Violent Extremism*, has no quantitative measures associated with it. Unusually, success or failure is self-assessed and judged on a subjective basis. The lack of more objective measures however undermines efforts to identify what is working and what is not. It becomes difficult to build momentum about effective initiatives (and to stop investment in failures). Almost none of the PREVENT projects and initiatives have been properly evaluated and to the best of my knowledge, in any case where a decent evaluation has been carried out the results have not been made public. The result is a profound lack of information on what actually works. Evidence-led policy becomes impossible. In such circumstances, a lack of further investment or indeed of a clear and detailed strategy framework is hardly surprising.

Yet, evidence in different forms is obtainable. In a battle for hearts and minds, psychology offers many insights as to how the struggle is progressing. Attitudes, for example, are frequently measured, surveyed and assessed on many other subjects and can readily be done so here as well. It is important, of course, to ask sensible questions. 'On a scale of one to ten, please rate the strength of your sympathy with al-Qaeda?' How likely is it that a strong supporter of the group would actually give an honest answer to such a question?

But more useful questions are possible. There are two sides in the battle for hearts and minds, and measuring support and sympathy for the government can be just as useful as measuring it for the terrorists. For example, a number of surveys have asked questions along the lines of 'Do you believe that the British government is anti-Muslim?' As a question, this is not as loaded as the previous one on al-Qaeda and arguably is more likely to obtain honest answers. Interestingly, surveys using such questions have found that among Muslim communities in the UK such beliefs have been declining in recent years.

For example, Anthony Richards in his chapter later in this volume notes that in March 2004 an ICM poll found that 64 per cent of Muslim respondents thought that UK anti-terrorism laws were being used unfairly against Muslim communities. A *Times* Populus survey in July 2006 found that this figure had dropped to 47 per cent, while a BBC poll carried out in June 2009 found that it had dropped still further: 'almost a third of respondents said they thought the police, government and British society were anti-Muslim'.

This type of data is helpful in understanding what is happening in the battle for hearts and minds, and it does suggest that the UK is indeed becoming an increasingly austere environment for al-Qaeda and its kin. Such a picture ties in with the declining number of plots, court cases and convictions. The threat is by no means over but the tide does seem to be ebbing. For now.

Naturally there are still problems. The surveys themselves are still very flawed in their current states. There have been very few to begin with, none have been tied in to specific initiatives and all have used different questions. This last point is crucial, as psychology has long learned that even very subtle changes in phrasing can dramatically affect the responses received. For example, three polls in 2006 asked Muslim respondents questions that could be related to sympathy or tolerance for al-Qaeda and acts of terrorism. One suggested a sympathy/approval rate of 20 per cent among British Muslims, another was very similar at 22 per cent, but the third suggested an astoundingly high 51 per cent. Variation in the type of questions used across the three surveys however seriously clouded the answers, hindering rather than helping efforts to understand what was really happening. What is needed is a more consistent use of such approaches in order to evaluate the impact of the small-scale projects that make up most PREVENT-related work in the UK. Consistency is needed both in a commitment to carry out such evaluations but also in the types of questions, attitudes and issues that are examined.

Are PREVENT projects changing people's attitudes? Or are wider forces – such as foreign policy and international events – the real driving forces behind any changes? The short answer is that at the moment there is not enough evidence to say for certain either way.

Unquestionably major challenges face counter-terrorism efforts in the UK and elsewhere. To start, there is a crippling lack of good evidence as to what actually works. This is particularly the case for work in the PREVENT strand ('hearts and minds'), where initiatives have usually not been properly evaluated. As a result it is difficult to judge what policies ultimately work and deserve further support and which are failures. Overall, policies frequently seem to be adopted or endorsed for uncertain political reasons rather than because there is compelling evidence that they are actually beneficial.

A second issue is that counter-terrorism is not the reserve of any one government department or agency, and counter-terrorism itself can involve a bewildering array of activities and policies. While there may be lead agencies in certain areas, the reality is that counter-terrorism as a whole involves a wide range of organisations. Most government departments and a wide range of different agencies will have at least some involvement. Even those very heavily committed to this area will usually still also have responsibilities for other activities and serious issues. One result of multiple actors and different layers of activities is that this can create confusion, competition and conflict over exact responsibilities and resources. At the least this can produce duplication of effort and wastage. At worst, it can seriously compromise the counter-terrorism work, making it less effective and more costly.

The final critical challenge is how to strike the right balance between the different aims of the counter-terrorism nexus. Inevitably there are tensions between some parts of the strategy. Some policies aimed at improving and increasing police powers, for example, also carry a risk of increasing animosity towards the state among the wider communities from which terrorists draw their support and recruits. Getting the balance right between different approaches is arguably one of the hardest obstacles facing the counter-terrorism community.

## Some Conclusions

In recent decades, psychology has provided one of the most useful frameworks for understanding terrorism and terrorists. As a discipline, psychology has particularly focused on explaining how and why people become involved in terrorist violence and also in understanding the psychological impact that terrorist attacks and campaigns have on victims and wider society (e.g. Silke, 2003; Bongar et al., 2007). Recent years have also seen a major growth in our understanding of the ways in which people leave terrorist groups and how campaigns of violence can be brought to an end (e.g. Bjørgo and Horgan, 2008; Horgan, 2009). Combined with this deepening understanding of many aspects of terrorism, there has also been a much greater awareness of the role that psychology and psychologists can play in counter-terrorism efforts. At times this has led to serious controversy, nowhere more so than in the heated debates over the potential role that psychologists have played in the interrogation and torture of terrorist suspects.

Ultimately, psychology can provide powerful insights for anyone who seeks to better understand terrorism and counter-terrorism. The aim of this volume is to help present an overview of this field at a time of major breakthroughs in our understanding as well as severe debate and controversy in how this understanding is applied (and could be applied). This book gathers together contributions from psychologists and writers who have direct experience of researching terrorism. Some of these authors have met actual terrorists; others have worked to assist those tasked with the serious responsibility of combating terrorism. In many cases, the authors combine academic credentials and understanding with substantial policy or practitioner experience. The ultimate aim is that this combination of perspectives will provide readers with a holistic and richly informed view of a controversial and critically important subject.

## Notes

1  http://www.ukpublicspending.co.uk/uk_year1990_0.html.
2  http://www.dasa.mod.uk/applications/newWeb/www/index.php?page=48&thisconten t=1600&pubType=1&date=1998-01-01&disText=1998&from=historic&topDate=200 8-10-01&PublishTime=00:00:01.
3  http://hansard.millbanksystems.com/written_answers/2000/feb/09/police-statistics;  Cain.ulst.ac.uk/ni/security/ni-sec-01-police-strength.rtf;  http://hansard. millbanksystems.com/written_answers/1992/jan/21/police-statistics.
4  hansard.millbanksystems.com/commons/1986/. . ./prison-staff.
5  A figure that does not include the considerable numbers working in other relevant departments such as the Home Office and the Northern Ireland Office, which were also active in counter-terrorism.
6  http://news.bbc.co.uk/1/hi/uk/8476381.stm.
7  http://www.telegraph.co.uk/travel/travelnews/6990006/Heathrow-in-security-alert-as-two-men-arrested-on-flight.html.
8  http://www.tsa.gov/what_we_do/layers/bdo/index.shtm.
9  http://homelandsecuritynewswire.com/behavioral-detection-tsa-officers-keep-watchful-eye-people-airports.
10  http://www.tsa.gov/press/happenings/boston_bdo_spot.shtm.
11  http://security.homeoffice.gov.uk/counter-terrorism-strategy/.
12  http://security.homeoffice.gov.uk/counter-terrorism-strategy/about-the-strategy1/four-ps/.
13  http://www.publications.parliament.uk/pa/cm200405/cmselect/cmhaff/165ii/165we25.htm.
14  http://security.homeoffice.gov.uk/news-publications/news-speeches/CONTEST_HS_statement_240309.

## References

Bjørgo, T. and Horgan, J. (2008). *Leaving Terrorism Behind: Individual and Collective Disengagement*. Abingdon, Oxon: Routledge.
Bloom, M. (2005). *Dying to Kill: The Allure of Suicide Terror*. New York: Columbia University Press.
Bongar, B., Brown, L., Beutler, L., Breckenridge, J. and Zimbardo, P. (2007). *Psychology of Terrorism*. Oxford: Oxford University Press.
Borum, R. (2004). *Psychology of Terrorism*. Tampa, FL: University of South Florida.

Bowden, B. and Davis, M. (2008). *Terror: From Tyrannicide to Terrorism*. London: Routledge.

Clarke, R. and Newman, G. (2006). *Outsmarting the Terrorists*. London: Praeger Security International.

Crenshaw, M. (1992). 'How terrorists think: what psychology can contribute to understanding terrorism'. In L. Howard (ed), *Terrorism: Roots, Impact, Responses*, pp. 71–80. London: Praeger.

Cronin, A. (2009). *How Terrorism Ends*. Princeton: Princeton University Press.

Friedland, N. (1992). 'Becoming a terrorist: social and individual antecedents'. In L. Howard (ed), *Terrorism: Roots, Impact, Responses*, pp. 81–93. London: Praeger.

Fromkin, D. (1975). 'The Strategy of Terrorism'. *Foreign Affairs*, 53 (July), pp. 692–693.

Gearty, C. (1991). *Terror*. London: Faber and Faber.

Horgan, J. (2009). *Walking Away from Terrorism: Accounts of Disengagement from Radical and Extremist Movements*. Abingdon, Oxon: Routledge.

Horgan, J. and Taylor, M. (1997). 'The Provisional Irish Republican Army: Command and Functional Structure.' *Terrorism and Political Violence*, 9/3, pp. 1–32.

Horgan, J. and Taylor, M. (1999). 'Playing The Green Card: Financing the Provisional IRA – Part 1.' *Terrorism and Political Violence*, 11/2, pp. 1–38.

House of Commons Communities and Local Government Committee (2010). *Preventing Violent Extremism: Sixth Report of Session 2009–10*. London: Stationery Office.

Hurst, J. (1993). *Nathan Bedford Forrest: A Biography*. New York: Alfred A Knopf.

Merari, A. (2000). Statement before the Special Oversight Panel on Terrorism. *Terrorism and Threats to U.S. Interests in the Middle East [H.A.S.C. No.106–59]*. Washington: U.S. Congress.

Rapaport, D. (1992). 'Terrorism.' In Mary Hawkesworth and Maurice Kogan (eds.), *Routledge Encyclopedia of Government and Politics*. London: Routledge.

Shafritz, J., Gibbons, E. and Scott, G. (1991). *Almanac of Modern Terrorism*. Oxford: Facts on File.

Silke, A. (2003). *Terrorists, Victims and Society: Psychological Perspectives on Terrorism and Its Consequences*. Chichester: Wiley.

Silke, A. (2004). 'Courage in Dark Places: Reflections on Terrorist Psychology'. *Social Research*, 71/1, pp. 177–198.

Taylor, M. (1988). *The Terrorist*. London: Brassey's.

Thiel, D. (2009). *Policing Terrorism: A Review of the Evidence*. London: Police Federation.

Victoroff, J. and Kruglanski, A. (2009). *Psychology of Terrorism: Classic and Contemporary Insights*. New York: Psychology Press.

Weston, K. (2005). UK counter terrorism policy. http://www.wun.ac.uk/security_seminars/seminars/weston.html.

Wilkinson, P. (2001). *Terrorism versus Democracy: The Liberal State Response*. London: Frank Cass.

# 2 Understanding terrorist psychology

*Randy Borum*

## Introduction

Behavioural scientists have shown a longstanding interest in understanding and describing the psychology of individuals who become involved in terrorism (Borum, 2004; Davis and Cragin, 2009; Horgan, 2005; Victoroff and Kruglanski, 2009). Understanding the causes, motivations and determinants of terrorist behaviour poses an enormous challenge, but pursuing this knowledge is vital to countering violent extremism's threat to global security. This chapter provides an overview of the major findings in this area and an account of our current understanding, introducing several concepts addressed in detail in subsequent chapters. It moves away from single-factor explanations and finger pointing at 'root causes', and aims toward a more diverse and dynamic view based on pathways into and through terrorist engagement and on how terrorist groups form, function, and fail.

## Motivation and mentation

Psychological researchers – like many in the general public – have been preoccupied with the notion of terrorist motivation (Crenshaw, 1986; Helmus, 2009; Hudson, 1999; Horgan, 2005; Victoroff, 2005). Acts of terrorism are relatively uncommon, often shocking, and sometimes self-destructive. They seem to defy easy explanation. No psychological theory has emerged to explain all types of violence, and terrorism is a distinct form of violence. It is most often deliberate (not impulsive), strategic, and instrumental; it is linked to and justified by ideological (e.g. political, religious) objectives and almost always involves a group or multiple actors/supporters (Crenshaw, 1986, 1988; Laqueur, 2003). These issues all add complexity to the construction of terrorism as a form of violence, and challenge the emergence of a unifying explanatory theory.

Even accounting for the influence of religion or ideology, it is vexing to discern how and why someone would come to adopt beliefs and behaviours that support his or her engagement in subversive and terrorist activity, particularly violence toward civilian non-combatants. Since the late 1960s, the academic research community has sought answers to these questions by analysing a variety of individual, interpersonal, socio-cultural, and even inter-state influences (Victoroff and Kruglanski, 2009; Horgan, 2005).

Early efforts tended to predominantly focus on the individual level, assuming that the aberrant behaviour so prominently associated with the dramatic consequences of terrorism must reflect some mental or personality abnormality (Schmid and Jongman, 1988). This thinking led some to propose clinical explanations and gave rise to a multitude of attempts to identify a unique terrorist profile. However, forty years of terrorism research has firmly debunked the notion that only 'crazy' people engage in terrorism and has yet to reveal a meaningful, stable, terrorist profile (Borum, 2004; Crenshaw, 1992; Horgan, 2008).

Research on the relationship between psychopathology and terrorism has been nearly unanimous in its conclusion that mental illness and abnormality are typically not critical factors in terrorist behaviour (Borum, 2004; Crenshaw, 1992; Horgan, 2008; Silke, 1998). Studies have found that the prevalence of mental illness among samples of incarcerated terrorists is as low as or lower than in the general population (Ruby, 2002). Moreover, although terrorists often commit heinous acts, they would rarely be considered classic 'psychopaths'.[1] Terrorists typically have some connection to principles or ideology as well as to other people (including other terrorists) who share them. Psychopaths, however, do not form such connections, nor would they be likely to sacrifice themselves (including dying) for a cause (Martens, 2004).

Research also has failed to find or produce any favourable prospect of identifying either a 'terrorist personality', or any accurate psychological 'terrorist profile' (Horgan, 2003). This consistent pattern of empirical findings probably comes as no surprise to many psychological researchers who are aware that personality traits alone tend not to be very good predictors of behaviour. Fortunately, with very few exceptions, most contemporary social/behavioural scientists studying terrorism have moved on (Silke, 1998; Horgan, 2005).

Building on prior studies, psychological researchers have realized that we are unlikely to find a new understanding of radicalization in static, 'trait-based' effects, but that viewing terrorism as a complex and dynamic 'process' is much more promising (Horgan, 2008). At this juncture, however, the exact nature of that process remains poorly understood.

Focusing on 'vulnerabilities' to terrorism seems to be more promising and useful than looking for unique personality traits. Vulnerabilities may be viewed as 'factors that point to some people having a greater openness to increased engagement than others' (Horgan, 2005, p. 101). Rather than being simple causes, these vulnerabilities may be leveraged as possible sources of motivation or as mechanisms for acquiring or hardening one's militant ideology. Three commonly occurring vulnerabilities are:

(1) perceived injustice/humiliation;
(2) need for identity; and
(3) need for belonging (Borum, 2004).

Social scientists have recognized perceived injustice and humiliation as central factors in understanding violence generally and terrorism specifically, dating back to some of the earliest writings. In the mid-1970s, Hacker (1976) concluded that 'remediable injustice is the basic motivation for terrorism'. Similarly, an individual's search for identity may draw him or her to extremist or terrorist organizations in a variety of ways. The absolutist, 'black and white' nature of most extremist ideologies is often attractive to those who feel overwhelmed by the complexity and stress of navigating a complicated world. Without struggling to define oneself or discern personal meaning, an individual may choose to define his or her identity simply through group membership, or identification with a cause (Taylor and Louis, 2004). Finally, in radical extremist groups, many prospective terrorists find not only a sense of meaning, but also a sense of belonging, connectedness and affiliation. Indeed, Crenshaw (1988, p.59) argues, 'for the individuals who become active terrorists, the initial attraction is often to the group, or community of believers, rather than to an abstract ideology or to violence.'

## Pathways to terrorism

The pathways to, and motives for, terrorism are quite varied and diverse. Different people connect with violent ideologies and groups for different reasons at different times. For the individual, the process is often framed as comprising phases of radicalization, engagement (in terrorism), and disengagement. At the group/organization level, the corresponding processes are recruitment, mobilization and demobilization. Understanding these processes of becoming and being a terrorist does not lend itself to simple, linear, sequential analysis (Horgan, 2008). Alternatively, by using a 'pathway' approach, terrorism is not viewed as 'the product of a single decision but the end result of a dialectical process that gradually pushes an individual toward a commitment to violence over time' (McCormick, 2003, p. 492).

Prior research also supports the general proposition that no single pathway or theory exists that would satisfactorily explain how all – or even most – people come to adopt violent extremist ideologies and engage in violent action (e.g. Borum, 2004; Horgan, 2008). Laqueur (2003, p. 22) has said of terrorism that the quest for a 'general theory' is misguided, because: 'Many terrorisms exist, and their character has changed over time and from country to country.' This seems to be equally true for the radicalization process itself. Moreover, researchers have begun to distinguish between reasons for joining, remaining in, and leaving terrorist organizations, finding that motivations may be different at each stage, and not even necessarily related to each other.

### *Conceptual approaches*

Several efforts have been made, however, to articulate a general sequence of stages, events or issues that might apply across and within group types. These are mainly conceptual models offering a logical narrative of a 'typical' transformative process, often with reference to a particular extremist group.

One conceptual approach, for example, describes a four-stage process of acquiring or developing a 'terrorist mindset' (Borum, 2003), understanding that this mindset may be the result, rather than the cause, of joining an extremist group. The individual-actor model attempts to explain how grievances and vulnerabilities are transformed into hatred of a target group, and how hatred is transformed – for some – into a justification or impetus for violence. Fundamentally, the process begins by framing some unsatisfying event, condition, or grievance (*it's not right*) as being unjust (*it's not fair*). The injustice is blamed on a target policy, person, or nation (*it's your fault*). The responsible party is then vilified – often demonized – (*you're evil*) which facilitates moral disengagement and drives an impetus for aggression. This particular model was developed, though, as a training heuristic for law enforcement, not as a formal social science theory.

Alternatively, Fathali Moghaddam (2005) uses the metaphor of a 'staircase' to describe the process of becoming a terrorist. Like most theories, feelings of discontent and perceived adversity/deprivation are a platform for stepping initially onto the path to terrorism, though fewer people ascend to each successive level. In the beginning, according to his model, an individual's attempts to alleviate adversity and improve her/his situation have been unsuccessful, leading to feelings of frustration and aggression, which are displaced onto some perceived causal agent (who is then regarded as an enemy). As anger toward the enemy builds, some become increasingly sympathetic towards the justifications for violence and toward the terrorist groups that act against the enemy. Some of those sympathizers eventually join an extremist group, organization or movement that advocates for, and perhaps engages in, terrorist violence. At the 'top' or final level are those who have joined, overcome barriers to violent action, and actually commit a terrorist act (Moghaddam, 2005).

The application of Social Movement Theory (SMT) to understanding terrorism represents an approach with a deeper theoretical grounding, greater social-contextual emphasis, and empirical support. Donatella Della Porta (1995) is among the first serious terrorism researchers to connect SMT concepts to violent extremism in her studies of the Italian and German militants. More recently, Quintan Wiktorowicz (2003, 2005) has applied SMT in extensive fieldwork in the UK to understand how people came to join a militant jihadist group (Al-Muhajiroun) based in a Western democracy.

Wiktorowicz concurs with the general principle that 'joining the jihad' and becoming a terrorist are processes that evolve over time. They rarely occur as a sudden, discrete decision. Importantly, he sees the process as one of persuasion involving ongoing interactions between the recruit and the members (Wiktorowicz, 2005). His SMT-based model has four key components. A breakdown at any stage can divert the individual from a path to joining or ultimately participating. Wiktorowicz describes those stages as follows:

1.   Cognitive Opening – an individual becomes receptive to the possibility of new ideas and worldviews;
2.   Religious Seeking – the individual seeks meaning through a religious idiom;
3.   Frame Alignment – the public representation proffered by the radical group 'makes sense' to the seeker and attracts his or her initial interest;

4.  Socialization – the individual experiences religious lessons and activities that facilitate indoctrination and identity-construction. The latter process often includes ideological precepts that tie the individual's self-interest to the risky activism of the movement.

(Wiktorowicz, 2005)

In addition to the conceptual models offered by social scientists, several law enforcement and security agencies have developed and disseminated their own ideas about the radicalization process. The US Federal Bureau of Investigation (2006) has described the radicalization process, based principally on how it might apply to converts to Islam within the US, as comprising four sequential stages: *Pre-radicalization*; *Identification*; *Indoctrination*; and *Action*. Similarly, the New York Police Department (Silber and Bhatt, 2007), with input from terrorism researchers and other experts, suggest that citizens of a Western home-country who ultimately adopt a *Jihadi–Salafi* ideology do so through a linear four stage process as follows: *Pre-radicalization*; *Self-Identification* (exploring and adopting the ideological tenets); *Indoctrination* (intensifies beliefs and commitment to the ideas); and *Jihadization* (believe they have an individual duty to participate in [terrorist activities]). Finally, the Danish Ministry of Justice's (2007) report on home grown terrorism and Islamist radicalization in Europe also asserts that radicalization occurs in four stages: *Pre-radicalization*; *Conversion and identification*; *Conviction* and *indoctrination*; and *Action*.

Though the conceptual models posed by each of these three agencies are certainly consistent with each other and have become quite popular among some law enforcement groups, they seem more appropriately to describe a linear sequence of stages rather than a 'process' or pathway. Moreover, the accuracy and stability of this type of sequence model has not been rigorously tested.

Two recent integrative approaches have been attempted. One is a general framework of political radicalization, based on social psychological principles (McCauley and Moskalenko, 2008). They identify key 'mechanisms' of radicalization at individual, group, and mass-public levels, concluding that the following twelve are most prominent:

- Personal victimization;
- Political grievance;
- Joining a radical group – the slippery slope;
- Joining a radical group – the power of love;
- Extremity shift in like-minded groups;
- Extreme cohesion under isolation and threat;
- Competition for the same base of support;
- Competition with state power – condensation;
- Within-group competition – fissioning;
- Jujitsu politics;
- Hate; and
- Martyrdom.

The second is a project by The Joint Military Information Support Centre (JMISC) of the US Special Operations Command to discern 'common factors' across different models of radicalization and terrorist psychology.

### Empirical research

Despite a surge in terrorism-related publications since 2001 and a burst of recent interest in radicalization, empirical studies are rare. Marc Sageman (2008), a forensic psychiatrist and former CIA Case Officer, has reviewed and collected information from media and open source documents (e.g. courtroom testimony) on a series of Al-Qaeda related cases, though the exact nature of the methodology employed is not immediately apparent from the published documents. He has discerned four 'prongs' of radicalization – a sense of moral outrage, a specific interpretation of the world, resonance with personal experiences, and mobilization through networks – but concludes that these do not comprise stages, nor are they necessarily sequential.

Similarly, Hegghammer (2006) analysed 240 biographies – including 70 'extensive' ones – of (post-2002) Saudi militants, compiled over a two-year period from a broad range of primary and secondary sources, mostly in Arabic. He also conducted numerous interviews with former radicals as well as families and acquaintances of militants. He framed the analyses to ask who joined 'al-Qaeda on the Arabian Peninsula' [QAP] and why, and – to facilitate comparisons – what radicalization and recruitment factors might be specific to Saudi Arabia.

With a more in-depth and individualized focus, John Horgan (2009), recently conducted a series of 52 semi-structured interviews (29 former terrorists and 23 of their supporters, family members and friends) over an 18-month period from late 2006 to early 2008, producing some deeply personal, detailed and complex portrayals of former terrorists in Belfast, Beirut, Oslo, London, Paris, Tripoli, Jakarta and elsewhere.

Perhaps the most systematic and comprehensive effort to date to develop 'data-based' knowledge on violent radicalization has been conducted not by academics, but by MI5's Behavioural Science Unit. Their analysis is based on in-depth case studies on 'several hundred individuals known to be involved in, or closely associated with, violent extremist activity', ranging from fundraising to planning suicide bombings in the UK. An overview of their findings was published in June 2008 in an 'operational briefing note' titled: 'Understanding radicalisation and violent extremism in the UK'. The document is marked as 'UK restricted', but its contents have been widely reported in the British media. Among their key findings, MI5 notes that no profile or single pathway to extremism existed. In most cases they note that some vulnerability existed that made the person receptive to the ideology, but as with earlier studies, the process of becoming 'radicalized' appears to have occurred over time (Travis, 2008).

## Terrorist ideology

Ideology is often defined as a common and broadly agreed upon set of rules to which an individual subscribes, which help to regulate and determine behaviour.

Ideology guides and controls behaviour perhaps by providing a set of behavioural contingencies that link immediate behaviour and actions to long-term positive outcomes and rewards, or it may best be viewed as a form of rule-following behaviour. Culture is also a critical factor in the development of ideology, but its impact on terrorist ideologies specifically, has not been studied (Borum, 2004).

Ideologies that support terrorism, while quite diverse, appear to serve some common functions: they must provide a set of beliefs that guide and justify a series of behavioural mandates; those beliefs must be inviolable and must be neither questionable nor questioned; and the behaviours must be goal directed and seen as serving some cause or meaningful objective. A related question is whether common structures or patterns might exist across violent extremist ideologies, even when the content of the beliefs is dramatically different (Borum, 2004).

One simplistic approach, developed more as a teaching tool than as a social science theory, discerned four main characteristics of these ideologies summarized with the acronym PATH:

- *Polarized*: The essence of this is an 'us vs. them' mindset, or what some would regard as in-group–out-group conflict.
- *Absolutist*: The beliefs are regarded as truth in the absolute sense, sometimes supported by sacred authority. This squelches questioning, critical thinking, and dissent. It also adds moral authority to framing us vs. them as a competition between good and bad (or evil).
- *Threat-Oriented*: An external threat causes in-groups to cohere. Good leaders know this intuitively, if not from reading social psychological research. They persistently remind adherents that the 'us' is at risk from the 'them'. Because the 'us' is seen as being good or right in the absolute sense, this works not only to promote internal cohesion but also external opposition.
- *Hateful*: Hate energizes violent action. It allows principled opposition to impel direct action. It also facilitates various mechanisms of moral disengagement – such as dehumanization – which erode the social and psychological barriers to engaging in violence that one believes is 'justified' (an important point, since many more people endorse the justification for extremist violence than actually commit such acts).

More recently, Gerard Saucier, a social psychologist at University of Oregon, and his international team of colleagues sought to investigate this same question somewhat more systematically and on a larger scale (Saucier et al., 2009). They began with a rationally derived 'working model of the major components of the militant-extremist mind-set', then collected books, printed and web-based material from militant-extremist individuals or groups to see how often certain themes appeared. The project wished to include a broad range of groups, so they deliberately chose at least one from each of seven world regions. 'To qualify, a group had to have been active within the last 150 years, had to fit the definition of militant extremism, and also had to have had a record of actual violence involving the death of multiple persons outside the group. A qualifying group also had to have sufficient written documentary evidence (i.e. original statements) that would clearly indicate its mind-set' (Saucier et al, 2009, p. 258).

The precise methodology and procedures used are a bit sketchy. Saucier scanned these extremist documents looking for the presence of themes, then judged which themes were present in multiple statements 'when, in Saucier's judgment, a reasonable person hearing the set of statements would acknowledge them to be making the same essential point' (Saucier et al, 2009, p. 259). It is not clear from the described methodology whether a coding scheme was used or whether any check was done on the inter-rater reliability of theme identification. Nevertheless, the authors identified 16 themes characteristic of a militant-extremist mind-set 'based on fairly obvious correspondences that emerged in repeated reviews of the extracted statements. Each of these 16 themes was found to occur in three or more groups' (Saucier et al, 2009, p. 259).

1. The necessity of unconventional and extreme measures.
2. Use of tactics that function to absolve one of responsibility for the bad consequences of the violence one is advocating or carrying out.
3. Prominent mixtures of military terminology into areas of discourse where it is otherwise rarely found.
4. Perception that the ability of the group to reach its rightful position is being tragically obstructed
5. Glorifying the past, in reference to one's group.
6. Utopianizing. There is frequently reference to concepts of a future paradise, or at least 'the promise of a long and glorious future'.
7. Catastrophizing. There is a perception that great calamities either have occurred, are occurring, or will occur.
8. Anticipation of supernatural intervention: Miraculous powers attributed to one's side, miraculous events coming to help one's side, or commands coming from supernatural entities.
9. A felt imperative to annihilate (exterminate, crush, destroy) evil and/or purify the world entirely from evil.
10. Glorification of dying for the cause.
11. Duty and obligation to kill, or to make offensive war.
12. Machiavellianism in service of the 'sacred'. This theme involves the belief that those with the right (i.e. true) beliefs and values are entitled to use immoral ends if necessary to assure the success of their cause.
13. An elevation of intolerance, vengeance, and warlikeness into virtues (or nearly so), including, in some cases, the ascribing of such militant dispositions to supernatural entities.
14. Dehumanizing or demonizing of opponents.
15. The modern world as a disaster. Among militant extremists, there is commonly a perception that modernity, including the consumer society and even instances of successful economic progress, is actually a disaster for humanity.
16. Civil government as illegitimate.

The authors suggest that militant-extremist groups use these thematic elements to craft a 'narrative' frame for their ideologies. Drawing on these 16 themes, they offer the following narrative of how they might cohere:

> We (i.e. our group, however defined) have a glorious past, but modernity has been disastrous, bringing on a great catastrophe in which we are tragically obstructed from reaching our rightful place, obstructed by an illegitimate civil government and/or by an enemy so evil that it does not even deserve to be called human. This intolerable situation calls for vengeance. Extreme measures are required; indeed, any means will be justified for realizing our sacred end. We must think in military terms to annihilate this evil and purify the world of it. It is a duty to kill the perpetrators of evil, and we cannot be blamed for carrying out this violence. Those who sacrifice themselves in our cause will attain glory, and supernatural powers should come to our aid in this struggle. In the end, we will bring our people to a new world that is a paradise.
>
> (Saucier et al, 2009, p. 265)

## Terrorist recruitment

Surprisingly little research or analysis has been conducted on terrorist recruitment (Daly and Gerwehr, 2006). Some debate even exists among contemporary scholars about the nature and extent of terrorist recruitment into militant jihadism. Marc Sageman (2004) and Scott Atran (2003), for example, both well-known terrorism researchers, have argued that there is no recruitment per se to jihad or to Al-Qaeda. They believe that 'enlistment' (because people want to join) is the mechanism by which new militants emerge. They report having data to show that nearly 90 per cent 'join the jihad' through friendship and kinship (Sageman, 2004). While it seems reasonable to assert that traditional recruitment – as the military does it, with a dedicated budget and personnel – may not be terrorists' *modus operandi*, it seems nearly incontrovertible that militants seek new supporters, activists and members and that they engage in active efforts to influence others to adopt their point of view. That is arguably just a broader conceptualization of recruitment. How they do it becomes a very different field of debate than whether they do it.

Social movement scholars have studied activist recruitment for decades. One of the prevailing concepts is that when members of the movement look to recruit others, they operate as 'rational prospectors' (Brady et al., 1999). They want to be efficient and effective, so they seek to identify those most likely to agree to act, if asked, and to act effectively to further the cause. They 'conceive of the recruitment process as having two stages: (1) Rational prospectors use information to find likely targets; (2) after locating them, recruiters offer information on participatory opportunities and deploy inducements to persuade recruits to say "yes"' (Brady et al., 1999, p. 154.) Central to both tasks is the existence and strength of relationships. Understanding relationships among potential prospects is critical to understanding recruitment networks.

## Terrorist mobilization

Ideology, by itself, is generally not sufficient to create a terrorist. Not all extremist ideologies facilitate violence, nor are all extremists violent. One potentially useful distinction to consider is the 'direction of activity': that is, whether the focus is more on promotion of the 'cause' or destruction of those who oppose it. Even within destruction-oriented extremism, however, it usually takes more than ideology to compel violent action.

Getting people to *act* in service of a cause, not just to espouse a set of beliefs or maintain nominal allegiance to a group (what some refer to as 'radicalization'), is a process that social movement theorists call *mobilization* (Zald and McCarthy, 1987). Working from the assumptions of a rational actor model of behaviour, mobilizing people to act involves increasing their perceived benefits and minimizing the perceived costs. These assumptions cohere with basic approach-avoidance psychological models of human motivation (Elliott and Church, 1997).

The perceived benefits or terrorism – such as a sense of belonging, personal meaning, and approval of god/others – were discussed earlier, but manipulating 'costs' is also a critical factor in mobilization (Munger, 2006). Many more people believe that violence in service of a particular cause is justified than actually commit acts of extremist violence. Activists must provide incentives, but also remove disincentives. They must leverage the psychological and social influences to erode the powerful, naturally occurring barriers that inhibit widespread human killing. The barriers often involve how we think others will appraise our behaviour as well as our own self-appraisal. The avenues of assault on those barriers may be external (i.e. the effects of the group or social environment) or internally driven (i.e. making an internal cognitive adjustment about how to perceive the environment or situation).

Four of the major group/external influences to reduce psychological 'costs' are diffusion of responsibility, de-individuation, obedience, and social identity. Diffusion of responsibility is a social-psychological phenomenon by which individuals feel less responsible (or less culpable) for transgressive behaviour when they commit it either in the presence of, or on behalf of a group (Darley and Latane, 1968). De-individuation is a state or situation in which the focus of judgment is on a collective rather than on an individual. This reduces an individual's inhibition or restraint either by reducing their self-awareness or by facilitating conformity to situation-specific norms (Silke, 2003). Obedience to authority is another phenomenon that diminishes personal responsibility because the actor transfers his moral agency from self to the authority (Milgram, 1983). Finally, social identities (Tajfel and Turner, 1986) – the ways in which we view ourselves in relation to social groups or categories – also can weaken individual responsibility by boosting the salience of group norms.

Eroding internal psychological barriers to violence typically requires modifying self-appraisals. Once humans have developed a basic capacity to control their behaviour and regulate their actions, their internal moral code typically guides their choices. Violating one's own moral code may bring negative self-appraisals and feelings of self-condemnation (Bandura, 1990, 2004). Psychologist Albert Bandura notes, however, that these self-sanctions can be selectively 'activated and disengaged' to facilitate behaviour that would otherwise violate one's own moral standard. He describes this process of breaking down barriers as 'moral disengagement', which can operate through a variety of processes. One way to remove the barrier of self-sanction is to change one's interpretation or appraisal of events so that they justify the act (moral justification). Terrorists typically have some justification for their action, whether it is personally construed or derived from the group's ideology. A second mechanism is 'blaming the victim', since targeting aggression at people who have caused harm or are considered blameworthy or deserving of retribution is more acceptable. Another mechanism of moral disengagement is to dehumanize the victims in one's personal appraisals. Della Porta (1992), for example, describes how Italian 'militants justified their use of political violence by depersonalizing their victims, defined in the documents of the underground groups as 'tools of the system' and, later as 'pigs' or 'watch dogs'.

## Terrorist group vulnerabilities

Terrorist groups, like all social collectives, have certain vulnerabilities to their existence (Cronin, 2006; Jackson, 2009). Some come from within the organization, some operate from outside. Internal mistrust, for example, can be a disabling affliction for a group. It causes members to focus energy inward and not externally toward operations or goal directed activity; it potentiates interpersonal tensions and strains relationships. Periods of boredom and inactivity can also threaten group cohesion. McCauley and Segal (1989, p. 177) note that 'without action and external threat, the group may destroy itself'. Internal competitions and power struggles can undermine group unity and effectiveness. Substantive disagreements about tactics, strategy or leadership are also frequent sources of vulnerability, particularly when they lead to factions.

External vulnerabilities include disruption in the support network, disapproval of constituencies, and conflicts with other groups. No political or ideologically driven organization can survive and thrive without a support network. 'The types of support are financial, training, weapons, organizational, and operational. A group must be able to raise the resources necessary to provide sufficient incentives to attract and maintain a membership' (Oots, 1989, p. 166). Beyond the instrumental support network is a broader social network of sympathizers, who comprise the constituency of a terrorist organization. Changes in the attitudes of the supporters can lead to changes in the organization (Cronin, 2006). Finally, conflicts that arise between groups can threaten the integrity or even the very existence of a terrorist organization as well (McCauley and Segal, 1987).

## Terrorist group functioning

Terrorist groups must be able to maintain both cohesion and loyalty to sustain their existence (Jackson, 2009). Leadership can be an important factor in that effort. While the prototypical terrorist group leader is believed to capitalize on his or her charisma, the truth is that extremist leaders operate in a variety of ways and sometimes change over time. Terrorist groups require that certain functions be served, regardless of how they are stylistically implemented. First, the group needs a guardian to maintain its collective belief system, to deter dissent, and prevent ideological or commitment drift. A related aspect of this function is diverting conflict externally and maintaining a persistent sense of threat from the adversary. Second, a group must have organizational routines that help to keep action going, since boredom and inactivity are enemies of cohesion. Third, the flow of communication through the organization must be managed and controlled, so that the group's identity and narrative are carefully preserved. Fourth, incentives must be managed and manipulated to attract new members and to keep existing members focused on group objectives and motivated to act (Borum, 2004).

## Conclusion on the state of research

Social science researchers in the field of terrorism studies are nearly unanimous in their conclusion that research in this field of study largely lacks substance and rigour (Gurr, 1988, Schmid and Jongman, 1988; Silke, 2001; Horgan, 2005; Victoroff, 2005; Victoroff and Kruglanski, 2009). Several fundamental problems remain unresolved. First, there still is no agreed upon definition of terrorism, though more than 100 different ones have been proposed in the professional literature (Levy and Sidel, 2003). Second, most of the existing research is not empirical or based on any data. Silke's (2001) review found that 80 per cent of terrorism research articles published between 1995 and 1999 were 'thought pieces', or based on information taken from media sources, with less than 20 per cent providing substantially new knowledge based on previously unavailable data. Third, psychological researchers who have more of an empirical orientation seem to focus on questions that either lose the focus on observable behaviour, or are disconnected from issues that are important to practitioners. This is not meant to suggest that only applied research in terrorism studies holds any value. Rigorous basic social/behavioural science research on terrorism-related processes would also be welcome, and might provide a foundation of knowledge for an empirically- informed psychology of counter-terrorism.

## Note

1 Psychopaths are persons who possess both a pervasive and persistent history of antisocial behaviour and severe, endogenous emotional/affective deficits such as callousness and lack of empathy and remorse.

## References

Atran, S. (2003). Genesis of suicide terrorism. *Science*, 299: 1,534–1,540.

Bandura, A. (1990). Mechanisms of moral disengagement. In W. Reich (Ed), *Origins of Terrorism: Psychologies, Ideologies, Theologies, States of Mind* (pp. 161–191), Cambridge: Cambridge University Press.

Bandura, A. (2004). The origins and consequences of moral disengagement: A social learning perspective. In F. M. Moghaddam and A. J. Marsella (Eds.), *Understanding Terrorism: Psychosocial Roots, Consequences, and Interventions*, Washington, D.C.: American Psychological Association.

Borum, R. (2003). Understanding the terrorist mind-set. *FBI Law Enforcement Bulletin 72* (July), 7–10.

Borum, R. (2004). *Psychology of Terrorism*, Tampa, FL: University of South Florida.

Brady, H., Schlozman, K. and Verba, S. (1999). Prospecting for participants: Rational expectations and the recruitment of political activists. *American Political Science Review*, 93, 153–168.

Crenshaw, M. (1986). The psychology of political terrorism. In M.G. Hermann (Ed.) *Political psychology: contemporary problems and issues* (pp. 379–413), London: Josey-Bass.

Crenshaw, M. (1988). The subjective reality of the terrorist: Ideological and psychological factors in terrorism. In R. O. Slater and M. Stohl (Eds.), *Current Perspectives in International Terrorism*, Basingstoke, Hampshire: Macmillan.

Crenshaw, M. (1992). How terrorists think: what psychology can contribute to understanding terrorism. In L. Howard (Ed.), *Terrorism: Roots, Impact, Responses* (pp. 71–80), London: Praeger.

Cronin, A. (2006). How al-Qaida ends: The decline and demise of terrorist groups. *International Security*, 31, 7–48.

Daly, S. and Gerwehr, S (2006). Al-Qaida: Terrorist Selection and Recruitment. In David Kamien, (Ed.), *The McGraw-Hill Homeland Security Handbook* (pp. 73–89), New York: McGraw-Hill Companies.

Darley, J.M. and Latane, B. (1968). Bystander intervention in emergencies: Diffusion of responsibility. *Journal of Personality and Social Psychology*, 8, 377–383.

Davis, P. and Cragin, K. (Eds.) (2009). *Social Science for Counter-terrorism: Putting the pieces together*, Santa Monica, CA: RAND.

Della Porta, D. (1992). Political socialization in left-wing underground organisations: Biographies of Italian and German militants. *International Social Movement Research*, 4, 259–4,290.

Della Porta, D. (1995). *Social Movements, Political Violence and the State*, Cambridge: Cambridge University Press.

Elliott A. and Church M. (1997). A hierarchical model of approach and avoidance achievement motivation. *Journal of Personality and Social Psychology*, 72, 218–232

Federal Bureau of Investigation Counter-terrorism Division (May 10, 2006). The radicalization process: From conversion to jihad. *FBI Intelligence Assessment.*

Gurr, T. (1988). Some characteristics of political terrorism in the 1960s. In Michael Stohl (Ed.) *The Politics of Terrorism* (pp. 31–58), New York: Marcel Dekker.

Hacker, F.J. (1976). *Crusaders, Criminals, Crazies: Terror and terrorism in our time*, New York: W.W. Norton.

Hegghammer, T. (2006). Terrorist recruitment and radicalisation in Saudi Arabia. *Middle East Policy*, 13 (4), 39–60.

Helmus, T. (2009). How and why some people become terrorists. In Paul K. Davis and Kim Cragin (Eds.), *Social Science for Counter-terrorism*, Santa Monica: RAND.

Horgan, J. (2003). The search for the terrorist personality. In A. Silke (Ed.) *Terrorists, victims, and society: Psychological perspectives on terrorism and its consequence* (pp. 3–27), London: John Wiley.

Horgan, J. (2005). *The Psychology of Terrorism*, London: Routledge.

Horgan, J. (2008). From profiles to pathways and roots to routes: perspectives from psychology on radicalization into terrorism. *ANNALS, American Association of Political and Social Sciences*, 618, 80–94.

Horgan, J. (2009). *Walking Away from Terrorism: Accounts of Disengagement from Radical and Extremist Movements*, Taylor and Francis: London and New York.

Hudson, R. (1999). *The Sociology and Psychology of Terrorism: Who Becomes a Terrorist and Why?* Washington, D.C.: Library of Congress, Federal Research Division.

Jackson, B. (2009). Organizational Decision-making by Terrorist Groups. In P. Davis, and K. Cragin (Eds.) *Social science for counter-terrorism: Putting the pieces together* (pp. 209–256), Santa Monica, CA: RAND.

Laqueur, W. (2003). *No End to War: Terrorism in the Twenty-First Century*. New York: Continuum.

Levy, B. and Sidel V. (2003). Challenges that terrorism poses to public health. In B. Levy and V. Sidel (Eds.) *Terrorism and Public Health* (pp. 4–18), New York: Oxford University Press.

Martens, W. (2004). Terrorist with antisocial personality disorder. *Journal of Forensic Psychology Practice*, 4, 45–56.

McCauley, C. and Segal, M. (1987). Terrorist individuals and terrorist groups: The normal psychology of extreme behaviour. In J. Groebel and J. H. Goldstein (Eds.), *Terrorism* (pp. 41–64), Seville: Seville University Press.

McCauley, C. and Moskalenko, S. (2008). Mechanisms of Political Radicalization: Pathways Toward Terrorism. *Terrorism and Political Violence*, 20 (3), 415–433.

McCormick, G. H. (2003). Terrorist decision making. *Annual Review of Political Science*, 6: 473–507.

Milgram, S. (1983). *Obedience to Authority: An Experimental View*, New York: Harper/Collins.

Moghaddam, F. M. (2005). The staircase to terrorism: A psychological explanation. *American Psychologist*, 60, 161–169.

Munger, M. (2006). Preference modification vs. incentive manipulation as tools of terrorist recruitment: The role of culture. *Public Choice*, 128, 131–146.

Oots, K. L. (1989). Organizational perspectives on the formation and disintegration of terrorist groups. *Terrorism*, 12, 139–152.

Ruby, C. (2002). Are terrorists mentally deranged? *Analyses of Social Issues and Public Policy*, 2, 15–26.

Sageman, M. (2004). *Understanding Terror Networks*, Philadelphia, PA: University of Pennsylvania Press.

Sageman, M. (2008). A Strategy for Fighting International Islamist Terrorists. *The ANNALS of the American Academy of Political and Social Science*, 618, 223–231.

Saucier, G., Akers, L., Shen-Miller, S., Knežević, G. and Stankov, L. (2009). Patterns of Thinking in Militant Extremism. *Perspectives on Psychological Science*, 4 (3), 256–271.

Schmid, A. and Jongman, A. (1988). *Political Terrorism: A New Guide to Actors, Authors, Concepts, Data Bases, Theories, and Literature*, New Brunswick, New Jersey: Transaction Books.

Silber, M. and Bhatt, A. (2007). *Radicalization in the West: The Homegrown Threat*. New York: New York City Police Department Intelligence Division.

Silke, A. (1998). Cheshire-Cat logic: The recurring theme of terrorist abnormality in psychological research. *Psychology, Crime & Law*, 41, 51–69.

Silke, A. (2001). The devil you know: continuing problems with research on terrorism. *Terrorism and Political Violence*, 13/4, 1–14.

Silke, A. (2003). Deindividuation, anonymity and violence: Findings from Northern Ireland. *Journal of Social Psychology*, 143/4, 493–499.

Tajfel, H. and Turner, J. C. (1986). The social identity theory of inter-group behaviour. In S. Worchel and L. W. Austin (Eds.), *Psychology of Intergroup Relations*, Chicago: Nelson-Hall.

Taylor, D. M. and Louis, W. (2004). Terrorism and the quest for identity. In F. Moghaddam and A. Marsella (Eds.). *Understanding terrorism: Psychosocial roots, consequences, and interventions* (pp. 169–185), Washington, DC: American Psychological Association.

Travis, A. (2008). MI5 report challenges views on terrorism in Britain. *Guardian* http://www.guardian.co.uk/uk/2008/aug/20/uksecurity.terrorism1.

Victoroff, J. (2005). The mind of the terrorist: a review and critique of psychological approaches. *Journal of Conflict Resolution*, 49, 3–42.

Victoroff, J. and Kruglanski, A. (Eds.). (2009). *Psychology of Terrorism: Classic and Contemporary Insights*, New York: Psychology Press.

Wiktorowicz, Q. (Ed.) (2003). *Islamic Activism: A Social Movement Theory Approach*, Bloomington: Indiana University Press.

Wiktorowicz, Q. (2005). *Radical Islam Rising: Muslim extremism in the West*, Lanham, MD: Rowman & Littlefield Publishers.

Zald, M. and McCarthy, J. (1987). *Social Movements in an Organizational Society*, New Brunswick: Transaction Books.

# 3    The psychology of violent radicalisation

*Brooke Rogers*

## Introduction

The terrorist attacks on the World Trade Centre in New York City on September 11, 2001 (9/11) signalled a step-change in the world of terrorist research, resulting in attempts to develop comprehensive, flexible psychological, sociological and political theories capable of explaining terrorist behaviour in a number of different cultures and settings. Despite this apparent 'step change', terrorism was still primarily understood by the Western world in terms of a threat originating outside Western borders (Danieli et al. 2005; Taylor and Horgan 2006; Rogers, Loewenthal et al. 2007). The Madrid bombings of March 11, 2004 did little to alter this conception. More recently, the London bombings of 2005, the attempted London/Glasgow bombings of 2007, and White convert Nicky Reilly's detonation of a bomb in a restaurant in Exeter (UK) in 2008 cast a shadow of doubt over the level of certainty that the threat of terrorism did, indeed, originate from outside our borders in the minds of policy makers and members of the public, alike. As a result, involvement in terrorism has increasingly been seen in terms of a radicalisation process with the potential to occur within Western borders. Following from the analysis in the preceding chapter by Randy Borum, this chapter aims to provide a summary of our understanding of the motivation for joining an extremist group or taking part in terrorist activities, followed by an account of the current understanding of the process of radicalisation. The author will re-visit the question of *why* individuals are drawn to terrorist groups before exploring recent empirical evidence targeted at understanding *how* the process of radicalisation is believed to occur.

## Why are individuals drawn to terrorist groups?

A growing body of research has the potential to indicate the edges of the violent radicalization puzzle (See Kushner 1996; Post 1998; Reich 1998; Crenshaw 1981, 1998a, 1998b; Silke 2006; Rogers et al. 2007; Neumann and Rogers 2008). Researchers have attempted to identify the underlying social and organizational drivers influencing the likelihood that an individual will undertake violent extremist behavior in order to better understand what drives individuals to resort to acts of terrorism. Whilst reviewing these theories, Silke (2003; 2006) repeatedly reminds us that it is important to understand that, regardless of how successful a terrorist group appears; even the larger and more popular terrorist groups represent a minority within their communities.

One of the more popular theories centres on the concepts of grievance and threat. This theory purports that, while violent extremism has assumed many forms, all appear to be driven by a sense of grievance experienced by the individual or community at large (Kushner 1996; Silke 2006). However, grievance and threat in, and of themselves, are insufficient as primary causes, as the majority of populations and individuals experiencing real or perceived grievances and threats remain non-violent. Additionally, the list of extreme grievance and threat supported by the literature (e.g. attempted genocide, loss of land essential to identity, etc.) does not typically belong to the life experiences of individuals living in and growing up in the cities and towns of Western nations (Rogers et al. 2007).

Poverty is also cited as one of the key social drivers of terrorism. The academic evidence tends to contradict this popular belief because the majority of countries encountering suicide attacks between 1980 and 2001 are generally recognized as 'middle income societies' (Pape 2003; 2005; Moghadam 2006; Von Hippel 2002). Far from being the poorest countries in the world, general life expectancies in these countries were very close to those of the United States (Pape 2005; Moghadam 2006). Additionally, terrorists have been known to come from a variety of backgrounds, including middle to high levels of socio economic status and education, as evidenced by the doctors involved in the attempted London/Glasgow attacks in 2007. In spite of this, there are still voices of dissent over the role of poverty in violent radicalization. Some researchers believe that the repeated focus on religious fundamentalism is often an excuse to avoid focusing on the real social issues, including the ever growing gap between groups of varying socio-economic status (Rogers 2006, Rogers et al. 2007).

If grievance, threat and poverty are unable to function as primary drivers of violent radicalisation within Western borders, how, then, do Western individuals share in the sense of injustice experienced by those living outside our borders? A number of social theories offer insight on the possible reactions to perceived intolerance of a belief system within a Western country, as well as a method for connecting with the experiences of those outside our borders, thus fostering a connection with outside issues that have the potential to shape internal Western experiences. Drawn from psychology and sociology, a number of these theories have contributed heavily to discussions concerning the origins and manifestations of violent extremism.

While the theoretical contributions of psychology are grounded in their shared scientific methodology, the general psychological schools of thought as applied to the study of terrorism are quite different in their understanding of the push/pull factors involved in the decision to join, remain in, or leave a violent radical organisation. These include: 1) the Psychoanalytic approach; 2) the Cognitive approach; and 3) the Social approach. In short, the key psychological approaches have the potential to overlap and inform one another, yet the proponents of each theory rarely agree on the key drivers of violent radicalisation. The following discussion will identify some of the key psychological and social theories and summarise their contributions to a greater understanding of the psychological and social drivers of violent radical organisations.

## The psychoanalytic approach

The psychoanalytic approach is built around the premise that psychological disorder can determine or explain behaviour and motives. Given that terrorist activity can be clearly defined as a form of 'abnormal' activity, the psychoanalytic approach should have much to contribute to the understanding of violent radicalisation. Unfortunately, researchers repeatedly conclude that the majority of searches for possible psychopathology among terrorists have not been altogether systematic and are often based upon second-, third- and even fourth-hand accounts of interactions with known terrorists. Those researchers and 'experts' who suggest that terrorists are psychologically abnormal tend to be the ones with the least amount of contact with actual terrorists compared to those with direct contact who find that suggestions of abnormality do not stand up to close scrutiny (Silke 1998). In spite of this, psychoanalytic theories abound, including: 1) Absolutist/ Apocalyptic Theory in which individuals exhibit absolutist moral polarization, impaired assessments of reality, the belief in conspiracies of evil, and the idealization of a messianic figure (See Adorno et al. 1950; Lifton 1961; Taylor 2004); 2) Narcissism Theory, which focuses on the concept of terrorists as timid and emotionally damaged individuals; and 3) Paranoia Theory, which suggests that paranoid suspicions justify self defence, some forms of which can be extremely violent. Paranoia theory has strong links with theories of group-think, which can be created within the dynamics of an isolated, extremist group. These trends also form links with the processes of splitting and externalization, traits that are reportedly seen in higher frequencies amongst members of extremist groups, though the extent of this elevated frequency is open to debate. Splitting and externalisation describe the process by which an individual breaks his/her personality into 'me' and 'not me', resulting in a personality incapable of integrating the good and bad parts of an individual. When this occurs, all of the positive traits equated with 'me' are projected onto the self, while all of the negative traits equated with 'not me' are projected onto someone else. In turn, these tendencies contribute to an image of an injured self, or narcissistic wounds (Post 1998). Splitting and externalisation are also commonly seen in individuals who have had their personality development impacted by damage or stress during childhood, lending support to the idea that grievance and threat play a role in motivating membership in a violent extremist group (Silke 2003; Rogers et al. 2007).

## The cognitive approach

The cognitive approach defines violent extremist behaviour as a logical response to the environment, or the final, rational choice in a sequence of choices (Beck

2002; Crenshaw 1990, 1998a). This approach suggests that, if we can understand that a violent response to the environment can be founded upon rationale reasons, we will then be able to understand the reasons behind the behaviour and motives of an individual engaging in violent extremism. This understanding is driven by a number of theories, including: 1) Rational Choice Theory (RTC) (Crenshaw 1998b), which purports that if we can understand that the response to the environment as rational, we will then understand the reasons behind the behaviour and motives of an individual; 2) Humiliation–Revenge Theory (Jurgensmeyer 2000), which defines violence as stemming from anger; and 3) Terrorism as an Expression of Strategy, which suggest that terrorism follows a logical process that can be discovered and explained. RTC is one of the more popular cognitive approaches, in spite of disagreements amongst researchers about how rational and purposeful the choice to enter into violent extremism truly is. For example, Crenshaw (1998b) proposes that the use of violent behaviour by terrorist groups is a wilful choice made by the organisation in order to accomplish political or strategic objectives, while Post (1998) argues that the decision is based upon the unintended consequence of psychological or social factors driving the group towards violence (Reich 1998, pp. 7–8). Crenshaw suggests that it is also important to identify the main non-psychological contributors to terrorism by examining the way in which terrorism can be understood as an expression of political strategy.

This approach to understanding terrorism has been echoed in other disciplines, including sociology. Social movement theory, especially Political Opportunities Theory, views political violence through the lens of the environment in which social movements must operate, rather than on the internal workings of the groups, themselves. This theory argues that, 'the behaviour of social movements is influenced by the broader political context that can facilitate or hinder political violence' (Karagiannis and McCauley 2006, p. 321). Karagiannis and McCauley argue that authorities responsible for responding to social movements must note that perceived repression has the potential to create martyrs and mobilise movement supporters (2006).

### *The social approach*

Finally, the social approach suggests that group membership and identity determine and explain the behaviour and motives of violent extremists. The social approach is built upon the concepts of ethnocentrism, or 'the view of things in which one's own group is at the centre of everything, and all others are scaled or rated with reference to it' (Sumner 1906, p. 13, cited in Hewstone and Cairns, 2001). This results in the development of biases and preference for in-group characteristics, products, customs, languages, speech styles, and more (Hewstone and Cairns 2001; Rogers et al. 2007). Social Identity Theory (SIT) (Tajfel and Turner 1979), and Realistic Group Conflict Theory (see Brewer 1979; Levine and Campbell 1972; Sherif 1966; and Rogers et al. 2007) influence the likelihood of an individual joining a violent extremist group, as well as the potential of a group resorting to violence in the face of perceived adversity. SIT suggests that individuals are attracted to extremist groups because group membership enables the development of a positive identity by allowing individuals to define themselves in terms of their group membership, which also enables them to assign value and emotional significance to their group membership and group goals. Because the group's social identity becomes a part of the self-concept, then a threat to the group is a threat to self (Tajfel and Turner 1979; Reich, 1998; Rogers et al. 2007). Membership in a violent radical group also has the potential to fulfil self-esteem needs, especially when new recruits find that they can influence like-minded individuals. In fact, membership in such a group might be the first time that a terrorist individual feels accepted, important or needed. The group might also address welfare needs, as illustrated by Ed Husain's experience as he trod his pathway to violent radicalisation:

> My disagreements with my parents were now so deep, their revulsion for my Islamism so powerful, and my commitment to ideological so uncompromising, that my father had little choice but to give me an ultimatum: leave Mawdudi's Islamism or leave my house.
>
> (Husain 2007, p. 44)

Ed Husain left his parents' house and was offered shelter, food and comfort by his radical friends.

Realistic Group Conflict Theory (RCT) suggests that group conflicts are rational because groups have incompatible goals and compete for scarce resources, resulting in a realistic conflict. In short, competition for resources, which can include power, land, natural resources and more, increases the likelihood of inter-group conflict. This approach has also been reflected in social movement theory. For example, Neumann and Rogers (2008) discuss Resource Mobilization Theory which suggests that political forms of violence are created when a group mobilizes to attack its opponent's resources, or when a group attempts to reclaim resources they believe that they have lost. Resources can be understood in terms of concrete resources such as land or space, or in terms of social resources, such as privilege. Karagiannis and McCauley (2006) summarized this dynamic thus:

> The ability of a group to challenge the authorities eventually would be determined by the extent to which it is in control of normative resources (commitment of members to the group, legitimacy, and identity resources), coercive resources (means of imposing its will on opponents, material, and organizational resources); and institutional resources (access to state agencies and elites, mass media resources).
>
> (p. 320)

### It takes all sorts

When it comes to selecting one of these theories as the primary explanation of violent radicalisation, a number of issues hold each theory back. In respect to the psychoanalytic approach, repeated attempts to identify a terrorist personality or mental disorder capable of explaining violent radical behaviour have led many researchers to conclude that terrorists are often psychologically healthier and more stable than the rest of the criminal population, or at least as no more likely to display signs of 'appreciable psychopathology' than other people (See Rasch 1979; Crenshaw 1981, 2000; Silke 1998, 2006; Lanning 2002; Ruby 2002; Atran 2003; Whittaker 2003; Ganor 2005; Rogers et al. 2007). In short:

> The perils are that (a) human variation is such a there is no single, 'typical' terrorist psychology (b) many terrorists are psychologically inaccessible and when accessible often secretive and non-yielding, and (c) Western psychological concepts and assessments often are not readily exportable and applicable to cultures very different from their own.
>
> (National Research Council 2002, p. 30)

Similarly, the cognitive approach fails to fully explain individual motivations towards violent radicalisation. In fact, the cognitive approach to understanding violent radicalisation is more appropriate when applied to group or collective objectives, rather than individual objectives, as the high cost of terrorist activity (i.e. death, injury, capture) cancels out the benefits of the behaviour (i.e. political or social change), suggesting that a rational person would not take part in terrorist behaviour unless the benefits are also psychological (Crenshaw 1998; Post 1998; Reich, 1998; Rogers et al 2007). Finally, while the social psychological approach is useful for describing individual reasons for joining a terrorist group (i.e. self-esteem) and the internal group pressures that maintain group membership and have the potential to inform more extreme beliefs and behaviour, it still fails to provide researchers with a method of truly understanding *why* certain individuals are more prone to extremist messages.

This summary of the origins and manifestations of violent extremism through the lens of the social sciences has illustrated that no single theory has proven itself to be absolutely reliable. Likewise, discussion of violent radicalisation through separate theoretical perspectives can be misleading, as no single theory or school of thought has proven itself capable of providing a 'catch all' answer. Instead, individuals tasked with providing answers to some of the questions driving the study of violent radicalisation should view the wide variety of approaches as useful tools that enable researchers to tailor their approach to specific groups operating in specific cultures and contexts. To apply a single theory to all types of terrorism, irrespective of group, place or time, is to enter into folly because terrorism has changed over time, as have the motives and causes of terrorism. Instead, a flexible, multidisciplinary approach is needed to understand violent extremism, as suggested by Cronin's (2004) conclusion:

> Terrorism is a multidisciplinary challenge: The study of sources of terrorism requires the ability to translate between the fields of criminology, comparative

politics, economics, history, international relations, psychology, sociology, theology, and arguably others.

(Cited in Cronin and Ludes 2004, p. 20)

## How do individuals become involved in terrorist groups?

At the very least the combination of drivers and theories mentioned in the previous section requires a group. Therefore, it is necessary to create a deeper understanding of the pathways to radicalisation, and the role of intervening factors or facilitators of radicalisation that enable individuals to engage with violent extremist groups. In doing so, the author will frame the discussion in the UK context in order to provide a snapshot of the changing trends and dynamics of violent radicalisation in a Western context. This requires a discussion of the current situation within the UK, the growing conservative trend in Western Muslims, and a discussion of community and institutional facilitators of radicalisation.

First, it is important to recognise that the author is framing this discussion within a pre-existing definition of Islamist militants:

> . . . Islamist militancy combines a strict, literalist practice of Islam (often referred to as Salafi or Wahhabi) with a revolutionary political ideology (Islamism), proclaiming a global community of believers (the ummah) to be liberated and/or united under Islamic rule, and the belief that the most effective way of accomplishing this aim is through violence or 'armed struggle' (often referred to as jihad).
>
> (Neumann and Rogers 2008, p. 7).

Second, it is important to recognise that all conversations about radicalisation trends for Islamist militants in the UK are complicated by the fact that the 'Muslim community' is incredibly diverse. There are approximately 2 million Muslims in the UK, predominantly of South Asian origin. This population belongs to around five or six different sects worshiping in over 1,600 mosques (Active Change Foundation, 2008). Keeping in mind that individuals willing to engage in violent acts of terrorism form a minority of any population, the search for a greater understanding of the process of violent radicalisation is akin to finding a needle in a haystack. As a result, experts are left scratching their heads over which haystacks they must search, as well as the reasons that these pointed needles made their way into the haystacks in the first place. We must begin our search somewhere.

### *International drivers*

The roots or origins of terrorism are traditionally sought at a local rather than a global level (Sedgwick, 2007). This is a reasonable starting point, but solutions to radicalisation and extremism lay beyond the scope of the individual, group and local level. Brighton (2007) suggests that, while it is important to understand radicalisation within local politics and community relations, we must also understand radicalisation and extremism through longer term work that addresses 'tackling inequality, discrimination, deprivation and inconsistent Government policy, and in particular, foreign policy' (p. 2). This view is shared by many, suggesting that local causes cannot provide the explanation for global waves of terrorism (Brighton, 2007; Sedgwick 2007; and Mirza et al. 2007). The apparent difficulty or unwillingness on the part of policy makers to situate Western foreign policy within an account of violent radicalization deprives us of a means of objectively assessing the contribution that Western foreign policy makes to the radicalization process. Instead, dialogues of integration and multiculturalism abound, resulting in a lack of understanding about the impact of foreign policy on violent radicalisation.

There are a number of justifications for these repeated omissions on the part of policy-makers. These include references to a pre-existing threat, as seen in the fact that Al-Qaeda and similar groups had both planned and carried out attacks on the west prior to the 9/11 attacks on American soil in 2001. The fact that America and its allies entered Iraq in response to the attack in 2001 encourages politicians to separate the London attacks of 2005 and attempted 2007 attacks in London and Glasgow from operations in Iraq. Additionally, Brighton (2007) suggests that policy makers try to exclude the London bombers of 7/7 from the concept of home grown terrorism because:

> ... individuals based in the UK had had links with Al-Qaeda, had been seeking to further the ideology now associated with it and had received training in camps sponsored by Al-Qaeda and other Islamist groups prior to 9/11 and the coalition response to those attacks.
>
> (p. 3)

These arguments are strongly contradicted through the anger at British Foreign policy expressed by Mohammad Siddique Khan and Shezad Tanweer in their martyrdom videos made shortly before the attacks in London on 7 July 2005 (Brighton 2007; Mirza *et al.* 2007).

In the midst of these policy contradictions, there is an undeniable growing level of religiosity amongst the younger generation UK Muslims, many of whom are rejecting their parent's cultural traditions and expressing a more politicised form of religion (Jacobson 1997; Mirza et al. 2007; Neumann and Rogers, 2008). Far from being a new trend, this process of rejecting parental beliefs, which are viewed as becoming culturally grounded, and accepting a more universal (and sometimes extreme) identity or belief system was also illustrated in Jacobson's (1997) study with young, second-generation British Pakistanis (Neumann and Rogers 2008, p. 31). Additionally, Neumann and Rogers (2008) identified a recent UK survey in which 86 per cent of British Muslims identified religion as the most important thing in their life. In this survey, Muslim respondents identified foreign policy as the most important issue or concern for Muslims overall, yet Muslim youths expressed a low level of knowledge about international issues when questioned by Mirza et al. (2007). In this case, Muslim youths reported that they were the angriest about foreign policy issues, but compared to older Muslims were half as likely to know the answers to policy questions. This led Mirza et al. (2007) to conclude that young Muslims were expressing emotional responses to images of victims and violence around the world rather than truly engaging with foreign policy.

These observations must be balanced by the understanding that, if foreign policy is a key contributor to violent radicalisation, it is not the only contributor. If these young Muslims are reacting to the plight of those outside the borders, how are they gaining this sense of responsibility from their life experiences inside the borders of Western countries? It is possible that, instead of experiencing a shared Islamic community tradition with their local peers, the diverse and fragmented Muslim communities in the Western world are more likely to find similarities in the global fact of an ideology that contains the concept of jihad. This provides an easily accessible, understandable, and easy to act upon ideology, regardless of location, and without the need for expert meditation or mandates delivered by higher authorities. The availability of this ideology is the secret of its success since

> the movement it inspires (. . .) is composed of globally dispersed supporters who have no shared history and whose wider community, those 'oppressed' and subordinated by the West, from whom they seek 'vengeance', are people encountered almost entirely through nightly TV news bulletins.
>
> (Brighton 2007, pp. 13–14)

Additionally, it is also likely that 'foreign' identities are being reinforced by the increasing availability of cheap travel and instant communication, resulting in a failure on the part of expectations that links between minority homelands and immigrant ethnic communities would decrease with the passing of the immigrant generation (Brighton 2007, p. 6, Mirza et al. 2007; Neumann and Rogers 2008).

## *Local drivers*

The increasing awareness of the relationship between foreign policy and radicalisation does not mean we can turn our attention away from local issues. Durodie (2007) turned the analytical lens onto the role of the communities and society as a whole in promoting or mitigating the process of violent radicalisation. Referring to a desperate and obsessive search for meaning and identity within society, he claims:

> The key is not what it is that attracts a minority from a variety of backgrounds, including some who are relatively privileged, to fringe Islamist organisations, but rather what it is about our own societies and culture that they fail to provide aspirational, educated and energetic young individuals with a clear sense of purpose and collective direction through which to lead their lives and realise

their ambitions, that they are left looking for this elsewhere, including for some, among various arcane belief systems.

(Durodie 2007, pp. 433–434)

During the course of their recent study exploring pathways into violent radicalisation, Neumann and Rogers (2008) suggested that the disconnect between young British Muslims is not simply a disconnect between the wider UK community and themselves, nor is it simply a disconnect between the first, second and third generations. Young British Muslims are also struggling with a disconnection between the cultural teachings of the mosques and their modern, Western questions and experiences. This is because the mosques tend to be culturally led and cater to the needs of the older generation, resulting in exclusion and a lack of opportunity for the younger generation, as illustrated by a British Community Leader's statement:

What you find is that a lot of mosques are culturally led. They are more interested in keeping ties of kinship and traditional values. This excludes the youth who follow in their footsteps. Many young Muslims in this country have dual identity. They are Muslim, but they are also British, with their British identity being more predominant. Their issues are not being addressed by most of the mosques.

(Neumann and Rogers 2008, p. 29)

However, these ideas are still hotly contested as evidenced by Mirza et al's. (2007) argument:

Contrary to expectations, the rising interest in religion amongst second and third generation British Muslims is not an outcome of parental or community influence. In particular, if one looks at young Muslims in the UK, they are not responding to familial or broader community pressure. They are returning to the Qu'ran and reading about religion of their own volition, often having experienced the modern, secular lifestyles available to most people of their age.

(p. 12)

Finally, community level discussions shed some light on the questions posed during the previous discussion of the role of grievance and threat in violent radicalisation. The grievances and threats might be different for Western Muslims, but they are certainly visible in the domestic community and centre on a lack of opportunity and frustrated ambition. Cronin (2004) suggests that, while the majority of a society impacted by deprivation is unlikely to resort to violence in order to address issues of grievance or threat, the extent to which societal conditions lead to a sense of indignation is a crucial factor that must be understood in order to counter violent radicalisation. 'In other words, the objective conditions that face an individual are not as important as the perceived difference between what one has and what one deserves (in either material or political terms)' (p. 5). Cronin (2004) goes on to suggest that it is possible to view the sense of anger experienced by individuals drawn towards violent radicalisation as a result of frustrated ambition. In these instances, upwardly mobile individuals are unable to realise their capabilities in the form of political power because of a lack of opportunity or active blocking of these attempts.

## Current trends in violent radicalisation

Understanding the role of society in influencing the likelihood of terrorist group membership is important, as home grown violent radicals are not growing up or living in a social vacuum. In the UK, the disparity between the choice of identities can result in young Muslims feeling caught between the Western ways at school, and culturally based practices at home. Neumann and Rogers (2008) believe that this places individuals in a position where they risk becoming more susceptible to extremist messages. Radical group members recognise this susceptibility and offer to fill the identify void through inclusion in violent radical groups. As a result, '. . . this has the potential to place an individual within an environment where the group processes and radicalisation messages (. . .) are both introduced and reinforced' (Neumann and Rogers 2008, p. 30).

The community can act as both a social driver of and a cure for violent radicalisation. Currently, the Muslim communities are becoming increasingly aware of the threat of radicalisation, and acknowledging that they can play a role in encouraging or countering violent radicalisation. Neumann and Rogers (2008) indicated that, in the UK there is a lot of internal policing taking place, and that this involves a battle within the local communities over the way in which Islam should be defined and the role of political Islam. The question of identity feeds into this, with many individuals questioning whether they are British or Muslim, or if they can, in fact, be both. However, these internal community policing techniques are not always successful in their attempts to decrease radicalisation. For example, a community might ask a particular individual to leave because they notice that s/he is promoting extremist views. Often, this only moves the problem on, enabling a radical individual to create links and ties in another community before being noticed and moved on again. This often leads to frustration on the part of policy-makers and security experts intent on improving community engagement in order to counter radicalisation. Despite the shared interest in cooperation between Muslim community leaders and members of the security services in the UK, it is also acknowledged that there are numerous factors that inhibit people from picking up the phone and reporting suspected radicalisation (Neumann and Rogers 2008).

Other changes are also taking place. Nowadays, recruitment has either been driven underground, or into the private sphere. In response to the events of 9/11 and 7/7 in New York and London, rapid and severe police crackdowns have driven the majority of recruitment activity away from the mosques, moving the battle into new territories, including the Internet, prisons and informal gatherings. Additionally, the Government and security services are aware of the growing need to work with the Muslim community to address the issue of violent radicalisation, as illustrated by the renewed focus on the PREVENT strand of the UK's CONTEST strategy.

In conclusion, the growth of violent extremism in the Western world must be interpreted in relation to political and social trends inside our borders, as well as in terms of the impact of our foreign policies outside of our borders. Government policies must continue to focus on the internal, community and local socio-political issues within their borders while learning to address the impact of outside policy issues on domestic life experiences, as well. This will enable them to clarify misunderstandings and focus in on the key issues fuelling the attractiveness of radical messages. A number of social facilitators aid potential recruits during their journey towards violent radicalisation. These include disillusionment with their parental form of religion, which is seen as being culturally grounded; and the cultural grounding of mosques that are seen as isolating and unapproachable by young Muslims. Communities and the security services are aware of these issues and working to address them together. In order to do so, trust must be built within the communities, between communities, and between communities and the security services (Cronin 2004; Brighton 2007; Mirza et al. 2007; Durodie 2007; Neumann and Rogers 2008).

## References

Active Change Foundation (2008). Presentation at closed conference. Details can be found at http://www.activechangefoundation.org/.

Adorno, T., Frenkel-Brunswik, E., Levinson, D. and Sanford, R. (1950). *The Authoritarian Personality*. New York: Harper.

Atran, S. (2003). Genesis of suicide terrorism. *Science*, 299, 1,534–1,639.

Beck, U. (2002). The terrorist threat: world risk society revisited. *Theory, Culture and Society*, 19 (4), 39–55.

Brewer, M.B. (1979). In-group bias in the minimal intergroup situation: A cognitive-motivational analysis. *Psychological Bulletin*, 86, 307–324.

Brighton, S. (2007). British Muslims, multiculturalism and UK foreign policy: 'Integration' and 'cohesion' in and beyond the state. *International Affairs*, 1, 1–17.

Crenshaw, M. (1981). The causes of terrorism. *Comparative Politics*, 13, 379–399.

Crenshaw, M. (1990). The causes of terrorism. In Charles W. Kegley, Jr. (Ed.), *International Terrorism: Characteristics, causes, controls* (pp. 113–126). London; New York: St Martin's Press.

Crenshaw, M. (1998a). Questions to be answered, research to be done, knowledge to be applied. In W. Reich (Ed.), *Origins of Terrorism: Psychologies, ideologies, theologies, states of mind* (pp. 247–260). Baltimore, MD: John Hopkins University Press.

Crenshaw, M. (1998b). The logic of terrorism: terrorist behavior as a product of strategic choice. In W. Reich (Ed.), *Origins of Terrorism: Psychologies, ideologies, theologies, states of mind* (pp. 7–24). Baltimore, MD: John Hopkins University Press.

Crenshaw, M. (2000). The psychology of terrorism: An agenda for the 21st century. *Political Psychology*, 21, 405–420.

Cronin, A. (2004). Introduction: Meeting and Managing the Threat. In A.K. Cronin and James Ludes (Eds), *Attacking Terrorism: Elements of a Grand Strategy* (pp. 1–45). Washington, D.C.: Georgetown University Press.

Cronin, A. and Ludes, J. (2004). *Attacking Terrorism: Elements of a Grand Strategy.* Washington, D.C.: Georgetown University Press.

Danieli, Y., Brom, D. and Sills, J. (2005). *The Trauma of Terrorism: Sharing knowledge and shared care, an international handbook.* New York, USA: Hayworth Maltreatment & Trauma Press.

Durodie, B. (2007). Fear and terror in a post-political age. *Government and Opposition*, 42 (3), 427–450.

Ganor, B. (2005). Terrorism as a strategy of psychological warfare. In Y. Danieli, D. Brom and J. Sills (Eds), *The Trauma of Terrorism: Sharing knowledge and shared care, an international handbook* (pp. 33–43). New York: Hayworth Maltreatment & Trauma Press.

Hewstone, M., and Cairns, E. (2001). Social psychology and intergroup conflict. In D. Chirot and M.E.P. Seligman (Eds), *Ethnopolitical Warfare: Causes, consequences and possible solutions* (pp. 319–342).

Husain, E. (2007). *The Islamist: Why I Joined Radical Islam In Britain, What I Saw Inside and Why I Left.* London: Penguin Books.

Jacobson, J. (1997). Religion and ethnicity: dual and alternate sources of identity among young British Pakistanis. *Ethnic and Racial Studies*, 20, 238–250.

Jurgensmeyer, M. (2000). *Terror in the Mind of God: The global rise of religious violence.* Berkeley: University of California Press.

Karagiannis, E. and McCauley, C. (2006). Hizb ut-Tahrir al-Islami: Evaluating the threat posed by a radical islamic group that remains nonviolent. *Terrorism and Political Violence*, 18, 315–344.

Kushner, H.W. (1996). Suicide bombers: Business as usual. *Studies in Conflict and Terrorism*, 19, 329–337.

Lanning, K. (2002). Reflections on September 11th: Lessons from four psychological perspectives. *Analyses of Social Issues and Public Policy*, 4, 27–34.

LeVine, R.A. and Campbell, D.T. (1972). *Ethnocentrism: Theories of conflict, Ethnic Attitudes, and Group Behaviour.* New York: John Wiley & Sons.

Lifton, R. J. (1961). *Thought, Reform and the Psychology of Totalism.* New York: Norton.

Mirza, M., Senthilkumaran, A. and Ja'far, Z. (2007). *Living Apart Together: British Muslims and the Paradox of Multiculturalism.* London: Policy Exchange (www.policyexchange. org).

Moghadam, A. (2006). Suicide terrorism, occupation, and the globalization of martyrdom: A critique of Dying to Win. *Studies in Conflict and Terrorism*, 29, 707–729.

National Research Council (2002). *Terrorism: Perspectives from the behavioural sciences.* National Research Council of the National Academies. Washington, D.C.: National Academies Press. (www.nap.edu).

Neumann, P. and Rogers, M.B. (2008). *Recruitment and Mobilisation for the Islamist Militant Movement in Europe.* Report submitted the Directorate General for Justice, Freedom and Security of the European Commission (http://ec.europa.eu/justice_home/ fsj/terrorism/prevention/docs/ec_radicalisation_study_on_mobilisation_tactics_en.pdf).

Pape, R.A. (2003). The strategic logic of suicide terrorism. *American Political Science Review*, 97, 343–361.

Pape, R.A. (2005). *Dying to Win: The strategic logic of suicide terrorism.* New York: Random House.

Post, J.M. (1998). Terrorist psycho-logic: Terrorist behavior as a product of psychological forces. In W. Reich (Ed.), *Origins of Terrorism: Psychologies, ideologies, theologies, states of mind* (pp. 24–40). Baltimore, MD: John Hopkins University Press.

Rasch, W. (1979). Psychological dimensions of political terrorism in the Federal Republic of Germany. *International Journal of Law and Psychiatry*, 2, 79–85.

Reich, W. (1998). *Origins of Terrorism: Psychologies, ideologies, theologies, states of mind*. Baltimore, MD: John Hopkins University Press.

Rogers, M.B., Loewenthal, K.M., Lewis, C.A., Amlôt, R, Cinnirella, M. and Ansari, H. (2007). The role of religious fundamentalism in terrorist violence: A social psychological analysis. *International Review of Psychiatry*, 19 (3), 253–262.

Rogers, P. (2006). Personal commentary during climate change: The global security impact, RUSI, London. 24 January 2006. Reproduced with permission.

Ruby, C. L. (2002). Are terrorists mentally deranged? *Analyses of Social Issues and Public Policy*, 2, 15–26.

Sedgwick, M. (2007). Inspiration and the Origins of Global Waves of Terrorism. *Studies in Conflict & Terrorism*, 30 (2), 97–112.

Sherif, M. (1966). *In Common Predicament: Social psychology of intergroup conflict and cooperation*. Boston, MA: Houghton-Mifflin.

Silke, A. (1998). Cheshire-cat logic: The recurring theme of terrorist abnormality in psychological research. *Psychology, Crime and Law*, 4, 51–69.

Silke, A. (2003). *Terrorists, Victims and Society: Psychological perspectives on terrorism and its consequences*. Chichester, UK: Wiley.

Silke, A. (2006). The role of the organisation in suicide terrorism. In M.B. Rogers, C.A. Lewis, K.M. Loewenthal, M. Cinnirella, R. Amlôt and H. Ansari (Eds), Proceedings of the British Psychological Society Seminar Series Aspects of Terrorism and Martyrdom, eCOMMUNITY. *International Journal of Mental Health and Addiction*.

Tajfel, H., and Turner, J.C. (1979). An integrative theory of intergroup conflict. In W.G. Austin and S. Worchel (Eds), *The Social Psychology of Intergroup Relations* (pp. 33–47). Monterey, CA: Brooks/Cole.

Taylor, K. (2004), *Brainwashing: The Science of Thought Control*. Oxford University Press.

Taylor, M., and Horgan, J. (2006). The psychological and behavioural bases of Islamic fundamentalism. In M.B. Rogers, C.A. Lewis, K.M. Loewenthal, M. Cinnirella, R. Amlôt and H. Ansari (Eds), Proceedings of the British Psychological Society Seminar Series Aspects of Terrorism and Martyrdom, eCOMMUNITY. *International Journal of Mental Health & Addiction*.

Von Hippel, K. (2002). The roots of terrorism: Probing the myths. *Political Quarterly*, 73, 25–39.

Whittaker, D. (2003). *The Terrorism Reader* (2nd edn). London: Routledge.

# 4 Why people support terrorism

## Psychological issues in understanding terrorism and attitudes towards terrorism

*Reena Kumari*

### Introduction

Psychologists have long attempted to understand the impact of terrorism both on individuals and on communities and this search has intensified since the events of 9/11 in 2001. Nevertheless there is a lack of good research into fully understanding causes and consequences, which have provided the opportunity for myths, prejudice and propaganda to dominate 'public and political discourse on terrorism' (Silke, 2001). While terrorism has been around for a long time surprisingly little is known about the psychological mechanisms involved in terrorist activity, hindering efforts to rehabilitate such individuals, or develop appropriate preventive actions and policies.

While there is no universal definition of terrorism (see Chapter 1 in this volume), there is a general consensus among most researchers that terrorism is an act of violence that attempts to influence public opinion by instilling fear in whole populations (Pape, 2003; Miller, 2002; Takooshian and Verdi, 1995). Although there is often no clear distinction between a criminal act and a terrorist act, terrorists do resemble criminals in the crimes they commit, though they may differ in terms of motivation. This particular chapter is sympathetic to Hallet's (2004) view that a terrorist incident is essentially a common crime, e.g. arson, kidnapping, murder, and as a result does not need a new category. Indeed, it could be argued that too often terrorism is misclassified as a sub-category of 'political violence' or 'war', rather than a specific crime in its own right. However we shall not delve further into the quagmire of the definitional debate.

Suicide terrorism is a growing phenomenon constituting an additional stage to the escalation of terrorist activities, attracting wide media coverage due to the particularly dramatic nature of the violence and the often large number of casualties involved. Although religious values and benefits of undertaking suicide actions are reinforced during terrorist training (at least within the context of jihadi-related extremism) these are merely facilitative factors and not the driving force (Silke, 2001). While female terrorist violence is only on a small scale compared to violent acts committed by males, there has been an alarming increase in the past decade. An increase in female violence is also becoming apparent in the context of suicide bombers, where for example female suicide bombers have carried out a significant number of attacks against targets in Sri Lanka and Russia (e.g. Speckhard and Ahkmedova, 2006). This prominence was demonstrated again in March 2010 when two female suicide bombers carried out attacks on Moscow's underground system killing 39 people. This was simply the latest in a long series of terrorist attacks in the Russian Federation where female suicide bombers were involved. To a lesser extent female suicide bombers have also appeared in other conflicts such as in Iraq and Israel, though their appearance has been much more isolated and sporadic.

As Silke (2001) states, potential suicide bombers usually join terrorist groups in an angry and vengeful frame of mind, with the intention of carrying out a suicide act. Similarly, women who have lost husbands and brothers in the war are desperate to seek revenge and therefore join such groups. Suicide terrorism is arguably the most aggressive form of terrorism, with the general idea of killing the largest number of people, hence gaining maximum concession from the terrorist act and high media attention.

According to Silke (2001) public opinions and views are somewhat 'ignorant' in terms of the understanding terrorism as a result of the media representation. For the terrorist, the media is an open channel to spread their message and image (Ditzler, 2004), particularly in circumstances where terrorist groups want to publicise their cause to the world. Bolz et al. (1996, cited in Miller, 2002) identifies the use of high media coverage as one of the activities that terrorists employ, thereby making terrorism a prime traumatic stressor even for individuals not directly involved in the attacks.

Research by RAND (Schuster et al., 2001), shows that on average adults watched approximately eight hours of TV coverage of the attacks on September 11, 2001. Generally the findings indicated that those who watched the most coverage of the horrific events reported the most stress. The report also explored the methods Americans used in order to cope with the tragic event. For some this was by turning to their religion or to other spiritual guidance. A study by Abdolian and Takooshian (2003), found that exposure to terrorism made victims more accepting of terrorism as a political tactic, and it was in fact mental health workers who suffered from high levels of Post Traumatic Stress Disorder (PTSD) as a result of interaction with traumatised clients.

While the concept of terrorism goes back to the French Revolution of the 1790s (McCauley, 2002), the terrorist attacks of 9/11 have had the greatest impact on civilians, particularly due to the enormity of death and destruction. This has led to an imbalance of normality and feelings of uncertainty, fear, anxiety, loss and perhaps eventually anger.

The 9/11 attacks resulted in a transition of attitudes and behaviours, particularly for those living in America. These changes existed in the form of both fear and cohesion. According to McCauley, (2002) the immediate response to the 9/11 terror attacks was the 'sudden increase in patriotic expression' as evidenced by the display of American flags and a pride in being American, and a public shift in identity. This public shift in identity was apparent immediately after 9/11 among Arabs, Muslims and Sikhs. For Sikhs, this was because Americans could mistake them for Arab or Muslim. While hate crimes were reportedly low these groups did not escape discrimination at work or school (Sengupta, 2001 as cited in McCauley, 2002). For African-Americans the shift resulted from acceptance from the white community, since they too have shared in the consequences of the terrorist attack.

Needless to say this is an area in great need of research and development. Very few studies have attempted to address the issue of attitudes towards terrorism in a systematic way and this is generally due to the difficulties in empirically quantifying feelings of hostility, aggression and attitudes towards violence (Takooshian and Verdi, 1995). Takooshian and Verdi (1995) developed a brief scale, which attempted to assess attitudes towards terrorism. The scale was used with a sample of undergraduate students, law enforcement personnel, and managers from federal and local agencies. They found that abhorrence was not the only public attitude regarding terrorism but a general acceptance or support was also evident across groups.

A particularly relevant study is by Abdolian and Takooshian (2003), who expand on the existing (Takooshian and Verdi, 1995) scale, extending it to 36 self-report items. A high score on the scale indicates high (a) authoritarianism, (b) acceptance of terrorism in general, (c) acceptance of al-Qaeda, and (d) a preference for individual liberties over needs. Although this survey was carried out after 9/11 the findings were generally the same as those reported by Takooshian and Verdi (1995). There was an acceptance of terrorism as a political tactic, however there was no clear support for al-Qaeda. Generally attitudes were best described as 'mixed, leaning toward non-acceptance'. Furthermore, people who were more supportive of individual liberties were considerably less authoritarian in personality, and more accepting of terrorism. In contrast, those more authoritarian in personality were less sympathetic towards terrorism. In addition, no correlation was found with regards to age, gender, educational level, and place of birth. However, there has been a shortage of research on attitudes in the UK, although since the 'War on Terrorism' was declared Britain has also been subject to terrorist threats.

This chapter now reports the findings from a study that aimed to examine public attitudes towards terrorism in the UK and seeks to investigate the relationship of gender, religion and ethnicity in relation to attitudes towards terrorism. The hypotheses are as follows:

1.  Membership of an ethnic minority group will be associated with positive attitudes towards terrorism. (These ethnic minorities are defined as Indian, Pakistani, and Bangladeshi.) ($H_1$)
2.  Males will be significantly more authoritarian in personality hence demonstrate a more positive attitude towards terrorism compared to their female counterparts. ($H_2$)
3.  There will be differences between groups in relation to religiosity, age and attitudes towards terrorism. ($H_3$)

# Methodology

## *Design*

The *dependent variable* in this analysis is the responses on the attitude towards terrorism questionnaires. The *independent variables* are ethnicity, age, gender, religion, and authoritarianism.

## *Participants*

Data were collected from a random sample of 92 participants with an attempt to include an equal number of female and male participants. In addition a special effort was made to include participants from different ethnic and religious groups. These religious groups were defined as Muslims, Christians and Sikhs.

## *Materials*

The study used a previously standardised 36-point scale questionnaire on attitudes towards terrorism developed by Abdolian and Takooshian (2003), which were administered to all participants. This was adapted to a 42 point scale in order for the questionnaire to be relevant to participants in the UK, and in order to sample attitudes towards suicide bombers. The questionnaire used a Likert scale Agree/Disagree format and all four 5-item scales were scored from 0 to 20, low to high:

  1–5   Authoritarianism
 6–10   Terrorism
12–16   Al-Qaeda
17–21   Liberties

A high score indicated a) authoritarianism; b) acceptance of terrorism in general; c) acceptance of Al-Qaeda, and d) preference for individual liberties over security needs (Abdolian and Takooshian 2003). Hence, scale scores could vary from 0 to 60 for attitudes towards terrorism. Each item was scored from 4 (A) through to 0 (D), with N or skip as 2. In addition a further 4-item scale measuring for attitudes towards suicide bombing was added (0–16). In the current study the Cronbach's alpha co-efficient was 0.76, indicating good internal consistency.

## *Procedure*

This was an intercept survey whereby participants were stopped during their daily activities and were asked to give their opinions on a survey. Data collection was carried out in 2004. All participants were provided with a consent form before being administered the questionnaire, which informed participants that they had the right to withdraw at any time during the experiment and included information regarding the nature of the questionnaire. Any additional comments made were transcribed verbatim.

Any questions that the participants asked were answered. Due to the nature of the questionnaire participants were provided with the opportunity to discuss any concerns regarding the survey once it had been carried out.

## Results

This study was carried out in an effort to examine public attitudes towards terrorism (ATT) in the UK. This was done by assessing participants' responses on the Attitude Towards Terrorism Scale (Abdolian and Takooshian 2003). Analysis was carried out to investigate relationships between ethnicity, age, religion and gender in relation to participants' scores on the ATT questionnaire. The results were statistically analysed and a Pearson Correlation was used to examine these relationships. The statistical test used was the one-tailed one-way ANOVA, and the level of significance was 5 per cent

The sample consisted of 51 per cent men and 49 per cent women. Age varied from 18 to 66 with a mean of 30.6 years. In addition a special effort was made to employ participants from different ethnic and religious groups, namely: Muslims, Christians, and Sikhs. In ethnicity 39 per cent described themselves as White, 29 per cent described themselves as Indian, 18 per cent described themselves as Pakistani and 14 per cent as Bangladeshi. In religion 37 per cent described themselves, as Christians, 26 per cent as Sikhs, 34 per cent as Muslims and 2.2 per cent were 'other'.

Responses from the 92 participants revealed a diverse range of attitudes towards terrorism. On the 0–60-point scale, individual scores varied from 5 to 56 with a mean score of 30.6. Presentation of single items revealed abhorrence towards terrorism, for example when asked if 'killing innocent civilians to achieve a political goal' was a morally acceptable tactic, 68.5 per cent said 'Never', but when presented as part of a 5-item scale the mean score of 92 people was 11 on the 0–20-point scale revealing a moderate general acceptance of terrorism as a political tactic

A similar pattern emerged with regards to support for Al-Qaeda in particular. On a 0–20-point scale 'measuring support for Al-Qaeda', people's views averaged from 0 (2.2 per cent) to 20 (1.1 per cent), with a mean score of 8.8, suggesting some support for Al-Qaeda leaning towards non-acceptance. Furthermore 80 per cent supported suspects' rights to an attorney, and 80 per cent were against the torture of US and UK detainees. However 66 per cent favoured security needs, supporting profiling people at US and UK airports. Table 4.1 reports the percentage and mean scores of the three 5-item scales. The four columns of numbers to the left indicate percentage of respondents who agreed with that view, from 0 (low) to 4 (high). The fifth column indicates the mean score for each item (0–4) or (0–20). Items marked (r) were reversed scored, so 'disagree' was scored high for that item. On inspection of these values it can be seen that 57 per cent agreed that 'Al-Qaeda have some legitimate basis for their anger at the United States, United Kingdom and its citizens'.

Again, public opinions on liberties were mixed leaning towards favour of civil liberties over national security. Scores varied from 2 (3.3 per cent) to 20 (2.2 per cent) with a mean score of 12.9 on a 0–20-point scale.

*Table 4.1* Public attitudes towards terrorism, Al-Qaeda and individual liberties

| *Percent* | | | | | | |
|---|---|---|---|---|---|---|
| *0* | *1* | *2* | *3* | *4* | *Mean* | |
| 68 | 17 | 11 | 2 | 2 | 0.6 | Terrorism as a morally acceptable tactic? (0–4) |
| 47 | 26 | 17 | 6 | 4 | 0.9 | Terrorism as an effective tactic? (0–4) |
| 20 | 36 | | 37 | 7 | 1.7 | Terrorists must be considered the enemy of civilised society, regardless of their motives. **(r)** |
| 17 | 35 | | 39 | 9 | 1.9 | It is sometimes understandable if people resort to terrorism as their only way to be heard. |
| 17 | 30 | | 35 | 18 | 2.2 | Only a cruel and cowardly group would resort to terrorism to achieve its goals. **(r)** |
| 12 | 31 | | 43 | 14 | 2.2 | Most terrorists seem like disturbed people. **(r)** |
| 19 | 35 | | 39 | 7 | 1.8 | Terrorism is sometimes morally justified. |
| | | | | | **11.0** | **Accept Terrorism (0–20)** |
| 12 | 49 | | 32 | 2 | 1.5 | They would have exploded nuclear weapons. **(r)** |
| 13 | 30 | | 45 | 12 | 2.1 | They have some legitimate basis for their anger. |
| 10 | 38 | | 41 | 11 | 2.0 | They are the enemy of all civilised people. **(r)** |
| 11 | 49 | | 29 | 11 | 1.8 | Outside the US and UK, the government should be aggressive to eliminate their network. **(r)** |
| 18 | 56 | | 16 | 10 | 1.4 | Inside the US and UK, the government should be aggressive to eliminate their network. **(r)** |
| | | | | | **8.8** | ***Accept Al-Qaeda*** |
| 14 | 52 | | 31 | 3 | 1.6 | 'Profile' people at US and UK airports and elsewhere if this can increase public safety. **(r)** |
| 5 | 33 | | 58 | 4 | 2.3 | Probe the otherwise private files of US and UK students and workers from suspect nations. **(r)** |
| 3 | 17 | | 51 | 29 | 3.2 | Torture US and UK detainees linked with Al-Qaeda if their information could save lives. **(r)** |
| 8 | 36 | | 47 | 9 | 2.1 | Expand wiretaps of suspects in the US and UK **(r)** |
| 1 | 13 | | 67 | 19 | 2.9 | Ensure the right to an attorney and other legal rights of suspects in US custody. |
| | | | | | **12.1** | **Favour civil liberties over national security.** |

Table 4.2 shows the mean scores for 'Bush and Blair's decision to invade Iraq'. This was scored on a scale of 0 (low)–9 (high) with 0 indicating disapproval of an invasion and 9 indicating strong acceptance of the decision to invade. Observation of the means show that there was a change in attitude after the invasion. Fifty one per cent opposed the decision to invade Iraq before the invasion. However after the invasion 57 per cent opposed the decision for the invasion of Iraq. The means for both before (2.03) and after (1.68) the invasion mean indicates that generally the sample opposed the decisions for the invasion of Iraq.

*Table 4.2* Mean scores for public opinions on invasion of Iraq, before and after

| | *N* | *Minimum* | *Maximum* | *Mean* | *Std. Deviation* |
|---|---|---|---|---|---|
| B4IN | 92 | 0 | 9 | 2.03 | 2.535 |
| AFTIN | 92 | 0 | 9 | 1.68 | 2.353 |
| Valid N | 92 | | | | |

## Ethnic minorities

Do the attitudes of ethnic minorities differ from the general White population? A one-way ANOVA was carried out to examine any differences between ethnic groups. These were defined as, White, Indian, Pakistani and Bangladeshi. The results revealed a significant difference between the groups $F(3, 88) = 18.07$; $p < 0.01$, with an overall mean acceptance of 30.6, therefore $H_1$ (hypothesis 1) can be accepted. Table 4.3 displays the descriptive statistics for the scores of the three 5-item scales in relation to each ethnic group. On observation of this table it can be seen that the total mean for the ethnic groups is 30.6, which suggests a general acceptance of terrorism, by all groups. There was also a significant difference between ethnic groups and support for Al-Qaeda $F(3, 88) = 9.06$; $p < 0.01$.

A Post Hoc Bonferroni test for multiple comparisons revealed that while Pakistani and Bangladeshi ($p < 0.05$) participants differed significantly from their white cohorts the Indian participants did not ($p > 0.05$). Differences within ethnic minority groups were also observed. Indian participants did not differ ($p > 0.05$) from the Bangladeshi cohorts but significantly differed from the Pakistani cohorts ($p < 0.05$). In general the Pakistani group differed from all cohorts and were associated with more supportive attitudes towards terrorism. Furthermore the one way ANOVA and Post Hoc Bonferroni tests revealed that Muslims were significantly more authoritarian $F(3, 88) = 4.52$; $p < 0.05$, supportive of Al-Qaeda in general $F(3, 88) = 7.50$; $p < 0.05$, and favoured individual liberties over national securities $F(3, 88) = 6.31$; $p < 0.05$).

## Gender differences

A part of the purpose of this research was to explore the relationship between male and female attitudes towards terrorism. A one way ANOVA revealed significant

*Table 4.3* Mean scores for the three 5-item scales in relation to each ethnic group

|  |  | N | Mean | Std. Deviation |
|---|---|---|---|---|
| ALQUADA | white | 35 | 7.1143 | 4.14283 |
|  | indian | 26 | 8.3846 | 4.16727 |
|  | pakistani | 17 | 12.8235 | 2.87740 |
|  | bangladeshi | 14 | 11.0714 | 4.63207 |
|  | Total | 92 | 9.1304 | 4.53368 |
| LIBERTIE | white | 35 | 9.9143 | 3.41598 |
|  | indian | 26 | 11.5000 | 3.00998 |
|  | pakistani | 17 | 14.8235 | 3.26411 |
|  | bangladeshi | 14 | 12.7143 | 4.21405 |
|  | Total | 92 | 11.6957 | 3.80497 |
| AUTHX | white | 35 | 10.81 | 4.094 |
|  | indian | 26 | 9.84 | 4.705 |
|  | pakistani | 17 | 15.47 | 4.033 |
|  | bangladeshi | 14 | 11.57 | 3.413 |
|  | Total | 92 | 11.51 | 4.559 |

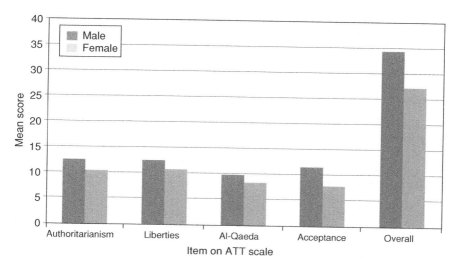

*Figure 4.1* Mean scores for each of the five 4-item scales on the Attitude Towards Terrorism Questionnaire showing the mean differences between male and female responses

differences between male and female responses on the 0–60 terrorist scale $F(1, 90)$ = 8.67; $p < 0.05$. Figure 4.1 displays the means for male and female responses in relation to authoritarianism (0–20), liberties (0–20), Al-Qaeda (0–20), terrorism (0–20) and overall acceptance of terrorism (0–60). Males were significantly more authoritarian in personality $F(1, 90) = 4.58$; $p < 0.05$, compared to their female counterparts. Furthermore males were significantly more supportive of individual liberties $F(1, 90) = 5.10$; $p < 0.05$ and more accepting of terrorism in general $F(1, 90)$ = 10.96; $p < 0.05$. Therefore $H_2$ can be accepted. However there was no significant difference between acceptance of Al-Qaeda and gender $F(1, 90) = 2.32$; $p > 0.05$.

A Pearson Correlation was carried out to analyse any associations between age, gender, ethnicity, religiosity, acceptance of terrorism, and education. The results from the analysis are displayed in Table 4.4. There is a positive correlation between religiosity and authoritarianism ($r = 0.22$; $n = 92$; $p < 0.05$). This positive association is also observed between religiosity and liberties, Al-Qaeda and acceptance of terror. This would suggest that the more religious an individual is the more like they are to endorse individual liberties, accepting of Al-Qaeda and supportive of terrorism in general. Furthermore, individuals who considered terrorism as an acceptable tactic were more authoritarian in personality.

### Suicide terrorism

This 4-item scale (0–16) attempted to measure opinions on suicide terrorism as a result of influence of religious extremists (low) or as a rational choice based

*Table 4.4* Inter-correlations of public's views (Pearson correlation)

|  | *Authorit* | *Liberties* | *Al-Qaeda* | *Terror* |
|---|---|---|---|---|
| **Authoritarianism** (0–20) |  | 0.110 | 0.261* | 0.415** |
| **Liberties** (0–20) |  |  | 0.458** | 0.515** |
| **Al-Qaeda** (0–20) |  |  |  | 0.607** |
| **Terrorism as acceptable** (0–4) | 0.305** | 0.263** | 0.296** | 0.500** |
| **Terrorism as effective** (0–4) | 0.110 | 0.158 | 0.355** | 0.491** |
| **Age** | –0.067 | 0.031 | –0.113 | –0.026 |
| **Education** | –0.050 | 0.007 | –0.253* | –0.106 |
| **Religiosity** | 0.221* | 0.384** | 0.394** | 0.465** |

Notes
* Correlations were significant at $p < 0.05$ (2-tailed).
** Correlations were significant at $p < 0.01$ (2-tailed).

on self-interest (high). As with the other four 20-point scales, opinions on this scale were also mixed attitudes, verging on acceptance of suicide terrorism as a rational choice. Individual scores varied from 0 (2.2 per cent) to 14 (2.2 per cent), with a mean of 7, almost half, indicating the diverse opinions across this scale. A one way ANOVA was carried out to analyse for any differences between gender, religion in relation to opinions on suicide terrorism, but no significant difference was found between gender and suicide $F(1, 90) = 1.22$; $p > 0.05$. There was also no significant difference between religion and attitudes on suicide terrorism $F(1, 90) = 1.83$; $p > 0.05$.

When asked if they 'would consider engaging in terrorist acts if they knew they could get away with it' on a four-point scale (0–4) 90 per cent said they would not consider engaging in terrorist acts, with 10 per cent saying that they would consider it. An independent t-test revealed that there is a significant difference between male and female responses $t(90) = 2.306$; $< 0.05$, and upon observation of the descriptive statistics (Table 4.5) it is clear that males were more likely to engage in a terrorist act compared to their female cohorts.

### *Where is at risk?*

Item 37 requested individuals to state which country they felt was at most risk of terrorism. Items were scored from 1 to 4, these were defined as 1 = Israel, 2 = USA, 3 = Ireland and, 4 = UK. Of the 92 participants, 49 per cent believed that USA was at most risk of a terrorist act, and 32 per cent considered UK to

*Table 4.5* Mean scores for 'engaging in a terrorist act', showing the differences between male and female responses

|  | *GENDER* | *N* | *Mean* | *Std. Deviation* |
|---|---|---|---|---|
| TERRORAC | Male | 47 | .62 | 1.344 |
|  | Female | 45 | .11 | .611 |

*Table 4.6* Mean and standard deviation on public opinion on which country is at most risk of a terrorist attack

|  | *N* | *Minimum* | *Maximum* | *Mean* | *Std. Deviation* |
|---|---|---|---|---|---|
| RISK | 92 | 1 | 4 | 2.50 | 1.104 |
| Valid N (listwise) | 92 |  |  |  |  |

be at most risk. Figure 4.2 displays the frequency score for each country while Table 4.6 displays the means and standard deviation.

While the USA was by far the country judged to be most at risk by the respondents, this 2004 perception has not been borne out by subsequent events. While US targets overseas have certainly been attacked (especially in the context of Iraq and Afghanistan), the USA has not suffered even one successful terrorist attack since 2001 within its own borders and even attempted attacks or plots have been very few. In contrast, both the UK and particularly Israel *have* experienced serious terrorist attacks within their borders in that period. Only Ireland has not seen any attacks – though this changes if one decides to include Northern Ireland within the 'Ireland' rubric. Of all four countries, Israel has suffered by far the highest number of terrorist attacks, especially if one counts rocket and mortar attacks launched from the Palestinian territories. Indeed, counting these, Israel has experienced several thousand terrorist attacks in the period between 2001 and 2010, yet the respondents placed the risk of attack facing Israel well below both the USA and the UK.

## Discussion

The aim of this study was to examine public attitudes towards terrorism in the UK particularly in relation to ethnicity, religion, age and gender. The results largely

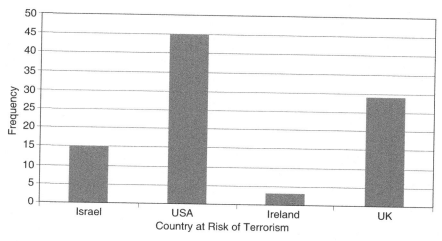

*Figure 4.2* Frequency of scores on public opinion regarding which country they feel is at most risk of terrorism

mirrored the findings reported by other investigators (Takooshian and Verdi, 1995; and Abdolian and Takooshian, 2003), displaying a wide range of attitudes towards terrorism. For all four 5-item scales, the general attitudes could best be described as showing mixed to non-acceptance of terrorism. Some items when presented individually indicated abhorrence, but when presented in a 5-item scale the mean scores of the 92 participants did indicate some acceptance of terrorism as a political tactic.

Similar observations were made with regards to public attitudes towards Al-Qaeda, with results indicating some support for Al-Qaeda. Considering the extent of death and destruction of the 9/11 attacks and media attention surrounding the tragic event – as well as the many Al-Qaeda linked attacks that have occurred since then – these findings were more unexpected. However this could be due to a collection of 'sympathy' that has generated since the invasion of Islamic countries – and particularly Iraq – as a result of the 'War on Terrorism'. In addition results from the analysis revealed that a majority of participants agreed that Al-Qaeda terrorists 'have a legitimate basis for their anger at the US, UK and its citizens', therefore suggesting that the public view terrorist acts as an act of retribution, rather than an attack on civilisation.

Further support of these findings comes from Finnegan et al. (2003) who contend that exposure to terrorism facilitates the process of acceptance of terrorism. However, one may wonder why this is, particularly since recently terrorists have been exposing the public to horrific images of hostage situations such as, for example, the graphic beheadings of some hostages as well as particularly shocking events such as the 2004 Beslan school massacre which saw over 330 people killed including 186 children.

The key finding that emerged from this study is that while there was a spectrum of attitudes towards terrorism from abhorrence to acceptance there were significant differences between ethnic minorities compared to their white cohorts. In general Pakistanis and Bangladeshis scored higher on all four 5-scale items. On further inspection of the results both ethnic minority cohorts belonged to the Islamic religion, and findings suggested that the Muslim participants were generally more sympathetic towards terrorism compared to participants from Christian or Sikh backgrounds.

In relation to gender differences, results indicated that males were more authoritarian in personality and generally were more supportive of attitudes towards terrorism than their female counterparts. This difference was observed for all four 5-item scales. So, are these patterns evident with regards to suicide terrorism? While the results indicated no significant differences between female and male responses with regards to acceptance of suicide terrorism as a rational choice, males scored significantly higher than their female counterparts when asked if they would consider in engaging in a terrorist act. Although there was no evidence to suggest that this was confined to one particular religious or ethnic group, these findings are still somewhat worrying, and there is a need for further research into this area. Why are males more predisposed to take part in such acts?

Contrary to findings reported by Abdolian and Takooshian (2003), statistical analysis revealed that participants who were authoritarian in personality were *more* accepting of terrorism as a political tactic. However in line with previous research, it seems that demographics such as age, gender and education are not significant predictors of attitudes towards terrorism, rather this should be based on lifestyle, personality, and personal experiences (Abdolian and Takooshian 2003). However one's religiosity appears to be a significant predictor of ones' authoritarianism, support for Al-Qaeda, acceptance of terrorism and favour of individual liberties.

Some respondents appeared visibly uneasy about answering questions about terrorism. This was particularly apparent in white individuals, with many refusing to take part. Those who did take part seemed reluctant to answer certain items on the questionnaire, particularly when responding to 'liberties'. This could be due to a fear of expressing views that may be considered as an attack on certain groups of individuals, leading possibly to respondents giving more socially desirable responses. However, on a more positive note Muslim participants were keen in taking the opportunity to express their opinions. This may be due to the fact that Muslims in general feel that they are being victimised with a belief that the so-called 'War on Terror' is in reality closer to a 'War on Islam', and feel the need to justify terrorist acts in defence of their religion. Not surprising, the issue of Palestine arose a few times. One participant stated:

> I am a born Muslim, who has grown up loving and believing in what the Quran & Sunnah says . . . I do not agree with any lives taken in an act of terrorism. However I do feel Muslims have been suffering for years and years. If Israel gets sorted, and the Palestinians are set free, we would have no problem . . . no innocent lives should be taken whether belief or not.

Another limitation was the item scoring for religiosity, as this was very subjective. When presented with this item, participants were somewhat confused as to where (on the scale of 0–9) to score their degree of religiosity. For some simply attending a place of worship occasionally was not considered religious, where for others this was fairly religious.

There was also a possibility of selection bias as the data collection method used was random. Furthermore due to the limited sample size it is not possible to generalise too strongly from the results, consequently only a limited number of correlations on demographics were established. Also the study was restricted to three religious groups. However, patterns did emerge as significant predictors between ethnic groups, religiosity and in some cases gender. While the results should not be generalised too much, they do draw attention to some potentially important issues. It is important to try and understand motivations of individuals who tend to become involved in extremism. While some researchers may minimise the role of religion and religiosity, it appears from these findings that this is an area that needs to be reconsidered as an important factor in facilitating the process of sympathisers.

Finally, while the attitude-towards-terrorism scale effectively measured individual attitudes towards terrorism, the question remains, could it predict behaviour?

## Conclusions

Ultimately, if we are to understand the complex behaviours surrounding terrorism it is clear that we will have to study it using a multi-disciplinary approach. Psychological explanations can help provide a starting point for identifying risk factors and in preventing and overturning negative attitudes towards terrorism. Encouraging individuals to substitute negative feelings with positive actions may facilitate the healing process for those who have been affected by terrorism. McGowan (2002) encourages forensic professions to 'lead by example, as they are the role models for other people'. As psychologists our primary goal is to prevent terrorism from recurring. As the prospect of this seems further away in the future, we must challenge our efforts in interventions for victims of psychological trauma.

Silke (2001) suggests six steps, which may improve prevention and flexible resolutions:

- Recognise that terrorists are normal people.
- Focus on the causes of terrorism, and not just the actors.
- Address the genuine grievances of minorities and other disaffected groups.
- Ensure that the security forces are restrained and disciplined in their responses.
- Effective polices are based on good understanding and good awareness. This needs to be cultivated both in government circles and among the public.
- A national or European centre for the understanding of terrorism should be created. (p. 581)

Overall the results here evidenced impressive differences between religious, gender and ethnic groups in terms of acceptance towards terrorism. There appears to be clear division between Muslim groups as particularly sympathetic towards terrorism. Findings were fairly consistent with those reported in the US with minor differences observed in terms of the relationship between authoritarianism and individual liberties.

There is a clear need for a deeper understanding of the psychological impact of terrorism and it is crucial for the recognition of extremism amongst minority groups. Findings indicate that psychological factors alone are not sufficient in explaining the behaviours involved in terrorist acts. Other disciplines need to be explored. It is also important always to consider each group in its particular context recognising that its characteristics, dynamics and context will not be shared by every other group, and that the role these factors play cannot be ignored.

# References

Abdolian, L. F. and Takooshian, H. (2003). The USA Patriot Act: Civil liberties, the media, and public opinion. *Fordham Urban Law Journal*, 3, 1,429–1,453.

Ditzler, T. F. (2004). Malevolent minds: The teleology of terrorism. In Moghaddam, F. M. and Marsella, A. J. (Ed) *Understanding Terrorism: Psychosocial Roots, Consequences, and Interventions*. Washington, D.C.: American Psychological Association.

Hallet, B. (2004). Dishonest crimes, dishonest language: an argument about terrorism. In Moghaddam, F. M. and Marsella, A. J. (Ed) *Understanding Terrorism: Psychosocial Roots, Consequences, and Interventions*. Washington, D.C.: American Psychological Association.

McCauley, C. (2002). Psychological issues in understanding terrorism and the response to terrorism. In Stout, C. (Ed) *The Psychological of Terrorism*. Pennsylvania: Greenwood Publishing.

McGowan, A. J. (2002). While waiting for the other shoe. *Forensic Examiner*, March/April, 38–39.

Miller, L. (2002) Psychological interventions for terroristic trauma: Symptoms, syndromes, and treatment strategies. *Psychotherapy: Theory, Research, Practice and Training*, 39 (4), 283–296.

Pape, R. A. (2003). The strategic logic of suicide terrorism. *American Political Science Review*, 97 (3), 1–19.

Schuster, M. A., B. D. Stein, L. H. Jaycox, R. L., Collins, G. N Marshall, M. N., Elliot, A. J., Zhou, D. E., Kanhouse, J. L. Morrison, S. H. Berry. (2001) A national survey of stress reactions after the September 11, 2001, terrorist attacks. *New England Journal of Medicine*, Vol. 345, No. 20, 15 November, 1,507–1,512.

Silke, A. (2001). Terrorism. *The Psychologist*, 14, 580–581

Speckhard, A. and Ahkmedova, K. (2006). The making of a martyr: Chechen suicide terrorism, *Studies in Conflict and Terrorism*, 29/5, 429–492.

Takooshian, H. and Verdi, W. M. (1995). Assessment of attitudes towards terrorism. In Adler, L. L. and Denmark, F. L. (Ed), *Violence and the Prevention of Violence*. Westport CT: Praeger.

# 5  The evolutionary logic of terrorism

## Understanding why terrorism is an inevitable human strategy in conflict

*Rick O'Gorman*

## Introduction

When I was growing up, one of the strangest concepts I encountered was the notion of 'rules of war'. Here is an arena of human endeavour in which people, usually men, attempt to kill each other, yet apparently it has rules. Eventually, I realised that such rules had a history to their existence and a broader setting beyond the conflict. Countries, nations, even empires, had (and of course have) rules that relate to concepts such as honour and chivalry that structure how they approach conflict. Terrorists seem to not embrace such notions. They violate our understanding of rules of conflict, and by doing so violate our greater sense of morality. And no form of terrorist activity seems more indifferent to life and all we hold dear than suicide attacks. As such, we equate terrorists with other individuals who eschew moral rules, such as those who commit incest or cannibalism.

Despite this perception, and the seamlessly endless willingness of politicians and other leaders to regurgitate a view of terrorists as monsters or madmen, evidence suggests that terrorists are both rational and strategic in their choice of actions. Terrorism is a strategy that is embraced only when there is a significant asymmetry in a conflict (Pape 2003; Whittaker 2003). I will examine terrorism from an evolutionary perspective, focussing on understanding the inevitable likelihood of humans acting rationally in conflict – albeit not necessarily from a subjective perspective, exploring why we are repulsed by their methods, and why they are motivated to act using the means that they do, in particular the extreme act of suicide terrorism, outlining how suicide terrorism can be understood from an evolutionary perspective.

## Terrorism as a form of war

If we examine the conflict techniques of humans in societies more akin to those in which we have evolved for most of our species existence (usually termed 'hunter-gatherer' societies and chiefdoms) then we find that there are no consistent rules for violent conflict (Knauft 1991; Turney-High 1949; Wrangham and Peterson 1996). Indeed, if there is a single thread, it is that stacking the odds in your own favour is paramount. Commonly, for example, aggressors will ambush opponents, often with several attackers against one victim (Wrangham and Peterson 1996). Interestingly, we can see similar intent in one of our closest biological relatives, the chimpanzee (Goodall 1986: 490–491):

> A patrol is typified by cautious, silent travel during which the members of the party tend to move in a compact group. There are many pauses as the chimpanzees gaze around and listen. Sometimes they climb tall trees . . . gazing out over the 'unsafe' area of a neighbouring community . . . [p]erhaps the most striking aspect of patrolling behavior is the silence of those taking part.

Usually when such patrols encounter a solitary stranger chimp, they pursue the individual, cornering him or her, and then cooperatively attacking. Blows rain down, bites are inflicted. The loss of a hand or foot is possible, in the case of male victims genitalia are often bitten off, and death is a not infrequent outcome (Wrangham and Peterson 1996). A female with an infant is an equally acceptable target. Importantly, such patrols occur intentionally from the get-go. The resulting attacks potentially can achieve several outcomes, including scaring (terrorising) the rival group into avoiding the boundary, thus allowing the protagonist group to expand its range.

While the types of actions by chimps and hunter-gatherers are not identical to modern terrorism, they share a similar intent, along with modern guerrilla warfare, of ensuring that the advantage lies with the attacker before engaging in conflict. Given this similarity with terrorism, can we then consider terrorism to be an extension of war? This depends upon your definition of war, and of terrorism. Defining the latter is an exercise that has consumed some quantity of woodland without reaching a consensus (Whittaker 2003). No doubt that is because it is a nebulous phenomenon, to start with. It does not help that its meaning has changed, more than once, from its early use (Whittaker 2003). Nonetheless, it is clearly a form of conflict, albeit with psychological goals rather than just territorial ones, and this chapter follows the general definition already laid out for this collection in Chapter 1.

Despite the scorn often directed toward terrorist organisations, the rationality of terrorism is not hard to discern. Whittaker (2003) identifies conditions where terrorism can seem a viable option, while Pape (2003) makes a strong case for the rationality of suicide terrorism, once certain parameters are recognised; in particular, these are the limits of organisational size and resources available to terrorist organisations. As Pape points out:

> The vast majority of suicide terrorist attacks are not isolated or random acts by individual fanatics but, rather, occur in clusters as part of a larger campaign by an organized group to achieve a specific political goal. Groups using suicide terrorism consistently announce specific political goals and stop suicide attacks when those goals have been fully or partially achieved.

(p. 344)

Atran (2006) argues that leading terrorist organisations have chosen suicide attacks as part of a strategy that has *prima facie* logic to it, however repugnant we find it. Atran quotes Al-Qaeda's Al-Zawahiri as stating that '[t]he method of martyrdom operations [i]s the most successful way of inflicting damage against the opponent and the least costly to the mujahideen in casualties' (p. 137). Similarly, Sheikh Hamed Al-Betawi of Hamas told Atran in an interview that '[o]ur people do not own airplanes and tanks, only human bombs' (p. 137). In the absence of an ability to inflict substantial harm using conventional techniques, using non-conventional means to inflict harm that not only disrupts an enemy's routine operations (military or civilian) but also impacts psychological harm on the enemy becomes a viable strategy. Why then, is it so repugnant to us?

## Terrorism is about morality

It is worth reflecting on why terrorism is so publicly reviled in the West momentarily, because revulsion and disgust are powerful emotions that can affect how we think about something. Yet the best way to counteract anything is to first understand it well. Terrorism is reviled because it breaks a moral code of combat, along with various laws that are in place (Whittaker 2003). That code states that civilians should not be targeted. In addition, there is probably a legacy effect of disdain for guerrilla tactics, something that has a long history of being condescended toward. At some level, there is a sense that they should 'come out and fight like a man'.

Evidence that terrorists are not viewed as equally moral is reflected in the pervasive view, held even among some researchers, that terrorists are psychologically aberrant (Silke 2008). Yet every study that has seriously examined the psychological state of terrorists finds that they fall within the bounds of normality (Silke 2003, 2008; Horgan 2005). The preceding discussion establishing the rationality that lies behind terrorist actions makes clear that these are individuals who are far from deranged. Nonetheless, their actions in targeting civilians, worse still by surreptitious means that seem irrational, breeches a central tenet of civilised behaviour, thus violating a moral code. This violation reinforces the 'otherness' of terrorist groups, allowing for their infra-humanisation, viewing them as less than human (Boccato et al. 2008). Haidt (2007) shows that such violations of a moral code prompt emotional reactions, such as disgust, while Wheatley and Haidt (2005) also show that disgust can prompt moral indignation. Thus, while terrorists clearly conduct illegal acts, the particular revulsion that is often felt may also reflect that they have breeched a sacred code, they are disgusting, and even less than human. That they are willing in the cases of suicide terrorism to 'throw their life away' reinforces this division.

Yet it is not only the victimised societies that are repulsed by the terrorists. Terrorists themselves often speak of the revulsion they feel for their targets. Terrorist groups usually articulate how their sense of morality is violated by the target group. Many terrorist groups during the 1960s and 1970s decried the excesses of capitalism. Members of such groups may feel that there is a serious inequality in the social system, a perceived violation of a norm of fairness. There is also evidence to show that humans do not like to be dominated (van Vugt et al. 2008) and seek an egalitarian system (Boehm 1993, 1999). In a hierarchical system, a perceived lack of reciprocity may incubate resentment. All of this may contribute again to infra-humanisation.

Additionally, many terrorist groups feel that their worldview or culture is being oppressed by another culture (Atran 2006). Most obviously, this revolves around a perception on the part of many terrorist groups that their homeland has been seized and violated (Pape 2003; Sosis and Alcorta 2008). One's homeland is often of symbolic importance and may even be in some sense sacred (Sosis and Alcorta 2008), and its appropriation by others is for this reason also felt to violate moral values. It is only a short extension to then see that the terrorists' revulsion is not that psychologically different from the revulsion felt toward them. We can now begin to see what it is that motivates terrorism. Moral violations produce emotional responses, particularly disgust. Disgust plays an important psychological role. We know that disgust serves a biological purpose of prompting us to avoid items that can harm us, such as faeces, rotting bodies, or contaminated foods (Curtis et al. 2004), but recently disgust has been shown to play a role in responding to outgroups, as they represent a risk of disease (Faulkner et al. 2004; Navarrete and Fessler 2006), and by extension to immoral individuals (Schnall et al. 2008).

## Terrorism is about revenge

However, disgust is not sufficient, as disgust prompts actions such as avoidance of the triggering stimulus, resulting in the social case of ostracism of offenders. It does not necessarily prompt aggression. What we see in the case of many communities originating terrorists is that there is often, due to the perceived cultural oppression and violation, a state of humiliation vis-à-vis the provocateur (Atran 2006). This is most clearly evidenced by Al-Qaeda, currently the single most threatening terrorist group facing the West. It is not only that the US (in particular) is seen to have intruded into the Muslim homeland, but also that this represents to many Muslims an effort to humiliate Islam (Atran 2006) or even to exterminate Islam (Scheuer 2004). Thus, a second key emotion that we must consider is resentment and anger, which engages more significant motivations pertinent to terrorism. Specifically, it can motivate revenge (McCullough 2008).

The psychology behind revenge is interesting because it has not received as much attention as it almost certainly deserves. One of the key recognitions that emerges from studying revenge is that it rarely produces people who run amok, lashing out at innocent bystanders (McCullough 2008). Those seeking revenge often methodically target those whom they see as having transgressed. However, revenge is responsible for many acts that are considered heinous. For example, approximately 10 per cent of murders in regions such as Ireland, Australia, and Hong Kong have been found to be due to premeditated revenge (where there is evidence of planning; Dooley 2001; Carcach 1997; Gaylord and Galligher 1994), while up to 20 per cent of homicides are likely due to revenge if more impulsive acts are included (Daly and Wilson 1988; Kubrin and Weitzer 2003). Even 20 per cent is likely to be conservative, as McCullough (2008) points out: Many murders are motivated by sexual jealousy or sexual infidelity, some of which also have a revenge component to them and which account for a substantial number of homicides. Many school homicides may also be triggered by revenge (McCullough 2008): In a survey of the period 1994–1999, 20 per cent of the killers were previously bullied by their peers (Anderson et al. 2001). Tying revenge to terrorism, McCullough provides data, drawn from a Bureau of Alcohol, Tobacco and Firearms study in 1999 that found that 27 per cent of bombing incidents between 1993 and 1997 showed evidence of revenge being a motive.

Human societies at the hunter–gatherer and tribal levels are marked by blood feuds that are essentially unending cycles of revenge (Boehm 1986). Wilson and Daly (1985) found, in a survey of 60 cultures, that 95 per cent had evidence of blood feuds. Cultures in the Middle East may be particularly prone to such revenge-motivated acts. Nisbett and Cohen (1996) showed that people drawn from a culture (in their research, the southern US) that pre-eminently values honour, termed *cultures of honour*, are more likely to act aggressively if transgressed in comparison to non-honour cultures (such as the northern US). They showed in laboratory studies that this difference manifests itself cognitively, hormonally, and behaviourally. They proposed that settlers in southern US were drawn from cultures that were sedentary pastoralists rather than farmers. Animals can be more readily stolen than can land, so herders need to develop a reputation for not being crossed, producing a culture of honour. Black-Michaud (1975) documented the presence of a similar culture of honour in the Middle East. As Atran (2006, p. 139) notes, 'Especially in Arab societies . . . the culture of honor applies even to the humblest family as it once applied to the noblest families of the southern United States.' Osama bin Laden stated in his 'Letter to America' (bin Laden 2002), in which he outlines his grievances against the West, that one of the motivations for attacking the US is revenge. Such is the psychological view from which Al-Qaeda operates.

McCullough (2008) has identified three functions for revenge:

1) Deterring aggressors from aggressing again.
2) Deterring other potential aggressors.
3) Deterring others from free-riding on cooperative endeavours.

In the case of terrorism, it is easy enough to see that the first function of revenge has a role. Terrorist groups see their aggressors as having to be pushed back, counteracted, or deterred from some current policy. However, the language, and often the actions, of terrorists often seem to go beyond deterrence and move into something stronger – a moralistic reaction to violations of norms and codes. Their actions are designed both to deter current wrongs and to deter future transgressions: They seek to punish (Pape 2003). Such motivation can lead not only to terrorist acts, but even to suicide attacks (Schmid and Jongman 1988; Silke 2008).

## An evolutionary framework

Existing explanations for terrorism using an evolutionary framework tend to either propose self-beneficial reasons or kin-beneficial ones. Self-beneficial explanations of course can only apply to non-suicide attacks. Warfare has a long presence in our society (Bowles 2006, Keeley 1996) and may even have driven facets of our intergroup psychology (van Vugt et al. 2007). Given that success in conflict has been essential, it is no surprise that those who contribute disproportionately are rewarded and fêted. Silke (2008) notes that terrorist groups and their members are often viewed as being courageous and honourable. Prestige (Henrich and Gil-White 1999), status and personal benefits (Silke 2008) is one route by which apparent altruism can actually gain such benefits to pay evolutionarily, allowing, on average over evolutionary timeframes, such traits to occur. These benefits in turn portray an image of excitement and risk-taking that is attractive to young males (Wilson and Daly 1985), driven possibly by trying to establish themselves within the adult population (Thayer and Hudson 2009), or as a means to garner the attention of the opposite sex (Wilson and Daly 1985). It has also been suggested that young single Islamic males may particularly be tempted to engage in terrorism because of the limited availability of brides (due to high cost of marriage and shortage due to polygamy), prompting both an attraction to risky behaviour, a feeling of lack of worth (at being unmarried) and the potential rewards awaiting them in heaven (Thayer and Hudson 2009).

However, often terrorists do not gain obvious advantages or benefits, and this is clear to them in advance. As Silke (2008) notes, '[h]ardship and suffering are seen as inseparable aspects of life as a terrorist' (p. 115–116). Furthermore, it is hard to justify, in the case of suicide terrorists, individuals sacrificing their lives for transient prestige. Nor do these theories explain the strong emotions of disgust and the desire for revenge that are related to terrorism. It is worth noting that, from an evolutionary perspective, carrying out terrorist acts offers potential benefits to the group or society on whose behalf the terrorist acts (at least, this is how the terrorists see it). Whittaker (2003) explicitly calls terrorists altruists (p. 9). But such acts carry with it risks to individuals that translate into evolutionary costs – terrorist acts have consequences that likely reduce survival and thus reproduction. We know from evolutionary theory that individuals should not want to engage in behaviours that reduce their fitness when it is to the benefit of others in the group (Williams 1966). Such acts are termed *altruistic* and we expect that humans, like any other form of life, will not engage in unconditional altruism (Wilson et al. 2008).

However, there are conditions under which altruism can evolve, which point to situations when individuals will be likely to act in a non-selfish manner (Wilson and Wilson 2007). The primary account for explaining the evolution of altruism is through inclusive fitness (Hamilton 1964), popularised by Dawkins as the *selfish gene* perspective (Dawkins 1976). Essentially, a genetic trait can evolve in a population – even if it is costly for an individual to possess that trait – provided the trait prompts the holder to bestow benefits upon others who are also likely to have the trait. This formulation has also been termed *kin selection* (Maynard-Smith 1964), as kin are most reliably going to share a trait, though it is an imperfect equivalence as will become clear momentarily.

Kin selection has been suggested by some as explaining suicide terrorists (Sosis and Alcorta 2008) and for altruism as found in human behaviour, generally (Alexander 1987). In both cases, the central tenet is that humans will act to benefit kin, and suicide terrorism may achieve this both in a narrow sense (by the family gaining in prestige or material benefits) and broadly, in that the suicidal act may strengthen the terrorist's community vis-à-vis the opposition. Certainly, in some communities and cases, suicide terrorism carries a positive view from within a community, but this is certainly not ubiquitous. And the loss of a productive family member may be more costly to offset than is achieved, even when a terrorist group compensates a family.

An alternative method to explain altruism, *group selection*, is also one that is dogged by controversy, having been rejected in the 1960s but having slowly been rehabilitated (Wilson and Wilson 2007). A framework that incorporates both individual and group selection, termed *multilevel selection* (Sober and Wilson 1998) provides a sound theoretical basis to understand altruism while inter-relating it with inclusive fitness.

Essentially, multilevel selection states that selection can happen at different levels – between genes, between individuals, between groups. Moreover, selection can occur simultaneously at multiple levels. The outcome depends on the overall net direction of the different selective pressures. In the case of altruism, within a group it will pay to be selfish (because altruism is costly, and mechanisms to guard altruism are costly) but groups with more altruists, or a greater overall altruistic tendency, will out-perform more selfish groups. Kin selection can be understood within this framework as a means by which a number of altruists could co-occur in a group. Thus, the framework is a different way to capture the same details as inclusive fitness (the two are mathematically equivalent; Hamilton 1975; Wilson and Wilson 2007).

## Costly punishment

So how does this relate to terrorism? Well, earlier I noted that some acts of terrorism are motivated by revenge and a desire to punish. Evolutionarily, a willingness to act on these emotions is altruistic: The act of punishing deviants (defectors) benefits the greater society but imposes a cost on those undertaking the risky behaviour. This pattern of behaviour has been termed by some as *strong reciprocity* (Gintis 2000), a willingness to act pro-socially and to punish those who do not act pro-socially. Unfortunately, because this concept combines two separate behaviours, I prefer to separate the behaviours involved and will refer to the punishment component as *costly punishment*.

Costly punishment has been demonstrated in numerous laboratory and field studies. Consistently, individuals will incur a cost to punish others who have failed to contribute appropriately to a public good (Gintis 2008). This is usually demonstrated in a structured interaction termed a *public goods game* in which participants are allocated a certain amount of resources, which they can either keep, or invest. If they invest the resource (or part thereof), the total invested by all the participants is increased some limited amount and then divided equally. The key aspect to this is that the increase is such that an individual never can earn back from their own investment alone as much as they put in. For example, participants might be allocated 20 points (which converts later to money). They can invest as much of this as they wish into the common pool, and the pool is then doubled (in many versions, the increase is only 60 per cent). Thus, an initial investment of 20 points can only yield back 10 points to the investor, because it is doubled and then shared equally. The gains are made when others make investments; the rational (and tempting) investment for oneself is always to invest nothing. Surprisingly, participants fairly consistently invest approximately half their allocation. However, these games are usually played in a series of rounds, and if someone does not contribute as altruistically in one round, others will be inclined to also not do so on the next round. And this is what we see in the games: contributions rapidly fall over rounds from the initial levels to very little.

The innovation that was introduced to these games (Fehr and Gächter 2002) was to allow participants, after the pay-off stage, to make deductions to other players at a cost to the punisher. If the cost ratio of punishing to imposed punishment is about 1:3 or stronger (Yamagishi 1986), participants will indeed take up the opportunity to punish, with the beneficial outcome that investments remain relatively high and profits are also higher. The system, despite seeming punitive, is preferred to no-punishment versions when players get to see both in action (Gürerk et al. 2006). Of course, there are individual differences in willingness to punish, as you might expect for an altruistic act (Wilson 1994), but that goes to the heart of this issue's relevance to terrorism. Importantly, for such a policing trait to evolve, group selection must have played a role in humanity's evolution (O'Gorman et al. 2008).

I should note at this point that not all researchers view this behaviour as worthy of being considered altruistic (Burnham and Johnson 2005; Hagen and Hammerstein 2006). There are a number of objections, but two primary ones, one methodological and one theoretical. The first one (methodological) is that, although these games are played anonymously, in practice this is not achieved. Research has shown, for example, that a cue as simple as seeing eyes in the background can increase altruistic behaviour in such games (Haley and Fessler 2005). While there is no doubting this phenomenon, it does not get us away from the willingness of humans to incur costs to punish others. It has even been shown to occur when a participant knows they are the only one able to make punishments, and thus justifiably able to claim that they would be shouldering the cost alone (O'Gorman, Henrich and van Vugt 2009). The second (theoretical) objection rests on the notion that we evolved in groups of highly interrelated individuals (essentially extended kin) and are not adapted to operating in an environment full of non-relatives (Burnham and Johnson 2005; Hagen and Hammerstein 2006). This remains a contentious debate.

Describing terrorists as evolutionary altruists may seem incongruous to say the least, but is clear when viewed from an objective perspective. In a sense, it is not that different from a soldier who throws himself on a grenade to save comrades (although morally not necessarily equivalent). It may be then that at least some acts of terrorism and particularly suicide terrorism, may be due to a psychological mechanism evolved to punish perceived wrongdoers. In most communities, as Haidt (2007) points out, '[a] moral community has a set of shared norms about how members ought to behave, combined with means for imposing costs on violators and/or channelling benefits to cooperators'. When a community or group find that they do not have their normal mechanisms to control what they perceive as wrongdoing, they fall back on other methods, but the desired outcome remains the same: to impose a severe penalty on the transgressors.

Why is it then that we do not see suicide terrorism more widely used? There are probably three key factors here. The first is the availability of recruits. Many terrorist groups such as ETA are relatively small organisations in terms of actual active duty members and so members are needed to carry out more than one action. If recruits are sufficiently easy to come by, then suicide acts may become viable. The second factor is the ability to strike at the enemy. If the ability to plant a bomb is restricted such that it has to be walked in and detonated immediately, then suicide tactics become more necessary. Finally, the cultural worldview, incorporating religious and other beliefs, may make the option of suicide attacks more or less appropriate. The fact that Islamic terrorist groups have become one of the prime users of suicide tactics may thus not be a coincidence. Islam requires a defensive jihad against those who attack Islam (Scheuer 2004; Silke 2008), while having at least some provisioning for militaristic martyrdom within the religion (Atran 2006; McCullough 2008; Sosis and Alcorta 2008). In addition, Bushman et al. (2007) present data that show that religion can exacerbate revenge motivations. The counter-example of suicide attacks as a strategy for the Marxist-oriented LTTE (Liberation Tigers of Tamil Eelam) might suggest that a religious worldview is not be essential; however Atran (2006) notes that LTTE suicide attack recruits may be coerced to follow through due to threatened reprisals against their families (Yoganathan 2004).

What then are the requirements for altruists to step forward to the degree that they are willing to sacrifice their lives? Firstly, the wrong or wrongs incurred must be sufficient to induce a very strong level of anger in a sufficient number of individuals. There are always individuals who are capable of becoming extremely angry in the face of a perceived transgression, but suicide terrorists must have a deep, steady anger that does not just explode spontaneously. The threat to the in-group must be perceived as extremely threatening, such that sacrificing your own life is worthwhile. In addition, research shows that people become more supportive of suicide terrorism, and more positively inclined to undertake such an act, when their mortality is made salient (Pyszczynski et al. 2006). Furthermore, this same stimulus prompts individuals to prefer a worldview that sees their culture as in a heroic struggle against evil (Pyszczynski et al. 2006), something common to terrorist groups (Sosis and Alcorta 2008). Furthering such a perception with ill-chosen words seems unwise to say the least. As noted earlier, a severe imbalance in power between the perceived aggressor and the terrorists' own group may also motivate: Humans dislike dominant individuals and appear to have evolved social control mechanisms to prevent individuals rising to dominance (Boehm 1999), including ostracism or assassination (Boehm 1985, 1993). There is no reason to think that group inequalities might not trigger the same response.

## The cure?

As Atran (2006) notes, 'it must be understood that terrorist attacks will not be prevented by trying to profile terrorists. They are not sufficiently different from everyone else' (p. 141). Even in light of the identified characteristics of suicide terrorists, profiling seems challenging. Simply put, not every strongly pro-social individual turns to terrorism – far from it. Individuals who are potential recruits must also harbour strong feelings of transgression, a particular view of the target group that allows for killing them arbitrarily, and a perceived greater need for them to act than to remain alive for the benefit of those around them. Nonetheless, we can begin to recognise how we might intervene to choke off the fuels that feed the desires for terrorist acts. Knowing that terrorist recruits, especially those for suicide attacks, are likely to be altruistically minded yet also moralistic, suggests that offering alternative channels for their motivations that can still address their desires for retribution may help alleviate the supply. As Atran notes (p. 141):

> What is needed is a subtle infiltration of opportunities to create chat rooms, as well as physical support groups, which advance causes that can play to ... sentiments but that are not destructive ... the aim should be to show how deeply held sacred values can be channeled into less-belligerent paths.

Alternative solutions are perhaps more challenging, in that they require either avoiding the transgressions in the first place, or moderating the desire for revenge. McCullough (2008) identifies the means by which forgiveness can be sought and obtained. They begin with signals to communicate a commitment to reconciliation. These signals need to be substantive to be convincing. According to Long and Brecke (2003), they should be beyond the normal type of signal, unconditional and costly for the offerer. Not surprisingly, such a process works best when the initiator is the stronger of the two sides. As McCullough notes, this is no trivial situation, because the stronger side has an incentive to not seek conciliation, having more to lose. That the stronger side may not perceive itself to have contributed to the problem to begin with may make offering unconditional compromises even more challenging.

Nevertheless, in a conflict with little sign of ending, or occurring with great cost to both sides, magnanimity is inevitably required to avoid the alternative method of resolving such disputes.

## Conclusion

An evolutionary approach to terrorism offers a number of contributions. Firstly, it offers us a deeper means to understand the psychological motivations for terrorist acts. Building on a growing recognition that terrorists are far from madmen and lunatics, evolution shows us that motivations to terrorism can actually be evolutionarily rational, even if not always beneficial for individuals. Moreover, it helps to point us in new directions to deepen our understanding of what is likely to trigger these motivations, which in turn can offer us ways to both undermine the ability of terrorist groups to recruit, and to determine means to resolve existing conflicts.

## References

Alexander, R. D. (1987). *The Evolution of Moral Systems.* New York, Aldine De Gruyter.

Anderson, M., Kaufman, J., Simon, T. R. et al. (2001). School-associated violent deaths in the United States, 1994–1999. *Journal of the American Medical Association* 286, 2,695–2,702.

Atran, S. (2006). The moral logic and growth of suicide terrorism. *Washington Quarterly* 29, 127–147.

Bin Laden, O. (2002). *Letter to America.* URL (accessed 26 June 2009): http://www.guardian.co.uk/world/2002/nov/24/theobserver.

Black-Michaud, J. (1975). *Cohesive Force: Feud in the Mediterranean and the Middle East.* Oxford, UK, Basil Blackwell.

Boccato, G., Capozza, D., Falvo, R. and Durante, F. (2008). The missing link: Ingroup, outgroup and the human species. *Social Cognition* 26, 224–234.

Boehm, C. (1985). Execution within the clan as an extreme form of ostracism. *Social Science Information* 24, 309–321.

Boehm, C. (1986). *Blood Revenge: The enactment and management of conflict in Montenegro and other tribal societies.* Philadelphia, University of Pennsylvania Press.

Boehm, C. (1993). Egalitarian society and reverse dominance hierarchy. *Current Anthropology* 34, 227–254.

Boehm, C. (1999). *Hierarchy in the forest.* Cambridge, MA, Harvard University Press.

Bowles, S. (2006). Group competition, reproductive levelling, and the evolution of human altruism. *Science* 314, 1,569–1,572.

Burnham, T. C. and Johnson, D. D. P. (2005). The biological and evolutionary logic of human cooperation. *Analyse & Kritik* 27, 113–135.

Bushman, B. J., Ridge, R. D., Das, E., Key, C. W., and Busath, G. M. (2007). When God sanctions killing: Effect of scriptural violence on aggression. *Psychological Science* 18, 204–207.

Carcach, C. (1997). *Youth as Victims and Offenders of Homicide* (No. 73). Canberra: Australian Institute of Criminology.

Curtis, V., Aunger, R. and Rabie, T. (2004). Evidence that disgust evolved to protect from risk of disease. *Proceedings of the Royal Society of London: B 271 Supplemental* 4: S131–133.

Daly, M. and Wilson, M. (1988). *Homicide.* Hawthorne, NY, Aldine De Gruyter.

Dawkins, R. (1976). *The Selfish Gene*. New York: Oxford University Press.

Dooley, E. (2001). *Homicide in Ireland 1992–1996* (No. 9435). Dublin: Government of Ireland.

Faulkner, J., Schaller, M., Park, J. H. and Duncan, L. A. (2004). Evolved disease-avoidance mechanisms and contemporary xenophobic attitudes. Group *Processes & Intergroup Relations* 7, 333–353.

Fehr, E. and Gächter, S. (2002). Altruistic punishment in humans. *Nature* 415, 137–140.

Gaylord, M. S., and Galligher, J. F. (1994). Death penalty politics and symbolic law in Hong Kong. *International Journal of the Sociology of Law* 22, 19–37.

Gintis, H. (2000). Strong reciprocity and human sociality. *Journal of Theoretical Biology* 206, 169–179.

Gintis, H. (2008). Punishment and cooperation. *Science* 319, 1,345–1,346.

Goodall, J. (1986). *The Chimpanzees of Gombe: Patterns of Behavior*. Cambridge, MA, Belknap Press of Harvard University Press.

Gürerk, Ö., Irlenbusch, B., and Rochenbach, B. (2006). The competitive advantage of sanctioning institutions. *Science* 312, 108–111.

Hagen, E. H. and Hammerstein, P. (2006). Game theory and human evolution: A critique of some recent interpretations of experimental games. *Theoretical Population Biology* 69, 339–348.

Haidt, J. (2007). The new synthesis in moral psychology. *Science* 316, 998–1002.

Haley, K. J. and Fessler, D. M. T. (2005). Nobody's watching? Subtle cues affect generosity in an anonymous economic game. *Evolution and Human Behavior* 26, 245–256.

Hamilton, W. D. (1964). Genetical evolution of social behavior. *Journal of Theorical Biology* 7, 1–52.

Henrich, J., and Gil-White, F. J. (2001). The evolution of prestige: freely conferred deference as a mechanism for enhancing the benefits of cultural transmission. *Evolution and Human Behavior* 22, 165–196.

Horgan, J. (2005). *The Psychology of Terrorism*. London: Routledge.

Keeley, L. (1996). *War before Civilization*. New York: Oxford University Press.

Knauft, B. M. (1991). Violence and sociality in human evolution. *Current Anthropology* 32, 31–428.

Kubrin, C. E., and Weitzer, R. (2003). Retaliatory homicide: Concentrated disadvantage and neighborhood culture. *Social Problems* 50, 157–180.

Long, W. J. and Brecke, P. (2003). *War and Reconciliation: Reason and emotion in conflict resolution*. Cambridge, MA, MIT Press.

Maynard Smith, J. (1964). Group selection and kin selection. *Nature* 201, 1,145–1, 146.

McCullough, M. (2008). *Beyond Revenge: The Evolution of the Forgiveness Instinct*. San Francisco: Jossey-Bass.

Navarrete, C. D., and Fessler, D. M. T. (2006). Disease avoidance and ethnocentrism: the effects of disease vulnerability and disgust sensitivity on intergroup attitudes. *Evolution and Human Behavior* 27, 270–282.

Nisbett, R. E., and Cohen, D. (1996). *Culture of Honor: The Psychology of Violence in the South*. Boulder, CO, Westview.

O'Gorman, R., Henrich, J., and van Vugt, M. (2009). Constraining free-riding in public goods games: Designated solitary punishers can sustain human cooperation. *Proceedings of the Royal Society* B 276, 323–329.

O'Gorman, R., Sheldon, K., and Wilson, D. S. (2008). For the good of the group? Exploring group-level evolutionary adaptations using Multilevel Selection Theory. *Group Dynamics: Theory, Research, and Practice* 12, 17–26.

Pape, R. A. (2003). The strategic logic of suicide terrorism. *American Political Science Review* 97, 343–361.

Pyszczynski, T., Abdollahi, A., Solomon, S., Greenberg, J., Cohen, F. and Weise, D. (2006). Mortality salience, martyrdom, and military might: The great Satan versus the axis of evil. *Personality and Social Psychology Bulletin* 32, 525–537.

Scheuer, M. (2004). *Imperial hubris: Why the West is losing the War on Terror.* Washington DC, Brassey's.

Schmid, A. and Jongman, A. (1988). *Political Terrorism* (2nd ed.). Oxford, North-Holland.

Schnall, S., Haidt, J., Clore, G. and Jordan, A. (2008). Disgust as embodied moral judgment. *Personality and Social Psychology Bulletin* 34, 1,096–1,109.

Silke, A. (2003). Becoming a terrorist. In A. Silke (ed.) *Terrorists, Victims and Society: Psychological perspectives on terrorism and its consequences*, 29–53. Chichester, Wiley.

Silke, A. (2008). Holy warriors: Exploring the psychological processes of jihadi radicalization. *European Journal of Criminology* 5, 99–123.

Sober, E., and Wilson, D. S. (1998). *Unto Others: the Evolution and Psychology of Unselfish Behavior.* Cambridge, MA, Harvard University Press.

Sosis, R., and Alcorta, C. (2008). Militants and martyrs: evolutionary perspectives on religion and terrorism. In R. Sagarin and T. Taylor (eds.) *Natural Security: A Darwinian Approach to a Dangerous World*, 105–124. Berkeley, University of California Press.

Thayer, B. A. and Hudson, V. (2009). *Suicide Terrorism in the Islamic Context: Insights from the life sciences on the importance of sex and marriage markets.* Unpublished manuscript.

Turney-High, H. H. (1949). *Primitive War: Its practice and concepts.* Columbia, SC, University of South Carolina Press.

van Vugt, M., De Cremer, D., and Janssen, D. P. (2007). Gender differences in cooperation and competition: The male-warrior hypothesis. *Psychological Science* 18, 19–23.

van Vugt, M., Johnson, D. D. P., Kaiser, R. B., and O'Gorman, R. (2008). Evolution and the social psychology of leadership: The mismatch hypothesis. In C. L. Hoyt, G. R. Goethals, and D. R. Forsyth (eds.) *Leadership at the Crossroads: Psychology and leadership* (Vol. 1), 262–282. Westport, CT, Praeger.

Wheatley, T., and Haidt, J. (2005). Hypnotically induced disgust makes moral judgments more severe. *Psychological Science* 16, 780–784.

Whittaker, D. J. (2003). *The Terrorism Reader* (2nd ed.). London, Routledge.

Williams, G. C. (1966). *Adaptation and Natural Selection: A Critique of Some Current Evolutionary Thought.* Princeton, NJ, Princeton University Press.

Wilson, D. S. (1994). Adaptive genetic variation and human evolutionary psychology. *Ethology and Sociobiology* 15, 219–235..

Wilson, D. S. and Wilson, E. O. (2007). Rethinking the theoretical foundation of sociobiology. *Quarterly Review of Biology* 82, 327–348.

Wilson, D. S., van Vugt, M. and O'Gorman, R. (2008). Multilevel selection and major evolutionary transitions: Implications for psychological science. *Current Directions in Psychological Science* 17, 6–9.

Wilson, M., and Daly, M. (1985). Competitiveness, risk-taking and violence: the young male syndrome. *Ethology and Sociobiology* 6, 59.

Wrangham, R., and Peterson, D. (1996). *Demonic Males: Apes and the Origins of Human Violence*. London, Bloomsbury.

Yamagishi, T. (1986), The provision of a sanctioning system as a public good. *Journal of Personality and Social Psychology* 51, 110–116.

Yoganathan, S. 1. (2004). *Rise and Decline of Suicide Terrorism in Sri Lanka*. Paper presented to the NATO Advanced Workshop, Lisbon.

# 6 The internet and terrorism

## Pathways towards terrorism and counter-terrorism

*Lorraine Bowman-Grieve*

## Introduction

The speed at which terrorist and extremist groups have embraced the possibilities offered by the Internet has been reflected in the sheer number of websites espousing support for various terrorist and extremist groups including white supremacists and radical Islamic militants, among many others. Levin (2002) partially explains the growth of Internet use by extremists and terrorists with reference to its economical and 'far reaching' nature. The speed of Internet acquisition may also be attributed to its inherent nature; it is easy to access with a chaotic structure that facilitates anonymity, and an international character that affords an easy and effective arena for action (Tsafti and Weimann 2002). While violence remains essential to the terrorist movement for the psychological impact of terrorism, the Internet provides a safe, easy and cheap means of communicating, disseminating propaganda, gathering intelligence, promoting support, demonising the enemy and raising funds.

Historically the Internet has been associated with military, scientific and academic institutions and communities, providing a particular historical and cultural context for online communication and membership. An important implication of this is that the Internet can be used to explore 'political action and affiliation online' (Kendall 1999, p. 63). 'Terrorist use of the Internet' provides a new solution to the old problem of communication. Where once terrorist movements were reliant on 'traditional' forms of media to bring their 'cause' to the public, the Internet now facilitates a broad spectrum of communication possibilities, ranging from websites to virtual communities. While websites serve the important function of providing a link between movement and supporter, it is the virtual community that allows for the construction and maintenance of political and ideological discourses in support of that movement, providing the 'public space' supporters crave (Arendt 1990). Virtual communities can be likened to 'communities of practice' (Lave 1988; Wenger 1998), informal social learning environments that facilitate increasing commitment of group members to movements, including those movements that justify the use of terrorism and political violence to achieve their goals (Hundeide 2003).

Virtual communities of practice are virtual spaces used effectively by members who interact in a meaningful community driven way. Regular community members pride themselves on their commitment to the community and the activities they pursue, for example communicating with others, disseminating their truth, creating a place where others can come to learn, and offering validation to others on their ideological beliefs. Discourses created within these communities provide validation, justifying and legitimising the use of terrorism. These discourses are central to the ways that the Internet can contribute to the facilitation of involvement either online (within the virtual community) or offline (in a potentially more active capacity). Involvement within a virtual community and potential involvement in offline activities thus presents itself as a potential pathway toward individual radicalisation. For the purpose of this chapter, 'radicalisation' is defined as an end stage on a continuum that spans from lower level support to the involvement or willingness to be directly involved in violent terrorist activities.

A crucial issue here is whether the Internet can be considered a catalyst for action by terrorists and their supporters. To try to understand this issue it is useful to begin by asking some key questions relevant to this; why do terrorist movements and their supporters use the Internet, i.e. what functions does it serve and what pathways toward involvement are facilitated?

## Why do terrorist movements and their supporters use the internet?

Much has been written on terrorist use the Internet in relation to the function of websites (see for example Whine 1998, 1999, 2000; Tsafti and Weimann 2002; Conway 2003; Weimann 2006a, 2000b). It is widely agreed that terrorist use of the Internet incorporates, but is not limited to, resource acquisition, intelligence gathering, propaganda (including auto-propaganda), support and recruitment. While the physical membership of core activists of most terrorist movements is kept to a minimum both because of the psychological premium associated with restricted membership and for security reasons, there is no practical limit to the numbers of supporters sought by any terrorist movement. The Internet can be used as a catalyst for fostering support and recruitment, the different levels of involvement that websites and online communities make available to the supporter facilitate involvement at various levels; a supporter can send a donation, buy merchandise, support prisoners, chat online, become more active and distribute propaganda/fliers, or attend marches/demonstrations. Both online research and a consideration of relevant psychological literature and theory can further inform us about this process of potential radicalisation.

## Resource acquisition

Many websites that support a terrorist movement link directly to online shopping facilities. Rather than serving as an income-generator that is of any real significance to the movement, in reality the symbolic nature of the products represent the true value of the commodities being offered. For example, via a right wing extremist online shop, browsers can purchase any of the following: music CDs (including entire collections of the music of famous Right Wing extremist music groups, such as Hammerskins), DVDs, flags, badges, pins, baseball caps, calendars, key rings, shirts, posters, and an extensive range of movement literature, including Hitler's *Mein Kampf*, MacDonald's *Turner Diaries* and Duke's *My Awakening* (see for example websites http://www.resistance.com/catalog and http://www.aryanwear. com/). The selling of such materials via websites is not limited to Right Wing Extremist sites, although these may be some of the most prolific.

Many websites also provide visitors with an option to directly donate funds, for example on opening the www.Kahane.org website,[1] a pop-up invites you to donate funds directly to the movement. Others provide addresses where donations can be sent, for example National Alliance at www.natvan.com. One of the more interesting examples of resource acquisition can be found on the Ulster Loyalist Information Services website,[2] the virtual home of the Loyalist Volunteer Force an extreme Loyalist faction based in Protestant areas of Portadown and Belfast. This movement quickly realised that not all its supporters 'feel comfortable in giving monetary donations', but encourages donations of unwanted items:

> *Want to help out LVPW, but don't feel comfortable* (sic) *with making monetary donations? You can also help by donating various items. Some of these items will be used for obvious uses, others will be packaged as Christmas gifts for less fortunate families of imprisoned volunteers or widows. Please review the list below, if you have any of the items and would like to donate them, please contact us at Projects.*
>
> • **Bullet Proof Vests** – *Any size, new or used. These can be found used at reasonable prices on eBay*
> • **Computers** *(Pentium II or newer), software of use, computer games*
> • *Items that would make nice **Christmas gifts** for children of all ages.*
> • *You may also make a monetary donation, via **PayPal** by following the link below.*

The purchase of items, often culturally significant to the movement, is important to a supporter providing a link to the organisation and its history, functioning not only as a means of donating some small amount to the organisation, but also serving to forge a tangible link between the supporter and the organisation. Donating money or goods to a movement may be seen as indicative of a belief that the goals of the movement are legitimate and that their means of achieving these goals, even through the use of violence and terrorism, are acceptable. This may be a first step on the pathway toward involvement. As one Right Wing extremist within the virtual community of Stormfront (www.stormfront.com) comments:

> I was on the internet one night looking for a song on some file sharing program. I came across one called 'White Power' by a band called Skrewdriver. I hated negroes, spics, gays, etc. and decided to download it. The second Ian Stuart shouted out 'White Power 1,2,3,4' I was HOOKED.

## Intelligence gathering

The Internet is also an unsurpassable tool for information gathering. This does not automatically bring us into the realm of how the Internet can be used to gather information, using tools such as Google Earth or The Anarchists Cookbook, to cause destruction to critical infrastructures (although this is of course possible), but can also be considered from another perspective. The Internet is by now well known as being a fast and efficient way to gather information on people, places and groups all over the world. As such, terrorist organisations can avail of the opportunity to keep well informed on up-to-the-minute news on how they are perceived by the mass media, as well as providing the group with information on their perceived enemies and allies. The Internet may also be a way for ideologically similar groups to forge alliances across international borders which are inconsequential online. 'Webrings' is an important feature that supports this, facilitating the networking of websites that are used to express similar views, perspectives and ideologies. They allow the user to work more efficiently through related sites and can serve to mark implicit affiliations between groups. Evidence for this can be found through an examination of the links between websites, for example current online links between the Ulster Volunteer Force and the Neo-Nazi group Combat 18, and online links between Aryan Unity and the British People's Party. Indeed, cyber-space is one place that serves as an ideal ground for contagion effects. Terrorist movements use websites to catalogue their successful operations. This is useful to boost member morale and can also serve as an effective tool to advertise successful violent campaigns. The Hizbollah websites for example, (www.hizbollah.org and www.almashriq.hiof.no/lebanon) provide coverage of successful operations as feature items.

## Propaganda

> Propaganda is an art requiring special talent. It is not mechanical, scientific work. Influencing attitudes requires experience, area knowledge, and instinctive judgement of what is the best argument for the audience.
>
> Bogart (1976, pp. 195–196)

A visit to any website proclaiming support for the actions of a terrorist movement will at once reveal its most immediate purpose, propaganda. Terrorist website homepages demonstrate that the Internet can serve as a valuable tool to disseminate information about the objectives, strategies, tactics and other features of the group to influence the public's perception of them, their ideology and goals. The instrumental nature of terrorist violence serves to perform a variety of functions that go some way towards explaining the attractiveness of the strategy of terrorism for isolated, marginalised political groups, and an important primary function is that of communication. For most sub-state terror groups, their tactics are predicated on attempting to overthrow or effectively destabilise a political authority. Winning hearts and minds is central to this, and terrorists must justify and legitimate their activity with facts. Alerting the world to the grievances of a particular movement, as well as documenting the history of injustices suffered (real or imagined) by a particular minority (depending on the kind of terror group) is of primary importance and is central to any attempt to gain support. The message of the terrorist organisation must be credible and believed by the user if it is ever to progress to some sort of support that may be measurable and tangible.

A pertinent example of this comes from the Hizbullah website (www.almasqriq. hiof.no/lebanon) which includes detailed statements outlining the ideology of the group and dealing with the perception of Hizbullah in the West as a terrorist organ-isation. The quotation below, for example, highlights the progression of the move-ment from 'turbulent' times of violence to its re-emergence as a 'pivotal force' in the Middle Eastern political arena. While recognising that the violent activities against Israel have been perceived as terrorism and thus condemned, it is defended as a 'natural human reaction' to the violence perpetrated by the Israeli occupy-ing forces. This statement highlights the importance of justifications bound in rhetoric of righteousness and rationality. Such justifications facilitate the call for violence and promote the legitimacy of the movement and the goals they seek to achieve.

> The prevalent perception of Hizbullah in the 'west' is of a militant, armed terrorist organization bent on abduction and murder. While the initial years of its emergence as a political movement in Lebanon were turbulent and con-trovertial (sic), The Party of God has matured to become an important and pivotal force in Middle East politics in general and Lebanese society in par-ticular. Hizbullah does not believe it is right for some people in the world to view the Zionist Jewish occupation as accepted violence and terrorism, while they condemn the counter-violence, which is a natural human reaction to the Zionist violence and terrorism.

On a related note, propaganda on websites can be used to actively promote violent activity against specific targets. For example, a website affiliated with the Animal Liberation Front, No Compromise (www.nocompromise.org), which defines itself as 'the militant, direct action news source of animal liberationists and their sup-porters' includes within its gallery archive, photographs of Federal Agents. The images included in this part of the site 'are photos of federal government offi-cials who have nothing better to do with their time than harass activists'. This website also provides access to a 'Directory of Abusers', which lists laboratories conducting animal testing including their addresses and the home addresses and telephone numbers of the directors and managers of these laboratories. Finding this type of listing on a website is especially interesting, particularly in terms of its similarity to what are known as the 'Nuremberg Files', a listing of abortion doc-tors in the US which was distributed online by anti-abortion extremists. Although the 'Nuremberg Files' were claimed not to be a death list, following its presence online a number of assassination attempts were made on abortion doctors, suc-cessful in the case of Dr. Selpian. Whilst court proceedings followed to ensure the removal of this list from the Internet, alternate versions of it can still be found on particularly extreme anti-abortion websites.

Websites are undoubtedly useful to terrorist movements in the orchestration of their propaganda campaigns. However, once a website of interest has been found by a supporter its role is limited and the role of the supporter remains relatively passive, limited to downloading information, and perhaps donating funds. This is where virtual communities in support of terrorist movements constitute a significant change in the role of the online supporter. Through involvement in a virtual community the online supporter can move from the passive onlooker toward a potentially more active role. This progression is certainly interesting from a psychological perspective, particularly in terms of how online activities might inform our understanding of processes of involvement and pathways toward radicalisation in the offline world.

## Facilitating involvement: considering virtual communities of terrorist support

The term virtual community is used here as an 'anchor', an already formulated notion of shared online space and communicative interaction between users. Community in cyberspace can be perceived in the same ways as communities in the physical world; they can be characterised by regular user interaction, most often with a sense of status associated with long-term membership, the construction of 'relevant' discourses with interactions adhering to community 'norms', with these often developed through a process of in-group monitoring.

Virtual communities vary in their levels of technological sophistication and of course in terms of the content of the discourses created within them, particularly in terms of ideology, current affairs and so forth. Similarities lie primarily in how these communities function in particular ways, both for the individual and the group, in terms of communication, information dissemination, propaganda, ideological development, the development of a negotiated political identity (individual and group), and increasing involvement in support activities over time. Furthermore, these functions are important in relation to the social and psychological processes to which they relate, such as how social interaction within the community can be viewed in terms of processes themselves; processes of communication (including propaganda), processes of identity negotiation and processes of involvement and increased support and activity over time.

Research in this area (Bowman-Grieve 2006) indicates that the discourses created within virtual communities are fundamentally similar; community members use their virtual community to discuss and debate, to praise and to criticise, creating discourses related to issues of importance to the movement. Such discourses often consider how the movement might move forward to achieve its goals and aims and it is often from this perspective that the decision to use violence or terrorism is discussed, with the choice to use terrorism often justified as the only viable course of action.[3]

## Identity negotiation, recruitment and radicalisation

> *Everyone, Republican or otherwise has their own particular part to play. No part is too great or too small, no one is too old or too young to do something.*
>
> Bobby Sands 1954–1981

### *Identity negotiation*

The negotiation of self-identity is an important function of the virtual communities and an important process for members, many of whom join the community with little sense of their position on various issues and who therefore negotiate their views over time and through interaction with other, often more experienced, community members. This process is also important in relation to the status of members, with older members (those who have negotiated their political identity) interacting with newer (or less sure) members and facilitating their identity negotiation and development. Similarly this process of negotiation allows for the justifications and legitimations of support to be verbalised and reiterated providing validation for members. In-group validation serves an important psychological function for group members contributing to their sense of community and of the validity of their views and opinions, which are often in the minority in everyday life outside of this virtual community. In these communities supportive views for extremist and terrorist movements are acknowledged and accepted, thus normalising these ideologies for the individual, and contributing to the creation and sustenance of strongly held views that are more resistant to change in the long term. The processes involved in community justifications and validations can also contribute to increased ideological control. Whilst community members are encouraged to negotiate their political affiliations and ideologies through on-going interaction, other community members also encourage them in either blatant or more subtle ways to demonstrate their commitment and support through action and involvement. Thus, the ideology of the group and group processes within the virtual community can contribute to increased ideological control in in-group members, particularly those who seek to 'prove' their commitment to the group.

Identity negotiation and ideological control occur over time, input from the individual community member and interaction with other community members. As such political identity is open to radicalisation within the online community. Wenger (1998) suggests that we experience identity in practice; that it is a lived experience within a specific community. Similarly the construction of identity can be viewed as a central part of learning (Lave and Wenger 1991; Packer and Goicoechea 2000). According to this argument, learning is viewed as social participation with the onus upon each individual to construct their own identity within the social space of the group. This occurs through processes of participation and interaction (Packer et al. 2000). Additionally, Wenger (1998) argues that we develop identity by assessing who we are in relation to the community in which we are practising members so that in a practical sense, identity development occurs through participation and interaction within the community. This negotiation of identity is a reflexive process, where individuals must be capable of considering and reflecting on the meaning of their own identity throughout the process of negotiation. In this sense identity construction is a careful negotiation between the individual and the community.

### Recruitment and radicalisation

The discourses created and sustained within the virtual communities are used to disseminate information, to communicate ideologies, to promote and propagandise, to encourage involvement and throughout all of these to potentially facilitate the radicalisation of individuals and groups. These discourses seek to dehumanise and de-legitimise the enemy and to justify and legitimise the ideology of the movement. Their sustenance contributes to the community of validation that exists for members of the movement and their content contributes to the justifications of the use of the terrorism (often despite in-group differences of opinion). These discourses in particular promote the notion of a 'right' to act in whatever way necessary in the face of an 'imminent' threat, always identified as some 'other' that is wholly 'evil'. Such ideals can contribute to the radicalisation process, making the decision to use violence or terrorism unavoidable and therefore the responsibility of the enemy.

Committed virtual community members exist in a pre- or semi-radicalised state. In this state individuals are aware of the 'conflict' and the goals of the movement. They are open to movement propaganda that espouses the movement's ideology. Through online interaction they have negotiated a position, perhaps even a role for themselves as a supporter. They may have become involved in support activities, on and offline. In this sense virtual community involvement can be viewed as a potential pathway toward radicalisation. Increased involvement over time may parallel increased ideological development and control (as a justification for actions *a priori* or *post hoc*). Processes of support and involvement, facilitated by online interaction, can contribute to ideological control and individual radicalisation, particularly when these are viewed as incremental processes, with each stage linked with the previous and demonstrating increased involvement in increasingly illegal or violent activities and behaviours over time. If involvement is considered in this way, as a process increasing over time, then particular interventions at any of the various stages might be open to development. Individual radicalisation (i.e. individuals becoming involved in the support of or the carrying out of violent activities) while not facilitated by online interaction alone, may be related to earlier stages of the support and involvement process and the formation of interpersonal bonds and relationships, an important factor in the recruitment process (della Porta 1988, 1992; Sageman 2004). Arguably, the most potent combination to facilitate radicalisation that incorporates use of the Internet will be exposure to radical ideology online, in addition to exposure to radical ideology and behaviour in the physical world.

## Countering terrorist use of the internet

### *Internet regulation and the role of civil society*

> *It is essential to appreciate the very strong collective ethos of the Internet. From its inception Internet users have always been passionately in favour of internal control and against outside influence. In effect, for many years the Internet has operated as a fully functioning anarchy.*
>
> Langford 1998, p. 98

Regulating, governing and possibly censoring the Internet is met with complex arguments both for and against any such moves, primarily because it is not a simple thing to apply the traditional laws of a state or international community to the Internet which, as a vast network, recognises no international borders. Unfortunately, because of the nature of the beast and the lack of international legislation regulating it, websites and virtual communities in support of terrorism proliferate online. It is important to note that while some websites can be easily found (because those who construct and maintain them want them found by potential supporters), others are more difficult to track, particularly those that seek to remain hidden to all but a select membership. Take for example the website 'Alneda.com': this is the name of the website believed to be the primary means of communication initially used by Al-Qaeda (currently over fifty websites in support of Al-Qaeda exist online (Weimann 2006a)). Legitimate service providers originally hosted Alneda. com and removed the site, having been alerted to its contents. Although ownership of the domain name was lost, Alneda.com continues to exist online according to Delio (2003). The website now appears to function as an Internet parasite, embedding itself within other websites without the owner's knowledge, for example by burying itself in sub-directory files. Although the site is not updated regularly it appears to be updated upon relocation, and its location is indeed difficult to ascertain at any given time and without the relevant knowledge. Generally, followers of the website are alerted to its newest location through posts on radical Bulletin Boards and particular mailing lists. As complicated as it may appear to regularly relocate a website and bury it within an already established (and apparently legal and unassociated) website, it is in reality a relatively uncomplicated manoeuvre manageable with 'cracking' tools that are currently available online (Delio 2003).

Internet regulation and legislation are important issues; however the question of who does the regulating remains pertinent. As the Internet is a public domain, many Internet watchdogs, human rights groups and other concerned citizens argue that any decisions made with regard to the issue of regulation and/or censorship must seriously consider the wider implications of such issues and the importance of the role of civil society in making these decisions.

Civil society refers to the arena of un-coerced collective action around shared interests, purposes and values. Civil society can be meaningful in contributing to the development of respect for diversity and tolerance and may be useful in bridging cultural divides (Shulman 2004). The institutional forms of civil society can be distinguished from those of the state and may include foundations, think tanks and other non-governmental organisations. Civil society as a concept has modernised over time and in relation to modernisation in our world. As such, the forms of civil society we see today offer new, alternative and innovative forms of solidarity, connectedness and civic and political engagement, in particular as these are now facilitated by the Internet (Ester and Vinken 2003). According to Shulman (2004) active civil society can enhance the vitality of democracy and may function as a means of easing interaction between the state and the individual. The Internet can facilitate a degree of organisational cohesion and coherence to groups outside of the political establishment who seek to orchestrate campaigns of political protest without relying on the traditional mass media (Reilly 2003). While civil society currently has positive connotations it is important to note that not all civil society is good, for example the Ku Klux Klan was a civil society organisation. In fact terrorist movements, according to Reilly (2003, p. 1), 'use the Internet like marginalised elements of 'civil society' to communicate with sympathetic diasporas, disseminate propaganda and issue statements unfettered by the ideological refractions of the mass media'.

Given the nature of terrorism, in particular the psychological element of this strategy with its aims of undermining public morale and creating an atmosphere of fear (which may incidentally lead to the acceptance of policy and legislation that effects public civil liberties over time, as has been seen post-9/11), it is important to recognise the role the public can play in counter- and anti- terrorism strategies, in particular the role of civil society. Because the Internet is a public domain offering almost unlimited access to the user, it is important that the public who use this technology are afforded the opportunity of monitoring this domain themselves. The appropriate role of civil society in addressing terrorist use of the Internet has not yet been clearly addressed. However, arguably its primary online role is in self-regulation; civil society can take the role of in-group monitors. However, as Jewkes (2002) points out, self-regulation too can be problematic, in some cases giving rise to online vigilantism. Nevertheless, civil interest groups have the potential to act in a real and useful way in attempting to limit the use of the Internet by deviant, extremist or terrorist movements.

Internet Haganah (Internet Defence) is a website dedicated to this purpose – researching, reporting and shutting down Internet websites currently being used to support terrorist organisations and their activities. Their focus is primarily on Islamist terrorist websites and the site itself is run on a voluntary basis. They argue that because the sites they target are usually in violation of their hosts' terms of service action can be taken to have them removed. According to the website, volunteers have succeeded in shutting down more than 700 terrorist support sites. All of the sites removed represented organisations designated terrorist by the US State or Treasury Departments. Of course due to the very nature of the Internet it is not unusual to see many of these sites back online in a short period of time. Nevertheless, this group of volunteers represents a form of self-regulation and self-governance online; a group of concerned individuals working to remove terrorist support sites making them less accessible.

## The internet and possible counter-terrorism initiatives

Apart from Internet watchdogs and the role they might play, both civil society organisations and the government can also play an active role in using the Internet to counter terrorism in other ways, for example by attempting to counter the propaganda campaigns of such movements. In fact, the UN has historically used this approach particularly in relation to combating racism. The Internet offers an excellent medium to launch such campaigns. Effective counter-propaganda campaigns can be conducted online, as terrorist and extremist movements have demonstrated through their own Internet use. Such propaganda campaigns must consider the importance of both the credibility of the communicator and the audience being targeted.

In considering this further it may be useful to incorporate former terrorists or former supporters of terrorism in the dissemination of anti-terrorist material and propaganda. The experiences and perceptions of former terrorists or supporters can lend credibility to the anti-terrorist argument and may be particularly useful in reaching those who have become more entrenched in the ideology and the group they support. Similarly, propaganda campaigns must recognise the various audiences being targeted and their levels of commitment to the movement or ideology, which range from those who are 'on the fence' to those who are supportive but not active in their support, to those who are actively involved. The effectiveness of counter-propaganda is dependent on various factors, such as the credibility of the communicator, the organisation of persuasive arguments, the use of fear arousing appeals, group and individual factors (Hovland et al. 1953). These factors warrant serious consideration in preparing and presenting such campaigns to public audiences.

Crelinsten and Schmid (1992), also suggest that particular communication strategies and psychological operations (PsyOps) can contribute to the fight against terrorism. Arguably such strategies can also be effectively promoted online. These communication strategies can be divided into those that are considered offensive or defensive operations, in other words those directed at one's own community or those directed at the constituency of the terrorists. In essence, any anti-terrorism propaganda campaign must be well structured, coordinated and integrated considering both the importance of the communicator and the importance of the particular audience being targeted.

Likewise, the Internet can be used by governmental and non-governmental organisations in positive ways to combat terrorism through educational campaigns, particularly those that promote non-violent forms of debate and dissent, such as those that encourage non-violent conflict resolution and promote negotiation and compromise (Weimann 2006a). Educational web campaigns can also actively challenge the 'morally disengaged rhetoric' of terrorist movements and 'can provide potential recruits with logical analysis of a group's purported grievances and activities' (Weimann 2006a, p. 240).

Finally, Internet use by terrorist and extremist movements can be used to gather intelligence necessary for counter- and anti-terrorism strategies. Intelligence relating to perceptions of successful attacks and acceptable targeting, for example, may be useful in preparing for counter- and anti-terrorism initiatives and in the planning of intervention strategies.

In conclusion, given the difficulty in tracking and tracing cyber communications, the lack of globally accepted processes and procedures for investigation and inadequate and ineffective information sharing between public and private sectors (Weimann and Von Knop 2008), it is apparent that in order to attempt in any real way to combat terrorist use of the Internet at the very least there must be an international recognition and agreed definition of the problem area. Such definition and recognition of an international issue is essential for the evaluation of the problem from an international perspective in order to develop international strategies to attempt to combat it effectively.

## Notes

1 www.Kahane.org is an Israeli Extremism website and the first website to be designated a terrorist organisation by the US Department of State, 2003.
2 This website no longer exists but it was previously located at http://www.ulisnet.com, which now appears to be a general information website made up of external links.
3 This relates to supporting literature that sees terrorism as a strategic choice, see Crenshaw 1990.

## References

Arendt, H. (1990) *On Revolution*. London: Penguin Books.
Bogart, L. (1976) *Premises for Propaganda: The United States Information Agency's Operating Assumptions in the Cold War*. New York: Free Press.
Bowman-Grieve, L. (2006) *Terrorist supporters and the Internet: An exploration of online 'virtual' communities*. PhD Thesis, Department of Applied Psychology, National University of Ireland, Cork.
Conway, M. (2003) *Cybercortical warfare: The Case of Hizbollah.org*. Paper presented at the European Consortium for Political Research (ECPR) Joint Sessions of Workshops, Edinburgh, UK.
Crelinsten, R. D. and Schmid, A.P. (1992) Western responses to terrorism: A twenty-five year balance sheet. In A.P. Schmid (Ed.) Western Responses to Terrorism. Special issue of *Terrorism and Political Violence*, 4 (4), pp. 322–323.
Crenshaw, M. (1990) The logic of terrorism: Terrorist behaviour as a product of strategic choice. In W. Reich (Ed.), *Origins of Terrorism: Psychologies, ideologies, theologies, states of mind*. Cambridge: Cambridge University Press, pp. 7–24.
Delio, M. (2003) Al-Qaeda website refuses to die. Available from http://www.wired.com/techbiz/it/news/2003/04/58356?currentPage=2 (accessed 10 March 2009).
della Porta, D. (1988) Recruitment processes in clandestine political organizations: Italian left-wing terrorism. *International Social Movement Research*, 1, 155–169.
della Porta, D. (1992) Political socialization in left-wing underground organizations: Biographies of Italian and German militants. In D. della Porta (Ed.), *Social movements and violence: Participation in underground organizations*. Greenwich, CT: JAI Press, pp. 259–290.
Ester, P. and Vinken, H. (2003) Debating Civil Society: On the fear for civic decline and hope for the Internet alternative. *International Sociology*, 18, 659–680.

88    *Lorraine Bowman-Grieve*

Hovland, C. I., Janis, I. L. and Kelley, H. H. (1953) *Communication and persuasion: Psychological studies of opinion change*. New Haven, CT: Yale University Press.

Hundeide, K. (2003) Becoming a committed insider: Acquiring skills through participation as an apprentice in a community of practice. *Culture and Psychology*, 9 (2), 107–127.

Jewkes, Y. (2002) Policing the Net: crime, regulation and surveillance in cyberspace. In Y. Jewkes (Ed.) *Dot.cons: crime deviance and identity on the Internet*, Devon, UK: Willan Publishing, pp. 15–35.

Kendall, L. (1999) Recontextualising 'cyberspace': Methodological considerations for online research. In S. Jones (Ed.), *Doing Internet Research: Critical issues and methods for examining the Net*. London: Sage Publications, pp. 57–74.

Langford, D. (1998). Ethics @ the Internet: bilateral procedures in electronic communication. In B. Loader (Ed.) *Cyberspace Divide: Equality, Agency and Policy in the Information Society*. London: Routledge, pp. 98–112.

Lave, J. (1988) *Cognition in Practice*. New York: Cambridge University Press.

Lave, J. and Wenger, E. (1991) *Situated Learning: Legitimate peripheral participation*. Cambridge: Cambridge University Press.

Levin, B. (2002) Cyberhate: A legal and historical analysis of extremists' use of computer networks in America. *American Behavioural Scientist*, 45 (6), 958–989.

Packer, M. & Goicoechea, J. (2000) Sociocultural and constructivist theories of learning: Ontology, not just epistemology. *Educational Psychologist*, 35, (4), 227–241.

Reilly, P. (2003) Civil Society, the Internet and terrorism: Two case studies from Northern Ireland. Presented at the European Consortium for Political Research Joint Sessions of Workshops, Edinburgh. Available from http://www.essex.ac.uk/ecpr/events/jointsessions/paperarchive/edinburgh/ws20/Reilly.pdf (accessed 16 January 2009).

Sageman, M. (2004) *Understanding Terrorist Networks*. Philadelphia: University of Pennsylvania Press.

Sands, B. (1981) The Prison Diary of Bobby Sands (14 March 1981). Available online at http://www.irishhungerstrike.com/bobbysdiary.html.

Shulman, M. R. (2004) Civil Society's response to the challenges of terrorism: A conference Report. From a meeting held at headquarters of the Luso-American Foundation, Lisbon, Portugal, 7–8 June.

Tsafti, Y. and Weimann, G. (2002) www.terrorism.com: Terror on the Internet. *Studies in Conflict and Terrorism*, 25, 317–332.

Weimann, G. (2006a) *Terror on the Internet: The new arena, the new challenges*. Washington, D.C.: United States Institute of Peace Press.

Weimann, G. (2006b) Virtual Disputes: The use of the Internet for terrorist debates. *Studies in Conflict and Terrorism*, 29, 623–639.

Weimann G. and von Knopp, K. (2008) Applying the notion of noise to countering online terrorism. *Studies in Conflict & Terrorism*, 31, 883–902.

Wenger, E. (1998) Communities of practice: Learning as a social system. *Systems Thinker*, June.

Whine, M. (1998) Islamist organisations on the Internet. Available from http://www.ict.org.il/Articles/tabid/66/Articlsid/716/currentpage/32/Default.aspx (accessed November 2, 2008).

Whine, M. (1999) Cyberspace: a new medium for communication, command and control by extremists. *Studies in Conflict and Terrorism*, 22 (3), 231–245.

Whine, M. (2000) The use of the Internet by far right extremists. In B. Loader and D. Thomas (Eds.), *Cybercrime: Law, security and privacy in the information age*. London: Routledge, pp. 234–250.

# 7 The impact of the media on terrorism and counter-terrorism

*Deborah Browne and Andrew Silke*

... I say to you: that we are in a battle, and that more than half of this battle is taking place in the battlefield of the media. And that we are in a media battle for the hearts and minds of our Umma.

Ayman al Zawahiri, (2005)

Victory in any terrorist conflict ultimately depends on two key factors. The first is the intelligence war; each side must protect its own secrets and plans while uncovering those of the other. The second is what has come to be called the battle for hearts and minds (Payne, 2009). Failure on either one of these fronts might not be terminal, but failure on both will ensure defeat. As is recognized in the opening quote, the power of the role of the media is in the fundamental part it plays in the battle for hearts and minds. Whoever communicates the most compelling message significantly improves their chances of winning. Yet the counter-terrorism strategies of many countries tend not to recognize this as promptly as their terrorist opponents. The irony of this has not gone unnoticed: many terrorist organizations are using the open media, which represents the values and institutions of the liberal-democratic nations they are targeting, for their own purposes (Ganor, 2005).

The opening chapter in this book highlighted some key aspects of successful terrorist campaigns – successful, that is, from the perspective of the terrorists. First, the terrorists need to provoke the state into responding in certain ways to their violence. Later, the terrorists and the state are locked in a blame game over who is responsible for the death, destruction and misery that ensue. Winning this blame game can be decisive.

The media play a necessary role in both of these stages. Terrorism, fundamentally, is about influence. It revolves around the attempt of a small group of people to profoundly influence the lives of considerably larger groups. Violence and the threat of violence is the method through which this attempt is made, but in order to have its desired impact, people need to be aware of what is happening. Without awareness, there can be no impact.

Brian Jenkins (1975, p. 15) famously observed that 'Terrorists want a lot of people watching and a lot of people listening, not a lot of people dead'. While 9/11 challenges the generality of the latter part of the sentence, the first element is unquestionably still true. Almost every terrorist group of the past century has been intensely concerned with the impact it has on the media. Most of them recognize that there is a vital media dimension to the conflict and, as has already been pointed out, terrorists usually recognize this earlier and more intensely than their government opponents. The opening quote above from al-Qaeda's second-in-command, illustrates that al-Qaeda – currently the world's most consequential terrorist group – is just as aware of this media 'battle' as many of its predecessors. Indeed, bin Laden also noted the magnitude of the impact of the media when he wrote to Mullah Omar 'it is obvious that the media war in this century is one of the strongest methods [of winning the propaganda struggle]; in fact, its ratio may reach 90 per cent of the total preparation for the battles' (cited in Payne, 2009, p. 110).

Why is the media so important? At one level, it is because terrorist conflicts are fundamentally not like other conflicts; victory here is not decided on the battlefield. In a conventional war, if you repeatedly destroy the enemy's armed forces in battle or advance a certain mileage per day, you will eventually win. The same, however, does not apply in a terrorist conflict. Winning a terrorist conflict or counterinsurgency campaign does not necessarily involve quantifiable indicators of success (Boettcher and Cobb, 2006), and the less tangible 'hearts and minds' factor plays a bigger role.

## A call to arms? The search for support and recruits

When terrorists attempt to use the media to communicate to wider audiences, a key element is to generate support and also to attract potential recruits and sponsors. A hope for many terrorists is that by becoming the focus of media coverage, an opportunity is created to explain and justify the violence. In covering a terrorist attack or incident, the media will often attempt to place the event in a context, and part of this context will be the rationale used by the terrorist group to sanction the campaign of violence. Thus, the terrorists' 'cause' as well as the violence receives attention.

Often such coverage of the 'cause' is superficial (and usually will be contrasted with government views on the conflict) but sometimes the media allows terrorists the opportunity to present much more detailed and sophisticated justifications for their actions. This is particularly facilitated by the Internet.

Contemporary terrorist groups make wide use of the Internet, and there are many web-sites linked to a wide range of terrorist groups and which go into great detail on the backgrounds to the conflicts and the motivations for the violence (at least from the perspectives of the terrorists). Besides being used as a vehicle for practical communication, Weimann (2006) noted that terrorist groups also use the Internet to debate and assess the conflict. These debates allow others the opportunity to get involved in discussion that allows rationalization of their cause and so potentially to the radicalization and recruitment of other individuals. Conway and McInerney (2008), for example, presented evidence to support the potential for online radicalization of YouTube users viewing jihadi martyr-promoting video material. They showed how users without any prior links to jihadists not only viewed these sites with interest, but formed virtual relationships with those promoting the videos.

Traditional media outlets have also been used to propagate justification and attract sympathy for the terrorist cause. One of the best-known examples of this was the publication of the Unabomber's manifesto by two major American newspapers in 1995.

By the time he was arrested in April 1996, the Unabomber was responsible for a 17-year-long bombing campaign. In that time, he had carried out a total of 16 attacks which left three people dead and a further 23 injured. Initially, the bomber targeted universities and airlines (hence the name Unabomber). Eventually, the range of targets grew and in the later years of the campaign several bombs were sent to people working in the computer industry.

This final attack saw the death of Gilbert Murray, a lobbyist for the timber industry who was killed when he opened a package sent to his office.

In 1995, the Unabomber announced that he would cease the bombing campaign if a 35,000-word manifesto called 'Industrial society and its future' was published. With the approval of the authorities this was published in September 1995, by both *The Washington Post* and the *New York Times*. The Unabomber saw the publication as an opportunity to justify his violence and rally support. In this case, however, that call to arms does not seem to have happened and indeed the publication played a key role in the capture of the Unabomber in April 1996. The bomber's brother recognized similarities in phrases and ideas in the 35,000-word article and the writings of Theodore Kaczynski. He consulted a handwriting expert who felt the concerns were well founded (Hubert, 1997). The authorities were contacted and shortly afterwards Kaczynski was arrested (with two more bombs almost ready for use).

Theodore Kaczynski was an isolated loner and while he attempted to exploit the media to spread his message and justify his violence, there is little sense that he succeeded in any meaningful way. In contrast, terrorist groups are often much more astute and sophisticated in how they attempt to generate and harness wider sympathy. In the early 1980s, Jeffrey Sluka conducted extensive fieldwork in nationalist areas of Belfast in an effort to understand the nature of support for and against the paramilitaries within their local communities. He quickly came to the conclusion that:

> Public support is absolutely vital to the guerrilla fighter because while a guerrilla campaign may be possible even without the active support of the majority of one's own people, it cannot survive their active hostility. The IRA and INLA cannot hope to win or even survive without the active or passive support of the majority of people in the communities in which they exist and operate.
>
> (Sluka, 1989, p. 65)

The crucial need for wider support is something that is well appreciated among active terrorists themselves and most terrorist groups have developed internal

rules designed to foster and maintain support among what they see as their con-
stituents. For example, the IRA's instruction manual to members, the *Green Book*,
explicitly warns that military success alone is not enough for the organization. In
order to achieve a strategic victory:

> The I.R.A. volunteer . . . must therefore . . . [enhance] our necessary stated
> task of ensuring that his conduct is not a contributory factor to the Brit attempt
> to isolate us from our people . . . [O]ur task is not only to kill as many enemy
> personnel as possible but of equal importance to create support which will
> carry us . . . through a war of liberation . . . IF, for example, we have an area
> with a unit of I.R.A. volunteers and nothing else: no Sinn Fein Cumann, no
> Green Cross committee, no local involvement etc., after a period, regardless
> of how successfully [sic] they have been against the Brits, they end up in jail
> leaving no structures behind: no potential for resistance, recruits, education or
> general enhancing of support.
>
> (Coogan, 1987, pp. 694–697)

This concern expressed in training manuals does seem to have transferred into a
very clear awareness among the more astute terrorists. Consider for example, this
very telling comment from Eamon Collins, who for several years was an intelligence officer in the Provisional IRA:

> The IRA – regardless of their public utterances dismissing the condemnations
> of their behaviour from church and community leaders – tried to act in a way
> that would avoid severe censure from within the nationalist community; they
> knew they were operating within a sophisticated set of informal restrictions
> on their behaviour, no less powerful for being largely unspoken.
>
> (Collins, 1997, p. 296)

The implication is that the terrorists must behave in an acceptable manner or else
they will be rejected by the people and thus unable to continue. Comments such as
Collins' above, clearly indicate that this is a fact very much to the forefront of terrorist thinking. Indeed, the quote from Ayman al- Zawahiri at the very start of this
chapter is taken from a letter he wrote to another terrorist commander criticizing
the excessive violence of some of that commander's attacks. Zawahiri himself has
ordered some extremely ruthless acts in his time, but he was trying to drive home
the damaging impact of the other commander's attacks in terms of undermining
wider support from the movement.

Support for terrorist groups can essentially be broken down in terms of *soft*
support and *hard* support (Silke, 2000). Soft support in practical terms can be
described as tolerance. Soft supporters of a terrorist group will not necessarily
publicly voice their approval of the terrorist group's actions or aims, and they
may not provide obvious tangible assistance to the group (e.g. in terms of financial contributions), neither would they necessarily vote for politicians connected
with the terrorist group. However, the value of soft supporters is that they tend

not to be willing to co-operate with the security forces in their efforts to police and apprehend the terrorists, failing to inform the security forces about the whereabouts or activities of members of the group, or alert the authorities if they saw suspicious activity in their neighbourhood. Such support is tacit and often even unintentional – 'looking the other way' may be seen simply as an easier option rather than something consciously deliberated. It is notoriously difficult to develop effective intervention for such support, despite recognition of its impact (Saggar, 2009). Indeed, Saggar (2009) noted that policy aimed at the supporters, including soft supporters, of Islamist-inspired terrorism could potentially have a boomerang effect, and damage the reputation of the government instigating the policy. Large numbers of soft supporters can be extremely valuable to terrorists, providing a community in which the terrorists can operate without much fear that the security and intelligence agencies will be made aware of what is happening.

Hard supporters represent a further level of commitment. Hard supporters *will* try to provide the terrorists with practical assistance. At a political level they will vote for terrorist candidates in elections and they will be prepared to take part in demonstrations and protests on behalf of causes linked to the terrorists' aims. They will contribute financially to the terrorist group by making donations, buying merchandise or perhaps subscribing to publications produced by the terrorists. More committed supporters will also be prepared to store and hide weapons and other contraband for the group and may also be willing to provide safe-houses for terrorists who are on the run or who are on 'active duty'. Hard supporters will also pass on intelligence about the security forces, possible targets or suspected informers to the terrorist group. While they may be a step away from being active terrorists, hard supporters are still integral to the effective running of any terrorist campaign.

For the terrorists, there is a relentless need to turn active non-supporters into soft supporters; and to then turn soft supporters into hard supporters. Examples of how this might be achieved include starting a campaign to improve the prison conditions for captured terrorists or by highlighting human rights abuses committed by government opponents. Such campaigns can work to create the impression that the terrorists are more widely supported than they actually are, and can also undermine the legitimacy of the government. This very point is explicitly raised by the IRA in the *Green Book*:

> Resistance must be channelled into active and passive support with an ongoing process through our actions, our educational programmes, our polices, of attempting to turn the passive supporter into a dump holder, a member of the movement, a paper-seller, etc., with the purpose of building protective support barriers between the enemy and ourselves, thus curbing the enemy's attempted isolation policy. And of course the more barriers there are, the harder it is for the enemy to get at us while at the same time we increase the potential for active support in its various forms.
>
> (Coogan, 1987, p. 695)

The media then provides an avenue for terrorists to try to convince opponents or neutrals to become soft supporters and then to convince soft supporters to become hard supporters (and then, if desired, to turn hard supporters into active terrorists). The media then is a critical arena in the battle for hearts and minds. This is something that is recognized by policy makers and policy analysts. The UK's Counter-Terrorism Strategy (CONTEST) includes a specific strategy (PREVENT) aimed at influencing how language is used as a means of combating radicalization. While policy makers may not be able to directly influence the language used by the news media, it is recognized that over time they tend to adopt the government's lead (Armstrong et al., 2008).

In the battle for hearts and minds terrorists are not only competing against the state, but they are also competing against other terrorist groups from among their own communities. Mia Bloom, for example, has highlighted that Palestinian groups such as Hamas, Islamic Jihad and Fatah are not only struggling against Israel, but are also very much in competition with each other for support and recruits among Palestinian communities. High-profile attacks against Israeli targets can quickly raise one group's prestige and standing compared to its rivals. A group that fails to carry out attacks while the others are engaged in high-profile campaigns runs the serious risk of being seen as weak and ineffectual and may struggle not only to attract new recruits, but may well lose current members and supporters who are attracted instead to a more 'successful' group. Bloom (2005) notes that when the groups are in more co-operative frames of mind, they will sometimes allow a rival organization to claim responsibility for an attack for propaganda purposes.

This internal competition is not restricted to Palestinian militant groups but can be found in most conflicts where several factions have emerged. The conflict in Northern Ireland, for example, has seen intense rivalries emerge among groups who are ostentatiously on the same side. Republican organizations such as the Official IRA, the Provisional IRA, the INLA, the IPLO, the Real IRA, and so forth, have waged bitter feuds amongst themselves as to which group is the 'true' representative of militant Irish Republicanism. These clashes have repeatedly led to violence and killing, but there has also been a sustained propaganda war as to which group was the most effective and powerful. This propaganda war was effectively won by the Provisional IRA between the 1970s and 1990s, but in the post-Peace Process era the battle has re-ignited as various dissident republican groups vie for the dominant role. Yet again, the key to this is seen to be through terrorist attacks, which generate publicity for the movement. The reward for the group that wins will be increased recruitment and increased sponsorship. On the loyalist side similar tensions have emerged with groups such as the Ulster Defence Association, the Ulster Volunteer Force, and the Loyalist Volunteer Force jockeying for position and power.

## The psychological impact of terrorist propaganda

As part of the media battle for hearts and minds many terrorist groups are extremely active in terms of developing and distributing material for propaganda purposes.

Indeed, most of the larger terrorist groups have internal departments dedicated to 'public relations'. The Provisional IRA for example had a Director of Publicity whose job among other things was to help produce a weekly newspaper in support of the movement (Horgan and Taylor, 1997). Al-Qaeda too has an 'Information Committee' whose task is to help organize and produce propaganda material on behalf of the movement (Burke, 2007).

In an internet age, the ability of terrorist-produced propaganda to rich a wide audience is exceptional and certainly far exceeds the possibilities terrorist groups from as little as twenty years ago could have dreamed of. Internet sites allow both the mainstream media and any curious members of the public to rapidly and easily find information on terrorist groups that has been placed online by the group itself or by individuals who have strong sympathies with the organization. Naturally this will present a very different account of the conflict from that provided through state or government sources. In the interests of providing a balanced account of events, mainstream media outlets can draw on this material in a way that would have been exceptionally difficult even fifteen years ago.

As well as allowing terrorist groups to more easily present their side of the story, propaganda also has an important recruitment function. Media material produced by terrorist groups often contain frequent and extensive calls for the reader or viewer to also join the movement and for them to carry out attacks similar to those being portrayed. Long established military emotive tactics aimed at uniting soldiers as a close unit are also utilized by terrorist groups in the form of pledging brotherhood not just to an individual terror cell but to an entire location, country and/or ethnic or faith group. This allows them to extend their pledges of loyalty to the 'fictive kin' (Speckhard, 2008, p. 130) of potential recruits. As an example, Speckhard (2008) refers to 'Azzam the American', who has been recorded acting a spokesman for Al-Qaeda, urging American Muslims to join the militant jihad. During his speech he is clearly differentiating between the outrages committed by the Americans and their allies, and the suffering witnessed by 'my brothers', 'our mujahedin'.

This sort of propaganda is evident in a great deal of the material produced by jihadi extremists over the past decade. Rallying calls are made both in many of the text documents (e.g. Osama bin Laden's *Declaration of War Against the Americans Occupying the Land of the Two Holy Places*) but even more dramatically in many of the videos now available, particularly on the Internet. In the videos, many of the filmed jihadis directly speak to the camera encouraging and extolling the viewer to join the jihad and to follow their example.

For example, in one film seen by the second author of this chapter, a series of clips show vivid footage of suicide bombings in Iraq. Prior to the attacks the bombers are interviewed on camera. All of the bombers separately call on the viewer to join their cause and carry out jihadi attacks. These calls are then followed by the dramatic footage showing the bombers' successful attacks. The calls follow a very similar theme which is well illustrated in the quote below, taken from one of the suicide bomber's speech to the camera just before he drove off on mission:

We call our brothers – by the will of Allah – to join us and to not delay in doing so. Everyone who watches this video should know that – by Allah – there is nothing between us and the Firdaws[1] except the pressing of a button. We ask Allah to grant us acceptance, success and correct aim, as well as to grant you the ability to join us.

These personal calls from each of the bombers are then backed up by a narrated call at the end of the video which emphasizes the similarities between the viewer and the bombers and again calls on the viewers to follow their example:

[these] are real events that have occurred and are continuing to occur in [Iraq] and the heroes [suicide bombers] featured in this production are people just like us. They had lives just like our lives, homes like our homes. They had sons and daughters, fathers and mothers. Some of them had universities that they were looking forward to graduating from with the highest of degrees, and some of them had businesses that they were preoccupied with expanding. However, they all refused humiliation and disgrace, weakness and degradation. They were pained by the weakness of the Islamic nation and the pouncing of other nations upon it . . . They were pained by the situation of the youth of Islam, and what they are in of misguidance and loss; the youth of Islam who used to pulverise the Kings of the East and the Caesars of the West; today find themselves lost between the pop stars of the East and the immorality of the West. So they decided to make Hijrah[2] for the sake of Allah and in order to give victory to this Upright Religion.

This type of content is typical of much terrorist propaganda material. Common themes in such material across different groups and conflicts will include (1) ideological and religious justifications for violent actions; (2) practical guidance on how to carry out terrorist attacks and campaigns; and (3) explicit calls for viewers to provide support for the campaign of violence and potentially even carry out attacks similar to those displayed and described. Throughout it all, is the underlying emotive appeal to the group-identity of the viewer, and to increasing their sense of belonging to the cause.

Given the nature of this material, an important question is to what extent can such material affect the attitudes and behaviour of viewers and readers? Ultimately, not everyone will be equally vulnerable to the effects of this material. Individual differences in cultural backgrounds, attitudes, values, personality styles, and vulnerabilities play a critical role in determining how people respond (e.g. Silke, 2003; Silke, 2008). To accurately predict any one individual's reactions, one would need to know a great deal about the person's worldview, sense of identity, as well as the situational forces currently prominent in the person's life.

Nevertheless, psychological research has identified a range of factors that are likely to play an important role in determining the impact of this type of material. These include:

- Identity;
- Perceived grievances/revenge motivations;
- Excitement;
- Mortality salience.

## *Identity*

Social science has long shown how an individual's identity can impact on a range of attitudes and behaviours. Identity has also been shown to provide valuable insight into explaining involvement in terrorism (e.g. Sageman, 2004). Before an individual will be prepared to join a terrorist group, they need first to belong to that section of society which supports or shares the aims, grievances and ambitions of the terrorist group (Silke, 2003). In the context of groups such as al-Qaeda, individuals need to have a strong sense of identity as a Muslim, and equally, to identify strongly with the wider Muslim community – the *Umma*. Prior to joining, recruits to Islamist movements such as al-Qaeda consistently report that they perceived they had a very strong connection to other Muslims across the globe. This wider connection brought with it a sense of responsibility for these other Muslims, even when the individual had never met them or travelled to their lands. Research has shown that individuals who rate their Islamic identity as being more important than their national or ethnic identity, express more positive and supportive views on topics such as martyrdom (Ansari et al., 2006). There are many intervening factors that might impinge on why such strong identities develop in certain individuals and not in others; Hammack (2008), for example, explains individual differences in cultural identity as a combination of cognitive, social and cultural factors, where personal narratives and paradigms are constructed and reconstructed throughout a lifetime of individual experiences and social interactions. This also suggests, however, that the experiences of the individual *before* they form a strong identity with such a group could be influenced to inhibit this identity developing, which supports the counter-terrorist PREVENT strategies that were mentioned earlier. It also supports the British counter-terrorism communication strategy of building an attractive concept of 'Britishness' as an alternative to Al-Qaeda's concept of an Islamist Utopia (Payne, 2009).

In the particular context of Muslim extremism, the material contained in the propaganda material is aimed explicitly at Muslims – it is not aimed at influencing non-Muslims. As was pointed out earlier, potential viewers are referred to as 'Brothers' (and less frequently 'Sisters') and reference is made repeatedly to the assumed shared Muslim identity that the viewers and individuals filmed share. References are made to the sense of duty Muslims owe to fellow Muslims who are oppressed or under distress and that the fate of the entire of Umma is the responsibility of every Muslim. Extensive reference is made to the noble benefits of assisting the Umma and of the religious rewards for Muslims who become martyrs through jihad. Individuals who do not feel that being a Muslim is a key component of their identity are less likely to be as strongly affected by this material (though it is worth noting that the mortality salience effects of much of the material – which will be discussed in more detail later – are likely to make being a Muslim a more important aspect of the identity of Muslim viewers). This is backed up by research that has shown that Muslims report a stronger sense of religious identification than Christians (Fischer et al. 2007). Fischer and his colleagues found that similar levels of threat to a person's religious identity had more of an impact on Muslims than on Christians.

Nonetheless, group identity clearly has an impact on pathways towards extremism (e.g. McCauley and Moskalenko, 2008) and similar effects are found for other terrorist movements. For example positive values and themes are pushed with regard to having an identity of white, non-Jewish ethnicity is seen as crucial for neo-Nazis, or seeing oneself as coming from an Irish Catholic background as a common shared factor for IRA members, or a shared Basque identity for members of ETA (e.g. Clark, 1983). If the cultural or ethnic values are not identified with to begin with, then the impact of any propaganda material based on such foundations will be limited.

### Perceived grievances/revenge motivations

Perceptions of grievance and a desire for revenge can be powerful motivations in any situation. Indeed, evolutionary psychologists explain this in terms of a response to a threat to perceived social status; value of social status is something that has evolved in humans and other primates because of its strong association with sexual selection. Competition for social status can lead to intense, and often violent, behaviours, usually in adult males (Gottschalk and Ellis, 2009). Psychologists have also shown that the individual seeking revenge demonstrates higher levels of goal fulfillment when they see their perceived offender suffer, and that the offender's understanding of why the revenge was sought is even more important (Gollwitzer and Denzler, 2009).

It is not at all surprising, therefore, that revenge is seen as a key factor influencing terrorism and communications of terrorist groups. A desire for revenge has been found to be a key factor in the radicalization process for many, if not most, extremists. In the context of jihadi extremism, the perception of a strong shared identity and link with the wider Muslim world has serious consequences when the individual perceives that some Muslim communities are being treated brutally or unfairly. Similarly it has been postulated that humiliation, shame and rage are potential trigger factors for pathways to a return to political violence in Northern Ireland (Alderdice, 2007). Radicalization has been explained in terms of a perceived threat to the in-group (McCauley and Moskalenko, 2008) (and here again the importance of group identity is highlighted) and so grievance and revenge motivations are important drivers of individual decisions to become involved in militant activism as well as motivating those already involved into action. A desire for vengeance has also been associated with symptoms of post-traumatic stress disorder (PTSD) in trauma survivors, and has been linked to involvement in Chechen terrorism (Speckhard and Ahkmedova, 2006). Catalyst events (i.e. violent acts that are perceived to be unjust) provide a strong sense of outrage and a powerful psychological desire for revenge and retribution (Silke, 2003). Significantly, these catalyst events do not need to be experienced first-hand to have this effect. For many individuals witnessing such events vicariously on television, the Internet or in propaganda, etc. can have an equally powerful impact and can provide a strong motivation to become involved.

Such exposure is frequently facilitated through viewing extremist propaganda. Importantly, one does not need to experience unjust events firsthand in order to feel sufficiently motivated to become a terrorist. Indeed, the events do not even have to involve friends or family members. For example, many terrorists report that they first joined the organization after witnessing events on television. They did not come from the area where the events occurred – or indeed even know the people who lived there – but at some level they identified with the victims. In this way it can be seen that two powerful psychological processes – identity with a particular group and a desire for revenge when it is perceived that this group, or the status of this group, is threatened or has been treated unjustly – combine to compel the individual to join a terrorist group in order to redress the balance.

One propaganda video seen by the second author dealing with Iraq, for example, opens with shots and pictures of alleged abuses by the American forces and their allies. In another tape, an alleged captured enemy soldier admits that his forces carried out abuses and atrocities against civilians. In another example, a Muslim woman gives an emotional account of the abuses and suffering she has experienced. Such propaganda may be extremely biased – and certainly does not seek to portray any atrocities or abuses carried out by the terrorists – but there is often still a basis of truth and reality in the events portrayed. For example, some of the footage is downloaded from mainstream media sources such as CNN or al-Jazeera.

Recruits to some terrorist groups are often extensively exposed to such propaganda material, with graphic images of abuses and violence. In the context of jihadi extremism such images can be drawn from a wide range of conflicts involving Muslim populations, including Kashmir, Chechnya, Bosnia, and the Palestinian Territories. US foreign policy is also heavily focused on, with recent propaganda focusing on the US invasion and occupation of Afghanistan and Iraq. In a number of public statements (including the last statements of suicide bombers) Islamists specifically draw attention to these conflicts as a justification for their own violence, and again the suicide bombers and jihadis filmed provide similar rationales. Psychologists have shown that it is not just the act of revenge and seeing the perceived offender suffer that is important, but that perceived victims obtain even more satisfaction when the offender signals that they understand why the revenge has been imposed (Gollwitzer and Denzler, 2009). The *message* of revenge, therefore, is probably even more important to the terrorist than the act as a means to an end in itself.

Not everyone though is equally content with the idea of vengeance or equally prepared to act in a vengeful manner. Some groups are more vengeance prone than others. Men hold more positive attitudes towards vengeance than women, and young people are much more prepared to act in a vengeful manner than older individuals (Cota-McKinley et al. 2001). Some evidence exists too to suggest that stronger religious belief also affects ones attitude to vengeance (e.g. Fischer et al, 2007), with more secular individuals showing less approval to vengeful attitudes. Thus one would expect young males who have stronger religious beliefs will feel a stronger need for and approval of vengeful behaviour in response to perceived injustices as is often portrayed in terrorist propaganda material.

## *Excitement*

Another factor that can play a role in violent radicalization is the perceived excitement and sense of adventure associated with the role. Research has long shown that young males in particular are much more attracted to high-risk behaviour than other segments of the population (Silke, 2003). The propaganda material routinely available on extremist websites clearly illustrates potentially exciting and certainly dangerous activities. For example, extremist jihadi websites frequently show videos of recruits training with a wide variety of weapons including assault rifles, machine guns, rockets and hand grenades. There is often also footage of actual attacks against enemy targets including combat with what appear to be US helicopters and forces in regions such as Iraq and Afghanistan.

Becoming a jihadi is a dangerous, high-risk decision. In the propaganda media, typically a very positive is painted of life as a terrorist (though the propaganda material will not use the term 'terrorist' but rather words such as 'soldiers', 'jihadis', 'volunteers', 'freedom fighters', etc. depending on the group and the cause). These accounts of life fighting for the cause may be rose-tinted and gloss over the mundane hardships experienced by recruits during training and in combat, but they are well pitched to create a sense of adventure and excitement associated with becoming involved. This is an appeal that is more prosaic compared to the religious or ideological incentives of joining the struggle, but arguably has at least an equal – if indeed not greater – role in attracting young males to the cause. In the modern context, this is certainly seen with regard to jihadi extremism where for on-line activity at least there is far more attention and interest invested in finding and viewing videos of attacks and combat, then of material which describes the religious and spiritual rationale for the struggle (Dienel et al., in press).

## *Mortality Salience*

When people are exposed to death-related thoughts or imagery this results in what psychologists refer to as a 'mortality salience' effect. Psychological research has shown that even very subtle cues relating to death can create a mortality salience effect – even when the cues are not consciously recognized by the person involved (Pyszczynski et al., 2002). The images of death, dying and killing that can be found on many extremist websites for example, are certainly sufficient to produce a mortality salience effect in viewers. Similarly, the strong focus in the material on what will happen to individuals in the after-life (e.g. the rewarding of martyrs, etc.) will also contribute to a mortality salience effect developing. Consider, for example, the death-related imagery in a quote from *The Islamic Ruling on the Permissibility of Self-Sacrificial Operations*, a document focusing on suicide attacks that has been posted on many jihadi web-sites:

> On the material level, these operations inflict the heaviest losses on the enemy, and are lowest in cost to us. The cost of equipment is negligible in comparison to the assault . . . The human casualty is a single life, who is in fact a martyr and hero who has gone ahead to the Gardens of Eternity.

News coverage of attacks and their aftermath – whether carried out by the terrorists or by the state fighting them – are also certainly capable of producing such mortality salience effects. A variety of research studies have shown that mortality salience generally increases identification with and pride in one's country, religion, gender, race, etc. (Pyszczynski et al., 2002). Crucially, mortality salience can lead to an increase in support for extremism when it is linked to group identity. For example, one study found that under mortality salience conditions, white Americans expressed more sympathy and support for other Whites who expressed racist views.

In mortality salience conditions, individuals experience exaggerated tendencies to stereotype and reject those who are different from themselves. Research has demonstrated that mortality salience produces especially punitive reactions to moral transgressions – for example, one study on court judges showed that they assigned far harsher penalties to an alleged prostitute after a brief reminder of their own mortality (Rosenblatt et al., 1989).

Research has established that subtle reminders of death produce increased clinging to and defence of one's cultural worldview (Pyszczynski et al., 2002). These tendencies include the following: greater affection for similar others or those who uphold cherished cultural values and greater hostility toward different others or those who violate cherished cultural values, heightened discomfort when handling cherished cultural icons in a disrespectful fashion, sitting closer to a person who shares one's culture and farther away from a foreigner, and increased physical aggression toward someone critical of one's cherished beliefs.

A crucial piece of research in this area was carried out by Pyszczynski et al. (2006). They found that Muslim college students who were reminded of death showed increased support for other students who voiced support for suicide attacks. Significantly, the mortality salient group also indicated that they would be more willing to take part in a suicide attack themselves.

Thus, the mortality salience created by the death-related images either in real life or through various media sources can be expected for many to lead to an increase in sympathy and support for militant groups who claim to defend important icons and tenets of identity. Further, there will also be increased hostility towards enemies of that identity (e.g. America and its allies in the context of jihadi extremism), and also to lead to an increased expressed willingness to engage in violence themselves.

The more important cultural icons and beliefs are involved (e.g. reference to the Qu'ran, the Prophet Mohammed, and other vital aspects of Islam in the context of jihadi extremism), the more pronounced that the effect is likely to be. As already indicated mortality salience leads to an increased attachment and protectiveness towards such beliefs and also produces increased hostility and aggression to others who appear to be denigrating or insulting such icons and beliefs. Extremist propaganda highlights and focuses on such issues. For example, jihadi web-sites often focus on the alleged abuse of copies of the Qu'ran committed by Americans in Iraq and the Guantanamo Bay prison camp, for example, and under mortality salience conditions such acts take on a more serious and provocative dimension.

## Does media coverage cause terrorism?

Given the different psychological effects that this chapter has already demonstrated can be associated with media coverage – and given how focal most terrorist groups view media coverage for the maintenance of their interests – perhaps the most fundamental question with regard to the media is whether media coverage of past terrorist attacks causes increased terrorism in the future? Certainly, in the literature on terrorism, there is often a common assumption that media coverage does indeed increase terrorism. This assumption is the result of a number of factors. The first of these is the simple fact that most terrorist groups are *so* interested in having a media impact. It seems clear that the terrorists themselves believe that media coverage is imperative. The more media attention the group and the conflict receive, then the more of an impact they are having.

For terrorists, an attack that receives a great deal of media attention is seen as much more successful than an attack which receives relatively little (even if the human casualties and physical damage caused by both attacks are similar). Indeed, even if an attack results in the death or capture of all the terrorists involved it can be still be regarded as highly successful if it has received intense international media attention. Consider the following assessment from Abu 'Ubeid Al Qurashi, an Al-Qaeda activist who was assessing the impact of the Palestinian attack on the 1972 Munich Olympics:

> . . . Seemingly, the [Munich Olympics] operation failed because it did not bring about the release of the prisoners, and even cast a shadow of doubt on the justness of the Palestinian cause in world public opinion. But following the operation, and contrary to how it appeared [at first], it was the greatest media victory, and the first true proclamation to the entire world of the birth of the Palestinian resistance movement . . . In truth, the Munich operation was a great propaganda strike. Four thousand journalists and radio personnel, and two thousand commentators and television technicians were there to cover the Olympic games; suddenly, they were broadcasting the suffering of the Palestinian people. Thus, 900 million people in 100 countries were witness to the operation by means of television screens. This meant that at least a quarter of the world knew what was going on in Munich; after this, they could no longer ignore the Palestinian tragedy.

Thus for many terrorist attacks a key aim is not simply to destroy or harm a particular target, but rather to attract and generate publicity. As discussed earlier, the message can be more important to someone seeking revenge than the act itself.

For observers why would the terrorists be so concerned about media coverage if it was not because it increased their support and thus allowed them to carry out more attacks and activities than before? However, evidence that increased media coverage encourages increased terrorism is much more mixed than many people expect.

Initial reviews of the evidence failed to find an impact. Robert Picard, for example, in a scathing review in 1986 drew attention first to the widespread assumption among many analysts and researchers that coverage did cause more terrorism, and then second to the serious lack of evidence that actually supported such widely held assumptions. The more rigorous research that followed initially failed to find the expected impact. Nelson and Scott (1992), for example, studied terrorism coverage in the media as well as recorded terrorist attacks (using the ITERATE database of international terrorism incidents). Examining data from 1968 to 1984 they failed to find a link between coverage and the number of attacks. When media coverage increased this was not followed by an increase in terrorist attacks.

Further research by Weimann and Winn (1994) shed more light. While an increase in the overall level of terrorism was not found with more coverage, there was a contagion effect: terrorism tactics that received more coverage were more likely to be copied in the future. The overall amount of attacks was unchanged, but the terrorist groups did show a shift towards those types of attacks that had received more coverage in the recent past. Other researchers have argued that this contagion effect can also be seen for example in recent years with the growth of suicide attacks as a more common tactic as well as an increase in practices such as the recorded beheadings of hostages by different groups.

While the early research failed to find that increased coverage was associated with an increase in terrorist attacks, more recent research has suggested a link. Rohner and Frey (2007) for example conducted a review looking at terrorist attacks from 1998 to 2004. The study found that there was a link between coverage and the number of attacks. Increased coverage was associated with a subsequent increase in attacks. Further, the link was reciprocal: more attacks led to more coverage, and more coverage was then followed by a further increase. In trying to explain why this finding was not found in earlier research, the authors highlighted that globalization was a potentially important factor particularly with regard to international terrorism. While a link was found between increased coverage and subsequent increased levels of terrorism, the authors highlighted that the evidence was not proof of causality. In other words, they could not be certain that the coverage caused the increase. There was a link, yes, but exactly how and why it worked was not clear and other factors might still be playing an unseen but vital role behind the scenes.

Overall, the evidence available today suggests that the assumptions Picard (1986) hotly criticized are probably broadly correct. It does seem that both a contagion effect exists – increased media coverage on a particular type of terrorist tactic, leads to an increase in similar attacks happening – and that a magnitude effect exists – more coverage is linked with more attacks happening overall. Exactly how strong these effects are is still not entirely clear, especially given the mixed nature of some findings. Nevertheless, given the intense interest the media often shows with regard to terrorism, the findings make for sobering thought.

## Does media coverage cause other harm?

While populations tend to cope fairly well with ongoing terrorist threats, media coverage often adds a destabilizing factor to the mix. Media attention certainly fosters a widespread belief that terrorist attacks are both more common and more dangerous than is actually the case. Psychologists have also found that intense media coverage by itself can have some damaging impact with some adults and children appearing to suffer serious psychological problems as a result of long exposure to media coverage of terrorist attacks. They often had trouble sleeping, suffered from nightmares, had anxiety problems or suffered depression. Yet, these people had not been at the scene when the attack occurred and they were not connected to direct victims. They had not lost family members, friends, neighbours or colleagues in the devastation, but they had witnessed a great deal of media coverage. Researchers found that in some groups of schoolchildren, media exposure alone seemed to be a primary cause of PTSD in the aftermath of the attacks (Pfefferbaum, 2003).

One survey of residents of Manhattan in the months after the destruction of the World Trade Center found that 7.5 per cent of the respondents reported symptoms consistent with PTSD and 9.7 per cent reported symptoms consistent with depression (Galea et al., 2002). There was a direct link between how close one lived to the Twin Towers and the likelihood that you would develop PTSD. Twenty per cent of those living in the vicinity of the World Trade Center showed signs of PTSD. The findings also emphasized the vicarious impact of the attacks: most of those displaying negative symptoms of PTSD and depression had not been physically at the Center when the attack occurred, they had not been in immediate danger and they were not related to direct victims. Instead, these people turned to television, radio, and the Internet, to learn about what had happened, and for some, the media had then become an extremely significant vector of fear.

At the time of writing, there have been no successful terrorist attacks in the US since 2001. Yet despite the absence of violence, terrorism has never left the public consciousness and has remained a high-profile political and public issue. Enormous debate and coverage is given to the issue of the threat of terrorism. Most people badly overestimate the likelihood that they will be killed or maimed in a terrorist attack. In the past ten years, the average American is much more likely to have been struck by lightning than to have been caught up in a terrorist attack. Such statistics appear to have done little to reassure however.

A further problem is the enormous attention given to terrorist alerts. Research in New York has found that changes in the colour-coded alert system are associated with increased signs of distress among a survey of nearly 2000 people. When the colour alert changed from yellow to orange these people showed increased levels of depression, anxiety, phobic responses and other signs of PTSD. When the alert levels dropped back, the symptoms again spiked indicating that public reminders of the danger acted as a stressor regardless of the direction of the change.

Reminders of the threat posed by terrorists however also bolsters society. Approval ratings for the President show a small rise every time the threat levels are changed – regardless of whether the level is increased or decreased. One explanation for this consequence is to return to mortality salience effects: when we are reminded of danger we tend to show increased support to our own group and to leaders of that group. This, naturally, has led to accusations that announcements regarding terrorist threats since 9/11 (including changes to the official threat levels) have occasionally been motivated by political motives (McDermott and Zimbardo, 2007).

Terrorism can be dangerous, callous and cruel, but in general the evidence is that society adapts. Even in very violent conflicts where terrorist attacks are happening sometimes on an almost hourly basis, society does not collapse under the psychological strain (e.g. Brandon and Silke, 2007). Most people adapt and cope, displaying remarkable resilience.

Indeed, the most psychological strain is often not seen when attacks are frequent and common, but rather when they are rare and unpredictable. In the latter circumstances it is harder to develop a sense of control over the situation, and in the end, having a sense of control is important – without it we are much more susceptible to our fears. In some respects, the US today faces the worst of both worlds. The welcome absence of any terrorist attacks in the homeland since 2001 at one level creates an impression of normality, yet this impression is constantly being jostled by the frequent warnings and public announcements of a continuing threat. It is an unhappy balancing act that shows no sign of ending soon.

## Counter-terrorism and the media

Media coverage of terrorist violence is generally a sensitive issue for governments. States often prefer that terrorist incidents receive no coverage at all, or else just coverage that is sympathetic and supportive of the government position. In contrast, the terrorist groups are generally very keen to attract as much media interest as possible (though there have been some exceptions to this rule such as the group Shining Path, which showed very little interest in the media). The result is that governments often use censorship to attempt to control the media coverage of a conflict. This censorship can take the form of legislation banning certain types of media reporting, to completely banning journalists from even travelling to the areas and regions where the conflict is taking place.

In the UK, the government introduced a broadcasting ban for the representatives of the paramilitary groups. This was particularly targeted at Sinn Fein, the political party affiliated with the IRA. Initially the ban was comprehensive and it prevented the UK media from broadcasting interviews or public statements from Sinn Fein members. The ban though did not prohibit Sinn Fein from publishing its weekly newspaper *An Phoblacht/Republican News*. Indeed, though banned from the radio and television, the censorship did not extend to print media and the paramilitary groups were able to publish their own magazines, pamphlets and newspapers. The most significant of these was (and is) *An Phoblacht/Republican News*. This weekly newspaper is published by Sinn Fein and has been sold openly in Catholic areas in Northern Ireland throughout the conflict (English, 2004).

As time passed, the broadcasting ban was gradually relaxed as the various media organizations began to systematically expose loopholes in the legislation. For example, the media were not allowed to broadcast the speech of Sinn Fein politicians though they could show their images. Broadcasters started to dub the images using actors' voices. A journalist would interview a Sinn Fein politician such as Gerry Adams, and then the interview would be broadcast with an actor's voice used instead of Adams' own voice. In the early phases this sometimes led to the disconcerting experience of someone with a polished English accent dubbing Adams, but quickly a small industry developed in Northern Ireland for local actors to carry out these duties.

There is something curiously half-hearted about the attempts of UK governments to censor the IRA and its political representatives. Other countries have taken far stricter attitudes. Sinn Fein and IRA, for example, were also the targets of a tough broadcasting ban in the Republic of Ireland. Irish governments were far more reluctant than their UK counter-parts to allow militant republicans access to the airwaves, and Sinn Fein members were entirely prevented from giving interviews either directly or indirectly, though again they could publish in print. The ban was only lifted with the advent of the peace process in the 1990s.

Other countries give us even more aggressive examples. Indonesia and Sri Lanka, for example, have both taken a particularly aggressive approach. For ten years between 1989 and 1998, Indonesia allowed no media access whatsoever to the troubled region of Aceh (Schulze, 2007). This severely restricted coverage of the conflict between the government and GAM being waged there. From 1999 on, the government relaxed media restrictions and coverage of the conflict increased enormously. However, in 2003, the government introduced fresh restrictions on the media making it again almost impossible for foreign journalists to visit the region. Indonesian journalists could travel to the area but primarily only if they were embedded with military units. Despite these fresh restrictions, media coverage of the conflict has remained relatively balanced as the media editors now have telephone numbers for many GAM representatives.

In other countries, the media are often surprisingly willing to self-censor. For example, this is very much the case in India particularly with regard to the Kashmir conflict. There is no serious attempt by the main media outlets to present a balanced account of this conflict and the general coverage is very pro-government (Bose, 2007). The government is primarily concerned with regulating and limiting the flow of information to the Indian public on the conflict, and media stories that are critical of government policies can provoke a serious reaction. For example, one journalist from *The Times of India* filed a story highlighting abuse of the electoral system in Kashmir with large numbers of people being forced to vote at gunpoint. Due to editors being absent, the story was included in the following day's issue. The journalist was recalled immediately from Kashmir by the paper and was forced to write a follow-up story denying the claims made in the previous piece. Thus, while there is no official censorship, self-censorship, combined with occasional government pressure, results in a very biased and controlled coverage of the conflict.

The situation in Israel is quite similar to that in India. Again, Israel has not imposed state censorship on the media but instead there is a high degree of self-censorship. Israeli governments attempt to manage the media rather than gag them (Gunning, 2007). After a major incident or event, the government will hold a well-organized press conference for journalists, supply them with information packs and also give them a list of contacts within government and the security forces who are available to be interviewed. On the Palestinian side there are rarely any co-ordinated press conferences and journalists can struggle to find contacts for interviews. They are also more likely to receive conflicting accounts about what has happened. The end result is that the government version of events tends, over time, to dominate (particularly in the domestic media).

In the UK, as has been set out earlier in this chapter, concerted effort has recently gone into designing counter-terrorist policy that aims to influence the language that politicians and the media use when communicating information that targets individuals at risk of radicalization (Payne, 2009). Drawing on psychological research, it is clear that such a policy has the potential to have a powerful influence on the audience.

## Conclusions

The impact that the media has in communicating messages that have the potential to increase or decrease support for terrorism cannot be underestimated. It is a power that is respected and exploited by terrorist groups, very often coming themselves from less democratic countries where the media is censored. The freedom of the press is a fundamental attribute that we value in liberal-democratic nations, but with it comes a responsibility to recognize how such a power can be utilized to the benefit rather than detriment of a more stable society.

In outlining the role that the media plays in influencing the 'battle for hearts and minds', this chapter has touched on a number of notable issues, each of which warrants more detailed attention in of itself. It has shown how the media have long been used to recruit and promote support for extremist groups across the globe. In particular in recent years, the Internet has successfully disseminated knowledge and information about the motivations of terrorist groups, and it continues to be a potential source of recruitment of new soft and hard supporters.

Policy aimed at targeting those at risk of radicalization already recognizes that how language is used by the media and by politicians can have an impact on those who receive the messages. However, more needs to be done to widen the scope of the influence of such policies. Terrorist groups themselves have recognized that the language they use in video and other propaganda material can resonate with individuals, drawing on their sense of identity and their reaction to perceived injustices to stimulate them into further involvement. Identity is something that continues to develop throughout a lifespan, however, and strategies aimed at communicating the attractiveness of belonging to different groups might have an impact.

Terrorist groups also use the media to communicate their message of revenge to target nations, and getting this media attention is very important to them. It has been pointed out in the chapter that this remains the case even if casualties are small and the terrorists themselves are killed or apprehended in the attack. For some observers, this has led to concerns that media coverage is having the impact of increasing the number of attacks. While this has not been conclusively demonstrated, enough evidence of an impact has been shown to mean that care needs to be taken in how attacks are portrayed and how the message of the impact of the attack is conveyed to those who might be swayed towards radicalization.

## Notes

1 Firdaws (سودرف) is the highest level of heaven in Islamic tradition. This is where the prophets, the martyrs and the most truthful and pious people dwell.
2 The Hijrah refers to the Prophet Muhammad's migration from Mecca to Madinah in 622A.D. The word hijrah means to leave a place to seek sanctuary or freedom from persecution or freedom of religion or any other purpose. Hijrah can also mean to leave a bad way of life for a good or more righteous way.

## References

Alderdice, Lord (2007). The individual, the group and the psychology of terrorism. *International Review of Psychiatry*, 19 (3), 291–209.

Al Zawahiri, A. (2005). In Laura Mansfield (trans.). *In His Own Words: A Translation of the Writings of Dr. Ayman Al Zawahiri*. TLG Publications.

Ansari, H., Cinnirella, M., Rogers, M. B., Loewenthal, K. M. and Lewis, C. A. (2006). Perceptions of martyrdom and terrorism amongst British Muslims. In M. B. Rogers, C. A. Lewis, K. M. Loewenthal, M. Cinnirella, R. Amlôt and H. Ansari (eds.) *Proceedings of the British Psychological Society Seminar Series Aspects of Terrorism and Martyrdom, eCOMMUNITY: International Journal of Mental Health & Addiction*.

Armstrong, J. Chin, C.J. and Leventer, U. (2008). *The Language of Counter-Terrorism: When Message Received is Not Message Intended. Report for the UK Foreign and Commonwealth Office*. Cambridge MA: Harvard Kennedy School of Government.

Bin Laden, O. (1996). 'Declaration of War Against the Americans Occupying the Land of the Two Holy Places.' Copy available at www.homelandsecurityus.net/osama%20posts/declaration_of_war_against_the_a.htm,

Bloom, M. (2005). *Dying to Kill: The Allure of Suicide Terror*. New York: Columbia University Press.

Boettcher, W.A. and Cobb, M.D. (2006). Echoes of Vietnam? Casualty framing and public perceptions of success and failure in Iraq. *Journal of Conflict Resolution*, 50 (6), 831–854.

Bose, S. (2007). 'JKLF and JKHM: Jammu and Kashmir Liberation Front and Jammu and

Kashmir Hizb-ul Mujahideen.' In M. Hieberg, B. O'Leary and J. Tirman (eds), *Terror, Insurgency and the State*, 229–256. Philadelphia: University of Pennsylvania Press.

Brandon, S. and Silke, A. (2007). 'Near- and long-term psychological effects of exposure to terrorist attacks.' In Bongar, B., Brown, L., Beutler, L., Breckenridge, J. and Zimbardo, P. (Eds.) *Psychology of Terrorism*, pp. 175–193. Oxford University Press.

Burke, J. (2007). *Al-Qaeda: The True Story of Radical Islam* (2nd Ed). London: Penguin.

Clark, R. (1983). Patterns in the lives of ETA members. *Studies in Conflict & Terrorism*, 6/3, 423–454

Collins, E. (with McGovern, M.) (1997). *Killing Rage*. London: Granta Books.

Conway, M. and McInerney, L. (2008). Jihadi video and auto-radicalisation: Evidence from an exploratory YouTube study. In Daniel Ortiz-Arroyo, Henrik Legind Larsen, Daniel Dajun Zeng, David Hicks and Gerhard Wagner (Eds.) *Intelligence and Security Informatics: First European Conference, EuroISI 2008, Proceedings*, 108–118. New York: Springer.

Coogan, T.P. (1987). *The IRA*. London: Fontana.

Cota-McKinley, A., Woody, W. and Bell, P. (2001). Vengeance: Effects of gender, age and religious background. *Aggressive Behavior*, 27, 343–350.

Dienel, H., Sharan, Y., Rapp, C. and Ahituv, N. (in press). *Terrorism and the Internet: Threats, Target groups, Deradicalisation strategies*. Amsterdam: IOS Press.

English, R. (2004). *Armed Struggle: The History of the IRA*. London: Pan.

Fischer, P. Greitemeyer, T. and Kastenmüller, A. (2007). What do we think about Muslims? The validity of Westerner's implicit theories about associations between Muslim's religiosity, religious identity, aggression potential and attitudes towards terrorism. *Group Processes and Inter-Group Relations*, 10 (3), 373–382.

Galea, S., Ahern, J., Resnick, H., Kilpatrick, D., Bucuvalas, M., Gold, J. et al. (2002). Psychological sequelae of the September 11 terrorist attacks in New York City. *New England Journal of Medicine*, 346, 982–987.

Ganor, B. (2005). *The Counter-Terrorism Puzzle: A guide for decision makers*. New Jersey: Transaction Publishers, Rutgers.

Gollwitzer, M. and Denzler, M. (2009). What makes revenge sweet: seeing the offender suffer or delivering a message? *Journal of Experimental Psychology*, 45 (4), 840–844.

Gottschalk, M. and Ellis, L. (2009). Evolutionary and Genetic Explanations of Violent Crime. In C.J. Ferguson (Ed.) *Violent Crime: Clinical and Social Implications*, pp 57–74. California: Sage Publications.

Gunning, J. (2007). Hamas: Harakat al-Muqawama al-Islamiyya. In M. Hieberg, B. O'Leary and J. Tirman (eds), *Terror, Insurgency and the State*, 123–156. Philadelphia: University of Pennsylvania Press.

Hammack, P.L. (2008). Narrative and the cultural psychology of identity. *Personality and Social Psychology Review*, 12, 222–247.

Horgan, J. and Taylor, M. (1997). The Provisional Irish Republican Army: command and functional structure. *Terrorism and Political Violence*, 9/3, pp. 1–32.

Hubert, C. (1997). Role in capture haunts Kaczynski's brother. *Sacramento Bee*, 19 January.

Jenkins, B. (1975). International Terrorism: A New Mode of Conflict. In David Carlton and Carlo Schaerf (eds.), *International Terrorism and World Security*. London: Croom Helm.

McCauley, C. and Moskalenko, S. (2008). Mechanisms of political radicalisation: Pathways towards terrorism. *Terrorism and Political Violence*, 20 (3), 415–433.

McDermott, R. and Zimbardo, P. (2007). The psychological consequences of terrorist alerts.

In Bruce Bongar, Lisa Brown, Larry Beutler, James Breckenridge and Philip Zimbardo (eds.) *Psychology of Terrorism*, pp. 357–372. Oxford: Oxford University Press.

Nelson, P. and Scott, J. (1992). Terrorism and the Media: an Empirical Analysis. *Defence Economics*, 3/4, 329–339.

Payne, K. (2009). Winning the battle of ideas: Propaganda, ideology and terror. *Studies in Conflict and Terrorism*, 33 (2), 109–128.

Pfefferbaum, B. (2003). Victims of terrorism and the media. In Andrew Silke (ed.) *Terrorists, Victims and Society*. Chichester: Wiley.

Picard, R. (1986). News coverage as the contagion of terrorism: Dangerous charges backed by dubious science. Paper presented at the Annual Meeting of the Association for Education in Journalism and Mass Communication, at Norman, OK, August 30, 1986.

Pyszczynski, T., Abdollahi, A., Solomon, S., Greenberg, J., Cohen, F. and Weise, D. (2006). Mortality salience, martyrdom, and military might: the great satan versus the axis of evil. *Personality and Social Psychology Bulletin*, 32/4, 525–537.

Pyszczynski, T., Solomon, S. and Greenberg, J. (2002). *In the Wake of 9/11: The Psychology of Terror*. Washington, D.C.: American Psychological Association.

Rohner, D. and Frey, B. (2007). Blood and ink! The common-interest-game between terrorists and the media. *Public Choice*, 133, pp. 129–145.

Rosenblatt, A., Greenberg, J., Somon, S., Pyszczynski, T. and Lyon, D. (1989). Evidence for Terror Management Theory I. The effects of mortality salience on reactions to those who violate or uphold cultural values.' *Journal of Personality and Social Psychology*, 57/ 4, 681–690.

Sageman, M. (2004). *Understanding Terror Networks*. Philadelphia PA: University of Pennsylvania Press.

Saggar, S. (2009). Boomerangs and slingshots: Radical Islamism and counter-terrorism strategy. *Journal of Ethnic and Migration Studies*, 35, 3, 381–402.

Schulze, K. (2007). GAM: Gerakan Aceh Merdeka (Free Aceh Movement). In M. Hieberg, B. O'Leary and J. Tirman (eds), *Terror, Insurgency and the State*, 83–122. Philadelphia: University of Pennsylvania Press.

Silke, A. (2000). Beating the Water: The Terrorist Search for Power, Control and Authority. *Terrorism and Political Violence*, 12/2, 76–96.

Silke, A. (2003). Becoming a Terrorist. In A. Silke, (Ed.). *Terrorists, Victims and Society: Psychological Perspectives on Terrorism and Its Consequences*, pp. 29–53. Chichester: Wiley.

Silke, A. (2008). Holy Warriors: Exploring the Psychological Processes of Jihadi Radicalisation. *European Journal of Criminology*, 5/1, 99–123.

Sluka, J. (1989). *Hearts and Minds, Water and Fish: Support for the IRA and INLA in a Northern Irish Ghetto*. London: Jai Press.

Speckhard, A. (2008). Understanding the psycho-social and political process involved in ideological support for terrorism. In M. Sharp (Ed.) *Suicide Bombers: The Psychological, Religious and other Imperatives*. Amsterdam: IOS Press.

Speckhard, A. and Ahkmedova, K. (2006). The making of a martyr: Chechen suicide terrorism. *Studies in Conflict & Terrorism*, 29 (5), 42–492.

Weimann, G. (2006). Virtual Disputes: The Use of the Internet for Terrorist Debates. *Studies in Conflict and Terrorism*, 29 (7), 623–639.

Weimann, G. and Winn, C. (1994). *The Theater of Terror: Mass Media and International Terrorism*. New York: Longman.

# 8   Disengaging from terrorism

*Neil Ferguson*

## Introduction

The field of terrorism studies has grown exponentially since the events of September 11, 2001 (Horgan, 2005), though much of the research that has been published since then has been poor (Silke, 2001; 2003), generally due to the reliance on secondary data and a lack of researchers working in the field. Nonetheless, there has been a growing awareness of the complexity of the challenge faced in understanding the psychology and motivations of the terrorist (Victoroff, 2005) and an increasing appreciation of the routes and processes involved in people engaging in terrorism or becoming radicalized to the point of engaging in armed violence to bring about political change (Horgan, 2003; 2005) and to a lesser extent the changes that take place once the terrorist becomes involved (Burgess et al., 2007). However, until very recently (Bjorgo and Horgan, 2009; Horgan 2009a) there has been a dearth of research exploring the processes and factors involved in disengagement from terrorist activities.

At first glance this seems surprising due to the obvious implications disengagement from terrorism has for counter-terrorism policy, the importance of issues around recidivism and rehabilitation as aspects of criminal lifestyles in Criminology (Kanazawa and Still, 2000) and the growing utilization of Disarmament, Demobilization and Reintegration (DDR) programmes in re-building post-conflict stability across the world. Counter-intuitively within the area of terrorism studies research exploring accelerators and barriers in the process of disengagement from terrorism are relatively unknown, yet the implications of this knowledge are enormous for anyone interested in counter-terrorism. Horgan (2009b) argues in part that this lack of interest stems from the 'new' versus 'old' terrorism divide, in which researchers and policy makers have been over eager to disregard terrorists and violent extremist groups who have already demobilized or embarked on the road to peace from the analysis of the 'new' terrorist threat we face post 9/11. Another reason for this deficiency of information could be related to the problems inherent in a field of study where the researchers are reluctant to actually meet and engage with current and former violent extremists.

This chapter will explore the processes of disengagement and will incorporate some of the findings from research[1] conducted in Northern Ireland with current and former members of the Irish Republican Army (IRA), the Ulster Volunteer Force (UVF) and Red Hand Commando (RHC) to illustrate the disengagement process.

## The process of disengagement

Just as with the process of engagement in terrorism, the process of disengagement from militant extremism is complex and incorporates interplay between micro, meso, macro and exo factors (for a discussion of exo, macro, meso and micro systems see Bronfenbrenner, 1977). This multitude of factors can crudely be divided into two main processes, either they (a) bring about individuals desisting from terrorism, or they (b) lead to groups disengaging from military operations. The reasons behind the individuals or groups disengaging from terrorism can be both voluntary (e.g. individuals become disillusioned, or groups voluntarily enter peace negotiations) and forced (e.g. incarceration) and the disengagement may be temporary or permanent. This chapter will primarily focus on individual disengagement, but as individual disengagement does not take place in a vacuum the chapter will also incorporate aspects of group level disengagement.

## The disengagement of individual terrorists

The two most commonly used approaches to bring about individual disengagement are incarcerating the terrorist for a period of time or permanently ending the person's involvement in terrorism by killing them. These approaches are perceived as effective and work on the basis that the more terrorists that are killed, especially seasoned combatants and leaders, the greater the impact this will have on the operational capacity of the terrorist cell or group. While incarcerating violent extremists is damaging to the capacity of the group, this impact may not be permanent. Additionally, incarcerating individuals or groups engaged in violent extremism has been shown to have two main effects (a) increasing their radicalization within the prison, or (b) bringing about their reform or rehabilitation (Pluchinsky, 2008). Obviously to counter terrorism, agencies need to aim to achieve the latter, rather than the former, making an understanding of the role of imprisonment a key aspect of any counter-terrorism approach. Pluchinsky (2008) believes there are fewer than 5,000 global Jihadists, not linked to groups involved in national struggles (e.g. Hamas, Hizbollah, etc) incarcerated across the globe at the moment, but this figure is difficult to confirm. Pluchinsky estimates that most Jihadists receive sentences of less than 20 years, with many receiving 10 years or less, leaving only 15 percent facing execution or life sentences. Therefore most incarcerated global Jihadists will eventually be free to reengage in extremist violence unless they are rehabilitated while in prison. Although there have not been any comprehensive analyses of recidivism rates among global Jihadists, there is much anecdotal evidence based on analyses of individual case studies to suggest a strong tendency towards recidivism.

Prisons and the prison experience of incarcerated militants are key parts of the battlefield for terrorist groups. For example, in Northern Ireland recruits to the IRA were routinely told how their involvement would mean incarceration or death. Terrorist organizations place a lot of emphasis on maintaining discipline, group cohesion, and group identity in its imprisoned members. Throughout the conflict in Northern Ireland the prisoners played a key role in both the maintenance of the conflict and the creation of the conditions for the fledging peace process. For the former prisoners we interviewed in Northern Ireland their removal from the conflict was key to both their radicalization and disengagement from terrorism, indicating that Pluchinsky's main effects of reform or radicalization are not necessarily polar opposites, but could take place simultaneously. In reality, a number of interviewees demonstrated that the prison experience provided them with the space to sharpen their political ideology and strategy while devising non-violent approaches to achieve their organisational and political goals. They also reflected how this would have been impossible if they were still involved in the military operations on the outside of the prison walls. The quote below is from a loyalist paramilitary who held a command position in the UVF and it illustrates how prison provides the space to debate and develop ideas, which would be unthinkable on the streets of Belfast:

> Some people say that the likes of the Maze [a prison in Northern Ireland] and places like that were universities of terrorism, they were terrorist training camps, but I actually believe that they were the university of peace, in terms of what we discussed in there, how we decided, how we came about in our discussions how do we get out of this? How do we get, you know, where is this all going?

So while the years spent in prison may not rehabilitate or de-radicalize the prisoner (indeed none of the former republican or loyalist prisoners interviewed in any way admitted to holding weaker attachments to their wider community, paramilitary organization or its goals), their conceptualization of the conflict and strategic vision was improved and crystallized by finding the space to think, rather than by simply reacting to events taking place around them. Another former UVF prisoner points out the role of going to prison in this process:

> I went to prison in 1980 and if you've any sort of grey matter in your head at all you have to start and analyse why you finished up in prison and just my thinking just reinforced the fact that everything wasn't as black and white as I had seen it. Prison just gives you an opportunity to be detached from the conflict, it's a dubious way to be detached but you're detached from it and it gives you time to think, you come out with pretty clear ideas in your head. It's pretty difficult after that period of time when you're away and you go back and see your friends and colleagues from before and some of them are thinking in exactly the same way as they did in the early seventies, how's this happening like, and then they think because you've been in prison it's softened you or broken you or whatever but that's not the case it's just common sense, pragmatism, you can't go on killing each other forever, some time you're going to

have to talk so why not do it now rather than go through another ten, twenty or whatever years of conflict.

The imprisonment of individual terrorists provides the desired goal of the temporary removal of combatants from the battlefield, the disruption of the group or cell's activities and capacity to engage in future terrorist attacks. However, the experiences of these and many other prisoners indicate that while this time in prison may provide neither the rehabilitating or de-radicalizing experience hoped for, it does provide members of the armed groups the much needed space to discuss and revaluate their armed struggle, which may begin a process of lessening the violent struggle or perhaps the renouncing of violence and the disarmament and demobilization of the armed groups they represent.

Obviously this outcome of prison providing the space to revaluate the conflict and strategy has implications for how the prisoners are housed during their incarceration. As terrorist prisoners are viewed as posing a potential radicalizing threat to other prisoners, many terrorists are held in solitary confinement away from other likeminded prisoners and potential recruits, however by doing so they reduce the likelihood that the prisoners will be able to create the critical mass necessary to reformulate their military and political strategy. The UVF commander quoted earlier discusses how they worked with members of Euskadi Ta Askatasuna (ETA) to debate this conundrum:

> And then they [Members of ETA] asked for a meeting and we went and talked to them and they asked for our help on how do we get out of the situation we are in. So I basically said to them look you have a big problem because if you have an active service unit that is caught maybe bombing in Madrid, say it's us three, you go to Barcelona, you go to Madrid and I'd probably go to Valencia. We never have the opportunity to discuss what we were doing. So what happens then is that another service unit comes up again, so there's no room for dialogue. So what we said to them was one of you should call a ceasefire, but have a condition within the ceasefire that after the ceasefire is held for so long that there is a repatriation of your prisoners into the one place, and then you start to debate and the discussion on how you move forward.

Being imprisoned is not the only way to create this space for reflection and debate, for some violent extremists (Garfinkel, 2007) getting away from the conflict for a period of time can help create the conditions to revaluate the armed struggle. Likewise for some of the Northern Irish paramilitaries we interviewed (such as the one quoted below) experiences of having to evade the police and leave Northern Ireland to live in exile accidentally provided the space to analyse the conflict and stirred them to return as community workers and peace activists rather than combatants.

> So you really understand what it's like [when you leave and look back at Northern Ireland]. And I think what you need to do is to take people out of

the picture and get them off their hides and have them look at it. I mean to try to give you an analogy of it, it's like watching your son grow up, or your child grow up, you never notice them growing from little child up to a man or a woman. You just don't notice it, and all of a sudden ten years later, wasn't that quick. How did you grow up so quick?

In addition to seeking a change of direction as a result of incarceration or removal from the conflict zone, the individual terrorist can desist from terrorism for a number of micro level intrapersonal reasons. Both Blee (2002) and Bjorgo (2009) in their research exploring involvement and disengagement from rightwing extremist groups such as neo-Nazi groups and skinhead gangs have uncovered a variety of similar *push* and *pull* factors involved in disengagement from extremist rightwing groups. Engagement with these groups as with other clandestine groups, usually involves cutting the ties to the rest of 'normal' society as they are socialized into the usually stigmatized, reclusive and closed racist groups and disengaging with these groups involves rebuilding a 'normal' life in mainstream society. Bjorgo (2009) charts a number of intra-individual or micro level push and pull factors that instigate disengagement such as (a) losing faith with the group ideology, (b) feeling that the violence is getting out of hand or becoming counterproductive, (c) growing disillusioned with the group mechanics or dynamics, (e) becoming burnt out, (f) getting too old, (g) changes in career or family situation.

These factors are also commonly reported in research exploring other violent militant groups, for example Horgan (2009a) describes how a member of Al-Qaeda disengaged from the movement while crossing into Afghanistan from Pakistan to fight US forces due to witnessing firsthand how his romantic and idealized vision of being a Jihadist is not replicated in the reality he is faced with. Previous research with members of the IRA and UVF (Burgess et al., 2005) has shown the importance both family situation and career prospects have on influencing people to engage in violence or take a more peaceful political approach. One loyalist interviewee indicated how age had an impact on a person's ability to physically conduct military operations: 'when you do thirteen years in prison when you come out you wouldn't be much use for doing anything else in that line of business', and suggested you would be better suited to taking up other roles in the organization (e.g. prisoner welfare). Incidentally a number of paramilitary interviewees reflected on how, rather than being *pushed* to leave because the violence was getting out of hand, they temporarily left their respective organizations because the violence was not intense enough or they felt the peace process was the wrong strategy at that particular place and time, as reflected in this quote:

I was . . . the sort of person who would have looked at school children, at a school, you committed an atrocity against us, we'll hit your school, what's more emotive than children? And if you hit children people will be so sick, you know children have been killed through the Troubles, been caught in bombs, things like that, but you get the one or two, if you get a mass incident then people's minds would maybe start to concentrate on exactly how to come to a solution.

Bjørgo also mentions the impact of 'burn out' on forcing an individual to reconsider their ability to engage in terrorism and as a factor which pushes the individual terrorist towards disengagement, indeed some of our interviews, members of the IRA and UVF discussed how there was intense physical, psychological and social pressures involved in being a terrorist, which left some traumatized, harbouring feelings of guilt and feeling morally disengaged (Ferguson et al., in press). These experiences of trauma have been seen as key antecedent aspects of the processes involved in the instigation and maintenance of violent extremism (Ferguson et al., in press; Speckhard, 2006). Garfinkel (2007) studied the psychological factors involved in the conversion of individuals from employing political violence to leaving violence behind and working to build peace. She interviewed seven former violent extremists from various conflict zones (Nigeria, Israel/Palestine, Kashmir and Lebanon) via the telephone. Her interviews explored the transition into violence and again out of violence, and she extrapolated a number of themes, one of which was that the experience of trauma is an important part of the process of change. For Garfinkel's participants the experience of trauma acted as a trigger to enable the individuals to begin the process of transformation from violent extremist to proponent of peace, which she views as a form of positive post-traumatic growth, a process that is evidenced in a variety of populations who have experienced traumatic events (Tedeschi and Calhoun, 1996). Thus traumatic experiences may play a key role in both initiating and terminating violent extremism.

Research with members and former members of armed groups (Brett and Specht, 2004; Ferguson et al., 2008) illustrated how exposure to critical and potentially traumatizing incidents was important in distinguishing between those who decided to join an armed group from those who didn't. These critical incidents were normally followed by a period of reflection (Ferguson et al. 2008) in which the individual goes through radical changes in their thinking during which they make a conscious decision to make the transition from civilian to violent extremist. Interestingly this process is also present in themes drawn from the narratives Northern Irish paramilitaries presented to us during interviews about disengagement, one of our loyalist interviewees explains how something switches on and you begin to realise you need to change and to encourage other colleagues to change.

> Something has to switch on, you know and I believe, I don't know whether it was the jail done that or what done that, maybe it was having the family done that or just basically going hold on a minute, where are we going here? But something switched on, you know and I know that I've seen it with other people, it switching on, you know and, we tried to expose as many people from our community as possible to that, hoping that this might be the thing that'll do, that'll switch them on.

For some of our participants this experience was being exposed to different people, ideas or seeing commonality or compassion in the enemy. Interestingly Garfinkel (2007) also drew this theme from her interviews with former violent extremists, as her sample comprised predominantly of religious extremists this turning point or critical moment tended to be recounted as a religious conversion or spiritual transformation that took place after meeting new people, moving away from the conflict, being exposed to new ideas or seeing compassion or commonality with the enemy.

This emerging research adds to the growing awareness that engagement in, involvement with and disengagement from violent extremism is a complex process and to understand these processes researchers need to explore the dynamics occurring at the intersection between individual experiences, their psychological dispositions, socialization processes and the external environment. It must also be remembered that for loyalists and republicans we interviewed or those ex-combatants who spoke to Horgan (2009a) or Garfinkel (2007) this process of disengagement from extremist violence does not mean de-radicalization. On the contrary, the majority, if not all of the participants in these studies still held the same political viewpoints, desired the same political goals and still worked to achieve these goals, but they had made a conscious decision to stop using violence (at least under the current circumstances) to realize their political goals.

Like the research exploring the process of individual engagement in militant violence (for example, see Ferguson et al., 2008; Victoroff, 2005) the emerging research on why people choose to disengage from violent extremism also demonstrates that terrorism is a nebulous activity, with many routes out, some of which will only lead to partial disengagement, with many of those engaged in terrorism today simply stepping back and taking up a variety of support roles (raising funds, recruitment, prisoner welfare, etc.) or potentially re-engaging in military activities in the future. However, the research does positively demonstrate that today's gunman can be tomorrow's community activist or peace worker.

## Organizational disengagement

Group level disengagement is a different process from individual level disengagement, but for many individual violent extremists, the disengagement of the group leads to their individual disengagement, so this chapter will also explore some aspects of organizational disengagement. Like the research exploring the individual processes involved in disengagement from militant violence the body of research on how terrorist groups decline is equally barren (Cronin, 2006; 2009).

Crenshaw (1991) builds on Ross and Gurr's (1989) comparative analysis of the declining incidence of domestic terrorism in Canada and the United States between 1960 and 1985 and develops a conceptual formulation of the decline of terrorist groups by exploring 76 terror groups from Europe, the Middle East, the Americas, Sri Lanka and the Philippines, which operated from 1950 until at least the end of the 1980s. Crenshaw (1991) related the decline of terrorist groups to three interlinked factors: the government response to terrorism, the strategic choices of the terror group and the group's organizational resources. Importantly she also notes that the decline of a terrorist group does not necessarily mean less terrorism, as groups can splinter and rival groups can form. For our paramilitary interviewees the fear of a split was one of the factors that contributed to the slow pace of organizational transition from violence to non-violence, as highlighted in this quote from a former UVF prisoner turned prisoners' representative and peace builder. He is discussing the difficulties the organization has in making the transition to non-violence and in particular the problem of what to do with the 'ceasefire soldiers' or the young volunteers in the organization:

> And that's the problem. And I know there are these thoughts within the organisation, how do we address these kids? How do we basically get rid of them, you know what I mean, without them falling into ruin the way the LVF [the Loyalist Volunteer Force, a dissident faction of the UVF] went, you know. It would be a tragedy to see another LVF or another group in that guise, who are only interested in gangsterism and drugs, you know what I mean. So its how do you keep them on board and how you disarm them gracefully and, that's what you're toying with the whole time.

Crenshaw (1999) explored the key variables involved in the decline of terror groups. Firstly she set out internal (e.g. organization decision making, perceptions of the outside world, internal rivalries and divisions) and external (e.g. outside support, comparative strength compared to state forces) factors that involve the terror group, and then she discerned the various tools a government can employ to counter the terrorist group, noting that these are not necessarily rival strategies, but can be pursed simultaneously, namely (a) military deterrence, (b) criminal justice powers, (c) defence through hardening targets and/or gathering intelligence, and (d) negotiating with the terrorist group. Crenshaw (1999) suggests the application of these tools to the terror groups will result in the following results, dependant on the internal and external factors presented in the terror group: complete success for the terror group, preliminary success, organizational collapse, dwindling support or take a new direction (e.g. into legitimate politics, widen the campaign into a full revolution).

Even within this limited typology, it is easy to see the multitude of potential combinations of strategies, variety of organization set-ups and outcomes, particularly if we remember that some of the tools and consequences can occur simultaneously. With this in mind, Crenshaw (1991, 1999) is keen to press the point to counter-terrorism policy makers that the picture is complex and challenging to analyse, and in particular to warn of the dangers inherent in 'getting tough' on terrorism.

Cronin (2009) conducted a review of previous studies exploring the decline of terrorist groups and discusses how and why some terror organizations ended their campaigns of violence providing a useful overview of why terrorist organizations end their military campaigns. Cronin builds on the work of Crenshaw (1991, 1999) and accepts the importance of the interplay of external and internal factors as crucial in the growth and decline of a terror group's capacity. She also notes the complexity of this interplay and how many of the factors which lead to the terminal decline of a terror group's effectiveness can be accidental or opportunistic rather than the result of any conscious counter-terrorism strategy. This analysis leads Cronin to develop seven broad critical factors inherent in the decline and disengagement of modern terror groups, namely:

(1) the death or capture of the leader,
(2) failure to transfer ideology the next generation,
(3) the group achieves their desired aims,
(4) transition to a legitimate political process,
(5) loss of popular support,
(6) repression through military force, and
(7) transition from terrorism to other forms of violence or criminality.

These seven critical factors are a useful summary of how many groups decline and desist in extremist violence, and indeed for many groups a combination of factors come into play. For example in discussions with our loyalist paramilitaries it was clear that many felt the group (UVF) had achieved its aims, in that the IRA had been unable to bomb the 'Brits' out of Ireland or that they had created an environment through their own violence that had brought the IRA to the negotiating table. There was also an acknowledgement that many of their former comrades in arms were now putting the skills learnt during the 'Troubles' to good use in organised crime as another former UVF prisoner succinctly puts it: 'the paramilitaries are disintegrating or mutating into gangs because since 1994 when the ceasefire was called, it's what do you do now mate, we're redundant aren't we.'

McCauley (2008) recently reviewed the literature on group level desistence from terrorism and pulled together key aspects from earlier studies to build a comprehensive overview of how desistence occurs at a group level. From this review he incorporates and builds on the work of previous theorists and researchers, including Crenshaw and Cronin, to build an inclusive model of group level disengagement. McCauley's model proposes the need to include actors (e.g. terrorist group, competitors, diaspora, governments), actions (e.g. increase violence, change in levels of support, government hardens targets) and outcomes (e.g. terrorists achieve final goals, transition into criminality, dwindling support) in developing a framework to understand group level disengagement. The dynamics of inter-relating all possible actor, action and outcome combinations would be difficult, and certainly impossible within the remit of a book chapter. Indeed McCauley acknowledges this complexity and argues that it would be impossible for a counter-terrorism initiative to pick a desired outcome (e.g. transition to non-violent politics) and then determine a formula of tactics (e.g. imprison terrorist leaders) that could *guarantee* that outcome. However, he believes that his model could help agencies (and terrorists) achieve their outcomes if they spent time considering how the various actors and actions impact on each other, for example, would hardening military targets cause more civilian casualties and as a by-product produce a reduction in sympathy for the terrorist group?

These analyses of organizational disengagement tend to underplay the role of leadership in the transition from violence to non-violence, except to acknowledge that the capture or killing of the leader or leadership could potentially destroy or destabilize the terror group. From the interviews we have had with former combatants and from research by academics with contact with armed groups (e.g. Edwards, 2009) it is clear that the role of terrorist leaders is crucial to any organizational transition towards exclusive non-violence. Indeed as McCauley (2008) notes it is almost paradoxical that terrorist leaders, who are often caricatured as the most radical, violent or fundamentalist, can be pivotal in pushing an organization towards disengagement. This pivotal role is illustrated in this discussion with one UVF commander about a key UVF leader who is trying to transform the organization into a new non-military civilianized role:

> He wants people to move forward now, and this is the type of guy who's worked all his life [in addition to being a member of the UVF]. He goes to his work and he said 'I don't like it when I walk along the Shankill Road and people say there's such and such, commander of the UVF. I want people to turn round and say there's such and such who works in such and such a factory, coz I don't want people to see me like that. You know not that I'm not proud of it, but we need to get back to normality'. We need to, and I think that's where we will be able to win the day within the UVF. The fact that there is enough good people at the top who are interested in moving forward. I wish I could say that for the whole rank and file, but I can't and I won't.

These models and examples from Northern Ireland clearly demonstrate that as with the processes in individual disengagement, the processes and routes to group level disengagement are complex and at times counterintuitive. However, they do provide ways of thinking about the problems and, at a minimum, provide those seeking to counter terrorism or insurgency with enough guidance to indicate that there is no one panacea for terrorism.

## Conclusions

The processes of disengaging from terrorism are complex, but through the case studies and literature reviewed in this chapter it is clear that there are common factors in the processes of both individual and group level disengagement which span different terror groups with varied structures and opposing motivations. This reminds us that lessons can be learnt from groups that have demobilized and entered the political mainstream, or are in the throes of transition from militant extremism to a more civilianized role. It must be remembered that terrorist organizations do understand the benefits of learning lessons from other conflicts and from other groups who do not necessarily share the same goals or ideology (e.g. both IRA and UVF members being invited to the Basque Country to advise ETA) so those interested in promoting disengagement from violent extremism would do well to do the same.

The emerging research around individual disengagement also demonstrates the importance of the prison experience and being removed from the heat of the conflict in order to facilitate the development of the strategic vision required in the transition to more non-violence approaches which still meet the group's desired goals. So it is important to understand the role of imprisonment and explore different approaches to housing violent politically motivated prisoners to develop best practice and additionally to explore how to provide and manage the space away from the conflict for terror groups to reflect on the dynamics of the conflict and develop more peaceful strategies. It must also be remembered that de-radicalization and disengagement are not equivalent and radicalization and disengagement may actually take place at the same time and in the same arena, if space is provided to allow this development.

Finally, the processes of both individual and organizational disengagement are complex; the activities involved in terrorism are nebulous and disengagement may be partial, temporal or simply the re-deployment to a non-military role. Incorporating this complexity makes it difficult to find a panacea for terrorism, but it is doubtful if any panacea truly exists. However, the developing research evidence and theoretic models discussed in this chapter and elsewhere in this book, do offer a means to conceptualize the scale and intricacy of the problem faced by agencies aiming to aid desistence from terrorism, which in turn should guide future research and policy, even if they often seem to lead to more questions than answers.

## Notes

1 Mark Burgess and Ian Hollywood also interviewed the paramilitaries during this fieldwork.

## References

Bjorgo, T. (2009). Processes of disengagement from violent groups of the extreme right. In T. Bjorgo and J. Horgan (Eds.) *Leaving Terrorism Behind: Individual and Collective Disengagement* (pp. 30–48). London: Routledge.

Bjorgo, T. and Horgan, J. (2009). *Leaving Terrorism Behind: Individual and Collective Disengagement*. London: Routledge.

Blee, K. M. (2002). *Inside Organized Racism: Women in the Hate Movement*. Berkeley: University of California Press.

Brett, R. and Specht, I. (2004). *Young Soldiers: Why They Choose to Fight*. London: Lynne Rienner.

Bronfenbrenner, U. (1977). Toward an experimental ecology of human development. *American Psychologist*, 32, 513–531.

Burgess, M., Ferguson, N., and Hollywood, I. (2005). A social psychology of defiance: from discontent to action. In M. Sönser-Breen (Ed.), *Minding Evil: Explorations of Human Iniquity* (pp. 19–38). New York & Amsterdam: Rodophi.

Burgess, M., Ferguson, N. and Hollywood, I. (2007). Rebels' perspectives of the legacy of past violence and of the current peace in post-agreement Northern Ireland: An interpretative phenomenological analysis. *Political Psychology*, 28, 1, 69–88.

Crenshaw, M. (1991). How terrorism declines. *Terrorism and Political Violence*, 3, 1, 69–87.

Crenshaw, M. (1999). Martha Crehsaw on how terrorism ends. In J. B. Alterman (Ed.), How terrorism ends. *United States Institute of Peace Special Report*, 48, May, 2–4.

Cronin, A. K. (2006). How al-Qaida ends: The decline and demise of terrorist groups. *International Security*, 31, 1, 7–48.

Cronin, A. K. (2009). How terrorism campaigns end. In T. Bjorgo and J. Horgan (Eds.), *Leaving Terrorism Behind: Individual and collective disengagement* (pp. 49–65). London: Routledge.

Edwards, A. (2009). Abandoning armed resistance? The Ulster Volunteer Force as a case study of strategic terrorism in Northern Ireland. *Studies in Conflict and Terrorism*, 32 (1), 146–166.

Ferguson, N., Burgess, M. and Hollywood, I. (2008). Crossing the Rubicon: deciding to become a paramilitary in Northern Ireland. *International Journal of Conflict and Violence*, 2 (1), 130–137.

Ferguson, N., Burgess, M. and Hollywood, I. (in press). Who are the victims? Victimhood experiences in post agreement Northern Ireland. *Political Psychology*.

Garfinkel, R. (2007). Personal transformations: Moving from violence to peace. *United States Institute of Peace Special Report*, 186, April.

Horgan, J. (2003). The search for the terrorist personality. In A. Silke, (Ed.), *Psychological Perspectives on Terrorism and it's Consequences* (pp. 3–27). Chichester, England: John Wiley & Sons.

Horgan, J. (2005). *The Psychology of Terrorism*. London: Routledge.

Horgan, J. (2009a). *Walking Away from Terrorism: Accounts of disengagement from radical and extremist movements*. London: Routledge.

Horgan, J. (2009b). Deradicalization or disengagement? A process in need of clarity and a counter-terrorism initiative in need of evaluation. *Revista de Psicologia Social*, 24, 2, 291–298.

Kanazawa, S. and Still, M. C. (2000). Why men commit crimes (and why they desist). *Sociology Theory*, 18, 3, 434–447

McCauley, C. (2008). Group desistence from terrorism: A dynamic perspective. *Dynamics of Asymmetric Conflict*, 3 (1), 269–293

Pluchinsky, D. A. (2008). Global Jihadist recidivism: A red flag. *Studies in Conflict and Terrorism*, 31, 182–200.

Ross, J. I. and Gurr, T. R. (1989). Why terrorism subsides: A comparative study of Canada and the United States. *Comparative Politics*, 21 (4), 405–426.

Silke, A. (2001). The devil you know: Continuing problems with research on terrorism. *Terrorism and Political Violence*, 13 (4), 1–14.

Silke, A. (2003). Preface. In A. Silke (Ed.), *Terrorists, Victims and Society: Psychological Perspectives on Terrorism and its Consequences*, (pp. xiii–xxi). Chichester, England: John Wiley & Sons.

Speckhard, A. (2006). Defusing human bombs: Understanding suicide terrorism. In J. Victoroff (Ed.), *Tangled Roots: Social and psychological factors in the genesis of terrorism* (pp. 277–291). Amsterdam: IOS Press.

Tedeschi, R. G. and Calhoun, L. G. (1996). The posttraumatic growth inventory: Measuring the positive legacy of trauma. *Journal of Traumatic Stress*, 9 (3), 455–471.

Victoroff, J. (2005). The mind of the terrorist: A review and critique of psychological approaches. *Journal of Conflict Resolution*, 49 (1), 3–42.

# 9 Terrorists and extremists in prison

## Psychological issues in management and reform

*Andrew Silke*

## Introduction

There is increasing recognition that prisons are a crucial arena in efforts to combat terrorism and bring about an end to terrorist conflicts. In most long-running conflicts, terrorist prisoners have become a critical factor in the conflict, one that often can hold the key to unlocking a solution to the violence. Ignored or mishandled, however, these prisoners have the capacity to turn a bad situation worse and to become a profound obstacle to progress in the world outside the prison walls. This chapter focuses on some of the key challenges posed by terrorists and violent extremists in prison. These range from critical issues as to how such prisoners can be safely and securely managed, whether it is possible to effectively deradicalise or disengage prisoners from campaigns of violence and also how to deal with concerns about the spread of radicalisation among prisoners and the recruitment of other prisoners to the terrorist's cause.

The first hurdle to be cleared in any effort for understanding extremists in prison is to clarify what exactly is meant by the word 'extremist'? This chapter follows the broad definition outlined at the beginning of this book, and is focused on individuals who hold extreme political/religious views and advocate the use of violence in furtherance of that agenda. Advocating violence is a crucial element. Individuals who hold radical views but who do not endorse the use of violence to further those views are not considered here. The chapter's definition, however, does encompass the members of terrorist organisations and also the members of groups such as animal rights activists who use violence as part of their campaigns.

It is important to also note that conviction under terrorist legislation is not a primary manner of identification. Many prisoners who were motivated by a political or religious ideology were convicted under criminal legislation rather than specialist anti-terrorism laws. For example, in England and Wales from 11 September 2001 to 31 March 2008, there were 196 convictions for terrorist-related offences, of which 102 were convicted under terrorism legislation and 94 under non-terrorism legislation.[1] Thus, many 'terrorist' prisoners have not been convicted under specialist counter-terrorism legislation, so one cannot define such prisoners based purely on the type of offences involved. Terrorism is also defined differently in different legal codes and by different countries adding to the complexity of the problem.

There is a small but growing amount of research literature relating to intervening with and managing violent extremists (e.g. Crenshaw, 1991; Jamieson, 1990; Bjørgo, 1997; Bjørgo, 2002; Bjørgo, 2005; Bjørgo and Horgan, 2008; Bates-Gaston, 2003; Horgan, 2003; Horgan, 2009; Silke, 2001; Silke, 2006; Silke, 2007; Speckhard, 2006; Speckhard, 2007; van Tangen Page, 1998; Victoroff et al., 2006). However, this literature is still small in comparison to research on other elements of terrorism and violent extremism. This shortage represents one of the most serious obstacles to developing effective management and intervention strategies for promoting and facilitating disengagement from terrorism. On many issues we currently have almost no published research, and much of what does exist is of poor quality.

Of particular note, throughout Europe today there is increasing recognition of the problem of militant jihadi extremists in prison and their ability to recruit new members among other prisoners. These are not the only politically motivated offenders in Europe's prisons but they are generally viewed as the most serious problem and are certainly the only one posing a simultaneous significant challenge to several European states. The numbers of such extremists are relatively low but grew significantly in the first six years after 9/11. There is evidence now that this growth has more or less stabilised and may in some countries (such as the UK) have now entered a period of slow decline.

A recent European Commission report found that prisons were becoming important centres of radicalisation. The report highlighted that prisons such as La Sante, in Paris, France, and the prison of Topas, in Salamanca, Spain, are examples of such centres of radicalisation (Areso, 2007). Indeed, a few terrorist plots appear to have been entirely based around networks that were radicalised in prison (Jordán and Horsburgh, 2006). The fear is that this trend will become increasingly common in the coming decade.

This fear is based on two factors. One is that the number of radicals in prison is increasing at a significant rate. Two, the Muslim population in many European prison populations is already very large and so presents a potentially large pool of recruits. Muslim prisoners make up at least 11 percent of the Spanish prison population, and 10 percent of the England & Wales population. In both cases this equates to over 8,000 prisoners. At the moment both Spain and England & Wales have approximately 100 to 150 militant jihadi prisoners, which is a very small number in the context of the overall prison population, but there are real concerns over the impact of these prisoners among other inmates.

A further issue relates to the role that Muslim converts may play. Conversion to Islam is already quite common in prison. Beckford (2005) calculated that 12 percent of Muslim prisoners in UK jails are white converts many of whom may have converted in prison. This potentially gives a current population in UK prisons of some 800 inmates who have converted to Islam while in prison. Concerns have been raised that converts form a disproportionably high percentage of militant jihadi groups.

Research by Sageman (2004) and Bakker (2006) suggest that Muslim converts comprise around 8 percent of the militant jihadis. The Spaniard José Emilio Suárez Trashorras, the British 'shoe bomber', Richard Reid, and the American José Padilla, convicted of trying to assemble a radiological bomb, were all converted to Islam and recruited into terror networks while in prison. This surprisingly high number of converts among militant jihadi ranks is explained by the converts lacking exposure to, and understanding of, mainstream Islam. As a result, they do not recognise that militant jihadi interpretations of Islam are isolated and radical and thus they are less prepared to resist or argue against such interpretation. Thus in an environment with a high level of conversion and a growing presence of militant jihadi radicals, there are obvious concerns that radicalisation has the potential to become a serious contemporary problem.

## Management strategies with extremist prisoners

The incarceration policies of most countries have tended to concentrate terrorist prisoners in a small number of high security prisons. This has been the approach adopted by countries such as the UK, Italy, Turkey, Israel, Columbia, etc (Heiberg et al., 2007). In almost every case however, such a concentration policy resulted in the development of 'universities of terror'. The incarcerated prisoners organised themselves, generally adopting the command structure seen in the movement on the outside. Once organised the prisoners created classrooms and lectures that focused on practical issues such as the construction of weapons, how to organise cells, surveillance, etc. Prisoners were also indoctrinated with regard to the history and politics of the movement. Indeed, many terrorists' understanding of the broader context and philosophy of their organisation were often extremely basic prior to prison. Further, the close proximity allowed the prisoners to co-ordinate escape attempts, protests and riots (von Tangen Page, 1998).

The isolated environment of prison settings, where the inmates are living in very close proximity, engendered powerful social pressures to conform to the group. The commitment of prisoners to the cause tended to increase considerably in such circumstances and indeed many innocent inmates – those who were innocent of involvement in terrorism prior to their arrest and imprisonment – became politicised and radicalised while incarcerated and had become committed supporters by the time of their eventual release. However in Chapter 8 of this volume, Neil Fergusson drew attention to prison providing an opportunity for terrorists to reflect on the conflict and to actually decide to favour a non-violent settlement. Interestingly, Fergusson's assessment was that the prisoners' commitment to the cause and to the group remained very strong (i.e. they were not deradicalised), but what changed was their belief that violence was the most effective way forward.

A few countries have gradually come to recognise that the disadvantages of concentrating so many political prisoners together outweighs the advantages. Spain is the most notable example of this. Up until 1986, ETA prisoners had been concentrated in only a few prisons. After 1986 however, the Spanish authorities started to distribute prisoners more widely throughout the Spanish prison system.

The dispersal strategy brought about several quick benefits. The number of prisoners who resigned from ETA increased considerably. There was no noticeable increase in recruitment or radicalisation among other prisoners who were now exposed to ETA prisoners for the first time. Overall, the organisation lost members rather than gained them. Further, the level of terrorism-related training and skills development the prisoners experienced while in prison declined considerably. Over a period of time, this eventually translated into a drop in the number and effectiveness of ETA operations on the outside.

In Indonesia, the authorities also initially concentrated prisoners who belonged to Gerakan Aceh Merdeka (GAM). This changed to a more dispersed policy especially for prisoners who had received sentences in excess of three years. This though seems to have been a response to accommodation issues rather than a conscious government policy on dispersal.

In most other cases however, states have tended to proceed with the concentration approach despite the many disadvantages. In Turkey, the state used dormitory-type prisons, which essentially became schools for the PKK. As happened with other groups, the PKK were also able to use the prisons to recruit and co-opt non-political prisoners with whom they came into contact. The high levels of abuse and torture in Turkish prisons did not undermine the commitment of PKK prisoners but instead was associated with an increase in prisoners' commitment to the group and the cause and an increase in their hatred for the government and the authorities. An indication of the importance of the social support prisoners gave to each other can be seen in the dramatic increase in suicide rates among prisoners when Turkey moved prisoners from dormitory arrangements to individual cells.

Israel too also followed a concentration approach and again suffered the disadvantages seen elsewhere. Mass incarcerations in the early 1980s radicalised an entire generation of prisoners and when these individuals were released en masse they became the leadership of Hamas.

Mass incarceration could also have other unexpected side effects. In 1989, mass sweeps allowed Israel to imprison most of the senior leadership of Hamas. However, the organisation remained relatively intact and the detentions allowed a younger and more aggressive leadership cadre to take control of the movement. The result was a significant increase in the level of violence.

Many states use detention as a way to recruit informers within the movements. As well as offering incentives to potential informers, states can use blackmail and threats. Israel for example has taken compromising pictures of prisoners (e.g. showing the inmate in an apparently homosexual activity) and threatened to release these images if the inmate does not co-operate.

Overall, the management of terrorist prisoners has been rather poorly understood by most states. Only in a few cases, notably Spain, did governments attempt to consciously tackle the *de facto* 'universities of terror' that are the result of a concentration approach. The Spanish dispersal policy did not destroy ETA but it did weaken the organisation. The policy led to a significant increase in the number of prisoners who left ETA and it also significantly hampered ETA's ability to train, supervise and motivate those prisoners who chose to remain in the organisation.

Thus, ETA experienced considerable obstacles, which were not faced by the IRA in Northern Ireland, for example.

## Recruitment and radicalisation of other prisoners

A key area of concern with the management of extremist prisoners is their ability to recruit other prisoners who they come into contact with. As indicated above, this is a recurring problem seen in almost every setting. In Northern Ireland, the paramilitaries were very active (and especially the Loyalist groups) in attempting to recruit other prisoners to join their groups. This is still a serious problem today, as both loyalist and dissident republican inmates recognise that the more prisoners who belong to their groups, the more control and influence they can exercise within the prison (Northern Ireland Affairs Committee, 2004).

One respect in which Islamist prisoners are more dangerous than IRA prisoners is that the Islamists appear more prepared and willing to recruit non-political prisoners who fall within their sphere of influence.

Most IRA prisoners, for example, were segregated from non-political prisoners at an early stage of their incarceration. IRA prisoners were typically housed on wings with other IRA prisoners at HMP The Maze and their interaction with other types of prisoners was limited. As an organisation, the IRA was not interested in recruiting other prisoners into its ranks (for obvious security reasons) but they were certainly prepared to work with other prisoners for mutual benefit (including joint escapes).

As already indicated a number of militant jihadi terrorists – including whole networks – have been radicalised and created within prisons. Spain in particular has had serious problems in this regard. For example, consider the case of José Emilio Suárez Trashorras, who was not religious or politically aware when he was jailed in 2001 for a drug offence. In prison he met Jamal Ahmidan, a young Moroccan living in Spain who had been convicted of a petty crime, but who also was not considered a radical by those who knew him before prison.

While in jail, Trashorras converted to a radical version of Islam and the previously non-observant Muslim Ahmidan also embraced radical Islamic fundamentalist beliefs. Both men were recruited into an al-Qaeda–linked Moroccan terrorist group, Takfir wa al-Hijra. Cuthbertson (2004) describes what followed next:

> The imprisoned Ahmidan quickly gained a leadership position in the cellblock, and on emerging from prison both men were absorbed into an extensive and well-organized radical Islamic organization that trafficked heavily in drugs to support its terrorist activities. Later, Ahmidan led the cell that carried out the Madrid bombings, while Trashorras supplied the explosives and helped plant the 13 backpack bombs that killed 191 people and injured hundreds of others on four Madrid trains crowded with early-morning commuters

The ability of extremists to attract new converts however seems to be related to the size of the group. Anecdotal evidence suggests that isolated extremists appear to have a poor record of attracting recruits (good evaluations on this issue are not available). In contrast, when they are present in numbers in one wing or prison, their ability to attract new members increases enormously. This was certainly the Spanish experience in dealing with ETA (von Tangen Page, 1998).

## Reform of extremist prisoners

People change, and this applies to terrorists as well. While there is a legitimate concern that prison will provide an opportunity for extremists to recruit new members, we should also recognise that some prisoners will move away from their former comrades. Knox (2005) found that 9.46 percent of the inmates who come into prison as gang members leave the gang while inside prison, and this is something that has also been seen among terrorist prisoners.

Historically, interventions with violent extremists have taken a variety of forms (Bjørgo, 2005). Some have focused on offenders in prison, while others have targeted individuals who are at liberty and are currently involved in illegal activity. The aims of the different interventions have also varied. Some simply try to reduce the size of a movement by reducing the number of active participants (e.g. the Child Combatant Programme as part of the Ministry of Interior and Justice's Reincorporation Programme in Colombia), and may require only a shift in attitude and behaviour away from violent extremism as the precondition for an individual to be released from prison.

Other approaches provide reduced sentences in exchange for testimony against former colleagues in a group. In Italy, for example, the *pentiti* system offered members of the Red Brigades as well as the Mafia reduced sentencing if they agreed to testify against their comrades. This system is widely considered to have played an important role in helping to disrupt both the Red Brigades and the Mafia in the 1970s, 1980s, and early 1990s (e.g. Ferracuti, 1990). It is worth considering these systems in more detail.

## Italian laws – *pentiti*

The Italian governments throughout the 1980s and 1990s, have consistently refused to provide amnesties to terrorist prisoners or to grant immunity from prosecution in return for co-operation. Italy did introduce a *pentiti* (repentance) system in 1979, which allowed for the early release of prisoners in exchange for co-operation in providing testimony against former comrades. As such, the scheme bore some similarities to the deeply troubled supergrass system in Northern Ireland. There were crucial differences however.

First, the *pentiti* were not offered immunity. Instead they were offered reduced sentences (generally cut by between 33 percent to 50 percent). They still had to face trial for their confessed crimes. Any agreements made between the prisoner and the authorities had to be openly declared in the court, and the Italians did not use a special court regime to try such cases.

*Pentiti* could be released on licence even earlier in their sentence if the prisoner's behaviour indicated genuine repentance (*ravvedimento*). In practice, most major *pentiti* served only two to three years before they were released from prison (von Tangen Page, 1998).

The Italians had to create separate compounds in prisons to hold *pentiti* prisoners (nine prisoners were killed in 1980 when their comrades suspected they had become *pentiti*). A witness protection programme was also established to protect *pentiti* after their release.

As with the supergrass system, there were real concerns that not all of the testimony supplied by *pentiti* were reliable and that some fabricated evidence in order to increase their value to the authorities. Ultimately the system may have collapsed in a similar manner to supergrass if it were not for a crucial second element to this approach described below.

## Italian laws – *dissociati*

As well as the more well-known *pentiti* system, Italy also introduced a scheme of dissociation – '*dissociati*'. This was a very different scheme, which did not offer prisoners as many benefits. The dissociated prisoner was expected to express genuine remorse for his/her actions, and to sever their links to the terrorist organisation. The prisoner also had to make a full and frank confession of the crimes in which they had been involved – including crimes for which they had not been convicted. The prisoner, however, was not required to testify against former comrades.

As time progressed, *dissociati* proved willing to testify against former comrades but only in cases where people had already been convicted based on other evidence. In essence, the *dissociati* would confirm what the police already knew, but they would not instigate new prosecutions or provide evidence that was not clearly supported by other sources.

As the 1980s progressed, it was clear that the terrorist campaigns in Italy were now in terminal decline. In 1987 a new dissociation law was introduced to help bring closure to the conflict. Prisoners were not released under this scheme, but were instead allowed to work outside prison while serving their sentence. The prisoners were thus allowed to put their past behind them and move to a less restricted prison regime, which also allowed them to begin to lay the groundwork for life after release.

The scheme was so successful that many terrorists who were still at large surrendered themselves to the authorities so that they could enter the scheme and close the chapter on their terrorist lives (von Tangen Page, 1998).

## Spanish laws – *social reinsertion*

The success of the Italian approach was noted in other European countries and especially in Spain, which was also experiencing a long-running campaign of terrorism waged by Basque nationalists. In 1982, the Spanish introduced a policy of 'social reinsertion', which bore much in common with the Italian *dissociati* scheme (Heiberg, 2007). The policy was first introduced when ETA-PM split into two factions, one advocating non-violence, the other a continuation of the terror campaign. Prisoners who identified with the non-violence faction could apply through the courts for early release. The prisoners were essentially given an amnesty for their crimes though this was not officially acknowledged (von Tangen Page, 1998).

The policy expanded and developed. 'Social reinsertion' quickly became one of the key elements of the Spanish counter-terrorism policy. Prisoners who had not been convicted of crimes involving serious injury or death were offered early release in exchange for three conditions:

1.  The renunciation of violence and the breaking of links with the terrorist organisation.
2.  A declaration that the prisoner would in future respect the law and democracy and an acknowledgment that they could be re-imprisoned if they did not.
3.  Recognition of the suffering that they had caused.

These three conditions were met through the signing of a legal document, which was presented to a judicial tribunal that would then allow their reintegration into normal society (von Tangen Page, 1998).

By the end of 1986, more than 300 prisoners had been released under the scheme. Active terrorist groups issued death threats against any prisoners who accepted the scheme. In September 1986, ETA killed a former leader, Maria Catarain, who had applied and been granted insertion. The high-profile killing temporarily halted the programme.

## The rehabilitation of militant Jihadis

There is a range of new programmes aimed specifically at militant jihadi prisoners and these are attracting increasing attention among researchers (Bjørgo and Horgan, 2008). Most of these programmes are based around the principle of exposing prisoners to mainstream Islam and highlighting the radical basis of the militant jihadi interpretation. This exposure is usually facilitated through meetings with experienced and respected Islamic scholars and Imams. The aim is to convince militant jihadis to move away from radical interpretations of Islam and to embrace more mainstream perspectives.

Many of these programmes also provide financial and other incentives and rewards for repentant militant jihadis. For example, prisoners who are judged to have changed are released early, financial support is provided to families while the prisoner is in jail, and the state provides prisoners with cars and employment on release. If the prisoner disengages from the programme then this support is withdrawn and the prisoner may be returned to harsher prison conditions.

While claims of success vary, the general assessment is that the militant jihadi programmes so far generally only work with 'soft-core' militant jihadis, and usually have little impact with leaders and hard-core members. No thorough evaluations of any of these programmes are available yet in the open literature.

Cuthbertson (2004) has argued that fighting militant jihadism in prisons requires both preventative and proactive measures. Key elements of a successful programme will be the isolation of 'potential radical leaders, cutting off the flow of incendiary fundamentalist propaganda, screening clerics and lay Islamic prayer leaders (both volunteers and prisoners), and effectively monitoring their sermons'. This alone is not enough, however, and Cuthbertson (2004) also argues for the following elements of what he refers to as an Educational Intervention Action System (some of which bear similarities with approaches to tackling prison gangs in the US):

(1) A training and educational program for government officials, prison administrators, prison staff, and civilians involved in prisoner welfare activities on Islamic religious precepts and practices and Islamic culture. Participants would receive instruction on the roots and nature of radical Islamic fundamentalism and its manifestations in Western societies and penal systems, and on the various conflicts in the Middle East. They would be taught how to identify and track the activities of radical fundamentalist Islamic groups and terrorist networks, both within the prison system as a whole and in individual facilities.
(2) An outreach educational program aimed at providing vocational and language skills to Muslim prisoners. Such a program might use the teachings of liberal Islamic scholars as texts for developing computer skills and in language classes. This might be seen as a first step in socializing Muslim prisoners, helping them to fit into the host society when they are released from prison, and as a means of inoculating individuals against the proselytising of radical fundamentalist ideologues.
(3) A more targeted program, led by local Islamic leaders, focused on weaning inmates from radical Islamic teachings through exposure to alternative interpretations of Islamic scripture and thought, coupled with socialization efforts.

Taarnby (2005) highlights the critical issue that when we think about implementing interventions we need to also very carefully consider how we can, and should, evaluate the success of those policies. For example, if even a few of the released militants return to wage jihad, does this negate an entire programme? What percentage should be considered an acceptable threshold for success?

## Conclusions

This chapter has highlighted that a range of different – and sometimes contradictory – approaches have been taken in efforts to effectively manage and intervene with extremist prisoners. Robust evaluations of these different strategies have by and large not been carried out and claims of success or failure must all be treated with caution. What is clear is that there is no magic formula for handling this problem. Likewise, there are no treatment programmes available 'off the shelf' that have a proven ability to work with terrorist prisoners.

Those faced with managing such prisoners are thus faced with a range of options – not all of which are compatible and with considerable uncertainty over what will work and what will not. Nevertheless, it is clear that many states – in Europe and beyond – are crossing a threshold on this issue as a major growth in militant jihadi prisoners in particular has occurred in recent years. Decisions made in the coming months and years will have impacts stretching over the next thirty years. What is clear from the experiences of other countries and other periods is that the wrong decisions will make the problem considerably worse.

There are many important questions that simply need better and more detailed answers: How do militant jihadis and other extremists organize themselves within a prison system, and how do they adjust their tactics to suit a particular prison's infrastructure and regime? How do such networks recruit, motivate, train, and retain new members? How do they provide support to recruits both in prison and when they are released?

Answers to questions like these are needed in order to allow the development of effective programmes in a wide variety of prison systems to counteract, disrupt, and ultimately eliminate extremism.

A linked and vital issue is that wherever possible, rigorous evaluation should be undertaken of any programmes that are now introduced. It is vital that we can determine what really works and what does not. As can be seen in this review, a major assumption of most current de-radicalisation programmes aimed at militant jihadis is that exposure to mainstream interpretations of Islam will have a positive effect. What is often overlooked is that major elements of these programmes frequently also include early release and considerable financial rewards for 'reformed' prisoners. It would be surprising if such elements did not play a considerable role in the success of such programmes. Linked to this, these programmes clearly struggle with the issue of failure. Entire programmes have been suspended or abandoned when it is discovered that one or a few prisoners who engaged with it were not actually reformed. Expecting 100 percent success is simply searching for failure, and it needs to be acknowledged and accepted that these approaches simply will not work with everyone. Realistic assessments and expectations have a vital role to play in any approach to tackling extremism in prison settings.

## Note

1  http://www.publications.parliament.uk/pa/ld200809/ldhansrd/text/90601w0011.htm

## References

Areso, J. (2007). *Analysis of Security Indicators: Terrorist threats against Europe*. A report for the European Commission for Freedom, Security and Justice.

Bakker, E. (2007). *Militant Jihadi Terrorists in Europe, Their Characteristics and the Circumstances in Which They Joined the Jihad: an exploratory study.* The Hague: Clingendael Institute.

Bates-Gaston, J. (2003). Terrorism and imprisonment in Northern Ireland: A psychological perspective. In A. Silke, (Ed.). *Terrorists, Victims and Society: Psychological Perspectives on Terrorism and Its Consequences*, pp. 233–255. Chichester: Wiley.

Beckford, J. (2005). Muslims in the prisons of Britain and France. *Journal of Contemporary European Studies*, 11/3, pp.287–297.

Bjørgo, T. (1997). Entry, bridge-burning and exit options: What happens to young people who join racist groups – and want to leave? In T. Bjørgo (Ed.), *Racist and Right-wing Violence in Scandinavia.* Oslo: Tano-Aschehoug.

Bjørgo, T. (2002). Reducing recruitment and promoting disengagement from racist groups. *Journal für Konflikt- und Gewaltforschung*, 4/1, pp. 5–31.

Bjorgo, T. (2005). Reducing recruitment and promoting disengagement from extremist groups: The case of racist sub-cultures. In C. Benard (Ed.) *A Future For The Young: Options for Helping Middle Eastern Youth Escape the Trap of Radicalization. A RAND Working Paper WR-354.* Washington, D.C.: RAND National Security Research Division.

Bjorgo, T. and Horgan, J. (2008). *Leaving Terrorism Behind.* London: Routledge.

Crenshaw, M. (1991). How Terrorism Declines, *Terrorism and Political Violence*, 3/1, pp.69–87.

Cuthbertson, I. (2004). Prisons and the education of terrorists, *World Policy Journal*, pp. 15–22.

Ferracuti, F. (1990). Ideology and repentance: terrorism in Italy, in W. Reich (ed.) *Origins of Terrorism*, (pp.59–64). Washington, D.C.: Woodrow Wilson Center Press.

Heiberg, M. (2007). 'ETA: Euskadi 'ta Askatasuna.' In Heiberg, M., O'Leary, B. and Tirman, J. (eds.). *Terror, Insurgencies and States: Breaking the Cycle of Protracted Conflict* (pp.19–50). Philadelphia: University of Pennsylvania Press.

Heiberg, M., O'Leary, B. and Tirman, J. (2007). *Terror, Insurgencies and States: Breaking the Cycle of Protracted Conflict.* Philadelphia: University of Pennsylvania Press.

Horgan, J. (2003). Leaving terrorism behind: An individual perspective, in A. Silke (Ed.), *Terrorists, Victims and Society: Psychological Perspectives on Terrorism and its Consequences. Chichester*: Wiley.

Horgan, J. (2009). *Walking Away from Terrorism.* London: Routledge.

Jamieson, A. (1990). Entry, discipline and exit in the Italian Red Brigades, *Terrorism and Political Violence*, 2/1, pp. 1–20.

Jordán, J. and Horsburgh, N. (2006). Spain and Islamist Terrorism: Analysis of the threat and response 1995–2005. *Mediterranean Politics*, http://www.informaworld.com/smpp/title~content=t713604487~db=all~tab=issueslist~branches=11 - v1111/2, pp. 209–229.

Knox, G. (2005). *The Problem of Gangs and Security Threat Groups (STGs) in American Prisons Today: Recent Research Findings From the 2004 Prison Gang Survey.* National Gang Crime Research Center.

Northern Ireland Affairs Committee (2004). *The Separation of Paramilitary Prisoners at HMP Maghaberry.* London: Stationery Office.

Sageman, M. (2004). *Understanding Terrorist Networks.* Philadelphia: University of Pennsylvania Press.

Silke, A. (2001). Terrorism: An action plan. *The Psychologist*, 14/11, pp.580–581.

Silke, A. (2006). Psychological counter-terrorism: What works, what doesn't. Paper

134   *Andrew Silke*

presented at Conference: Fighting Terrorism: Critical Lessons and Key Issues for the 21st Century, 15 September 2006, University of East London, London.

Silke, A. (2007). Risk assessment of terrorists and politically-motivated offenders. Invited paper presented at the Aggression & Violence: New Approaches New Directions Conference, 4 April 2007, University of Central Lancashire.

Speckhard, A. (2006). Defusing human bombs: Understanding suicide terrorism. In J. Victoroff (Ed.) *Tangled Roots: Social and Psychological Factors in the Genesis of Terrorism*, pp. 277–291. IOS Press.

Speckhard, A. (2007). De-legitimizing terrorism: Creative engagement and understanding of the psycho-social and political processes involved in ideological support for terrorism. *Connections*, Winter Issue (I).

Taarnby, M. (2005). Yemen's Committee for Dialogue: the relativity of a counter terrorism success, in C. Benard (Ed.). *A Future For The Young: Options for Helping Middle Eastern Youth Escape the Trap of Radicalization. A RAND Working Paper WR-354.* Washington, D.C.: RAND National Security Research Division.

Victoroff, J., Hafez, M., Post, J., Kruglanski, A., Barber, B., Speckhard, A., Akhmedova, K., Celinska, B., Ahmad, C. and Mednick, S. (2006). Preventing substate terrorist groups from recruiting and retaining young members. *Tangled Roots: Social and Psychological Factors in the Genesis of Terrorism*, pp. 438–442. IOS Press.

Von Tangen Page, M. (1998). *Prisons, Peace and Terrorism: Penal Policy in the Reduction of Political Violence in Northern Ireland, Italy and the Spanish Basque Country, 1968–97.* Palgrave Macmillan.

# 10 Interrogation tactics and terrorist suspects

## A categorisation process

*John Pearse*

## Introduction

The purpose of this paper is to outline some of the psychological processes at work during the interrogation of terrorist suspects and to try and improve our understanding of what it is that is taking place in the confines of the interrogation arena. For example, what can the psychological literature tell us about the transformation in behaviour from 'normal' human beings to violent and aggressive prison guards administering beatings and forcing detainees to perform humiliating and gross acts? Is it possible to categorise the many tactics reported in the literature, especially those reports of abuse and torture emanating from the Abu Ghraib prison compound in Iraq and from Guantanamo Bay in Cuba? Is there a difference in the impact, on a detained person, between the use of physical violence and threats of such violence compared to a quieter, more subtle approach?

To provide a suitable context for readers this chapter will make use of the published literature on the police interrogation of suspects and will also examine the legal and practical differences that have emerged between the tactics employed in the United States (US) and those reported in the United Kingdom (UK). In particular I will emphasise the advantages gained by some interrogators in manipulating the detainee's perception of the consequences of their decision-making and how anxiety levels can be exploited to maximise impact and effect. Of course, it is acknowledged that in terms of severity what takes place in the harsh and often extreme confines of a war zone or military conflict far exceed the public's perception of what takes place in a conventional US or UK police interrogation.[1]

It would be unrealistic, in this short chapter, to attempt to deal with all the influential psychological forces at play in this type of interaction. For example, the overwhelming power of the situation is ever present and plays a very dominant role in moulding the behaviour and attitudes of the participants, especially in recognised war zones. Each interrogator also brings with them their own preconceptions, biases, stereotypes and belief systems. In addition, the detainees – about whom we have only limited information – will also be made up of a broad spectrum of personality types with some more able than others to manage their environment and the rigours of the interrogation process. For these groups it will only be possible to provide a brief overview of the key psychological factors.

## Allegations of abuse at the Abu Ghraib prison compound in Iraq and from Guantanamo Bay in Cuba

It would be difficult to discuss the interrogation of terrorist suspects at this period in time without reference to the allegations of abuse at the Abu Ghraib prison in Iraq and at the American detention centre in Guantanamo Bay, Cuba, that have made headline news across the world. James Meek (2005) in his description of the allegations of abuse and torture at these locations provides one of the most disturbing summaries available in print. He starts by attributing the upsurge in torture and humiliation at the Abu Ghraib prison to Major-General Geoffrey Miller, the commandant in charge of detainees at Guantanamo Bay. It was the subsequent implementation of Miller's Guantanamo policy of using the guards to 'soften' up the detainees prior to any interrogation that led to the following description of events:

> Prisoners were hooded, threatened with rape, threatened with torture, had pistols held to their heads, made to strip naked, forced to eat pork and drink alcohol, beaten till they bled – sometimes with implements, including a broom and a chair – hung from doors by cuffed hands, deceived into thinking they were to be electrocuted, ducked in toilet buckets, forced to simulate masturbation, forced to lie naked in a pile and be photographed, urinated on, menaced and, in one case, severely bitten by dogs, sodomised with a chemical light, ridden like horses, made to wear women's underwear, raped, deprived of sleep, exposed to the mid-day summer sun, put in stress positions and made to lie naked in empty concrete cells, in complete darkness, for days on end.
>
> (p. 4)

I propose to make use of this harrowing summary to stimulate debate throughout this chapter. In the first instance I aim to begin to explore how psychological research can inform our understanding of some of the forces at play that can change apparently law abiding, 'normal' human beings into individuals capable of the most aggressive and degrading behaviour. Secondly, this same passage also represents a challenge for us to try and make sense in psychological terms of the likely impact of such tactics on the behaviour and actions of those detained.

Major-General Miller was the link between Guantanamo Bay (or Gitmo, as it is more commonly referred to) and Abu Ghraib. He had assumed command at Gitmo in November 2002 with the express objective of increasing the allegedly poor intelligence yield produced by the previous regime (Rose, 2004). Miller, a former artillery officer with no previous experience of intelligence gathering or the supervision of detainees, claimed that by July of the following year the amount of intelligence extracted from detainees each month had increased by 600 per cent – in quantitative terms. As the author David Rose (2004, p. 84) noted, 'For him, intelligence was a matter of volume, of productivity, much like artillery: shells on target; statements made.'

His efforts were recognised by his superiors who sent him, in the summer of 2003, to the Abu Ghraib prison to review operations there with a view to producing the same rapid increase in intelligence reports. He recommended adopting the system that was working so well for him at Gitmo, where he had merged the functions of two previously distinct sections, the guards and the interrogators; allowing the guards to 'prepare' the detainee for the interrogation process.

In effect the guards became subordinate to the interrogation officers. The powerful environmental forces had now been set and the results were broadcast to an astonished public by a voracious media campaign. But what can account for the guards' violent and aggressive demeanour, why is it that their personalities were able to change or be altered so dramatically?

## The Stamford University prison experiment

Perhaps the most relevant psychological research that addressed the drastic change in human behaviour in a prison environment was that carried out by Philip Zimbardo, at Stanford University in 1971. Zimbardo created a mock prison in the basement of his psychology building and selected 24 mature, emotionally stable, intelligent young men (out of 70) for the study. With the flip of a coin some were designated as 'prisoners' the rest served as 'guards.' The prisoners were stripped, given a uniform and number, and placed in a cell with two other inmates. They were told the cell would be their home for the next two weeks. The guards were informed that they had the authority to make up their own rules for maintaining law and order, and respect in the prison and were free to improvise new rules at any time during their eight-hour shifts on duty.

The experiment was supposed to last for two weeks but had to be stopped after only six days because, according to Zimbardo (1971, p. 4):

> . . . it was no longer apparent to most of the subjects where reality ended and their roles began. The majority had indeed become prisoners or guards, no longer able to clearly differentiate between role playing and self. . . . In less than a week the experience of imprisonment undid (temporarily) a lifetime of learning; human values were suspended, self-concepts were challenged and the ugliest . . . side of human nature surfaced. We were horrified because we saw some guards treat others as if they were despicable animals, taking pleasure in cruelty, while the prisoners became . . . dehumanized robots who thought only of escape, of their own individual survival and of their mounting hatred for the guards.

Some of the prisoners became severely depressed, confused, or hysterical and had to be released after only a few days. Many of the guards became tyrants, arbitrarily using their power and enjoying the control they had over others. Other guards were not as brutal, but they never intervened on behalf of the prisoners and never told the other guards to 'ease off'. This landmark research unequivocally demonstrated that individual behaviour can be controlled by social forces and that, given specific environmental circumstances individuals can create the very social forces that come to shape their behaviour. It was the subjects themselves who created the reality of their roles and therefore defined the power that the prison structure exerted over them (Zimbardo, 1971; Haney et al., 1973).

Whilst the study had a number of limitations (it could be argued that the guards were role playing what they thought was typical prison officers' behaviour – given the declared influence of the recent Paul Newman film *Cool Hand Luke*) these findings do not appear out of place when set against the circumstances currently under discussion.

## Psychological research on the impact of the physical environment and interrogator bias

The power of the situation and the ability to create their own social forces was clearly evident in relation to the behaviour of the subjects in the Stamford experiment and the psychological literature also provides some insight into the debilitating impact of oppressive prison regimes such as those believed to be practiced at Gitmo and Abu Ghraib. Gudjonsson (2003), for example, discusses the ways in which the physical environment can affect the psychological state and well being of detainees. It is recognised that all forms of sensory deprivation, fatigue, social isolation, hunger, sleep deprivation and physical and emotional pain or the threat of such pain can exert a very powerful and debilitating influence on the resolve and subsequently the decision making of detainees. For example, sleep deprivation impairs mental functioning, especially if it is maintained for more than two or three days. The symptoms include lack of motivation; attention problems, cognitive confusion and slowness of thought. Research has identified that the optimum period for these problems to occur is between 4 am and 8 am (Mikulincer et al., 1989).

Other studies have long confirmed that confessions can be extracted very effectively, without any special equipment, by using sleep deprivation, prolonged wall standing, and solitary confinement in cold or cramped conditions, and such practices tend to leave no physical after-effects (e.g. Hinkle, 1961; Shallice, 1974). As an aside, the preferred interrogation technique of Matthew Hopkins, England's most 'successful' seventeenth-century Witchfinder General was also sleep and food deprivation.

Having examined the impact of harsh physical regimes it is also important to understand some of the internal psychological processes that may influence interrogators' thoughts, attitudes and behaviour. According to a recent excellent summary of US and UK research into the psychology of confessions, modern interrogation is defined:

> . . . as a guilt-presumptive process, a theory driven social interaction led by an authority figure who holds a strong a priori belief about the target and who measures success by the ability to extract an admission from that target.
>
> (Kassin and Gudjonsson, 2004, p. 41)

From this standpoint we also need to add many other identified biases that have been unearthed by empirical research and that are acutely relevant to the interrogation of suspects. These include, the 'confirmation bias', a powerful distortion of the normally discriminative cognitive process that makes beliefs resistant to change even when presented with relevant and credible evidence. So for example, research has shown that once an individual forms a belief they will continue to find ways to support that belief, i.e. they will selectively interpret new data and accept what conforms to their pre-established belief and tend to reject information that challenges it. Such thought processes in turn influence our behaviour and we tend to act in ways that support this belief – a phenomenon normally referred to as the self-fulfilling prophecy (Kassin and Gudjonsson, 2004, p. 41).

Moving back to the Abu Ghraib and Gitmo detainees, there are many reports of prisoners handed over to US forces in Afghanistan with accompanying (unsupported) stories of the prisoner's alleged association with Al-Qaeda, or their attendance at terrorist training camps. Such information secured the $5,000 reward for the mercenary group disposing of the prisoner, but what impact did this information have on the receiving US forces during the interrogation process that were under the impression that they were interrogating a committed Al-Qaeda terrorist? Or how is an officer likely to respond to information from a source as authoritative as the then US Defense Secretary, Donald Rumsfeld, who labelled the detainees as 'among the most dangerous, best trained, vicious killers on the face of the earth' (Rose, 2004, p. 8).

Whilst it is not possible, within the constraints of this one chapter, to do justice to all the powerful psychological forces inherent in the concepts of bias, attribution error and stereotyping (especially when exacerbated during an armed conflict) I am sure that readers will appreciate how such universal processes can be manipulated with malevolent and dire consequences.

I would now like to return to Meek's catalogue of tactics and in order to improve our understanding of the psychological impact of such action I would like to suggest a suitable typology to make sense of what is taking place, to compartmentalise the many activities in order that we can better assimilate the totality of the process that is unfolding. In order to do that I need to very briefly outline what is known in the field of police interrogation.

## Police interrogation tactics: US–UK practices

It is a legal requirement throughout the UK that all police interviews with suspects are recorded,[2] and this accurate and transparent account of events has proved a very valuable and reliable research facility for psychologists. Initially recording took place on audio-tapes and more recently video recording has appeared at a number of sites for use with some witnesses and victims as well as suspects.[3] There is no such requirement in the US although, four states, Alaska, Illinois, Maine and Minnesota, have begun to adopt this practice.

Let me briefly summarise the reported work on what is known in the field of police interrogation in the UK. I apologise in advance for the rapid nature of this brief guide to police interrogation in the UK which is not meant to underscore the many impressive articles in this field. It will however be sufficient for our purposes and allow me to provide the necessary context.

The first authoritative research that capitalised on audio and video recorded records of police interrogation was published in 1993 by Professor John Baldwin, who had access to over 400 tapes of interview. His view of police interrogation can be summarised as:

> . . . inept and poorly prepared.
>
> (Baldwin, 1993)

A later study by Robertson, Pearson and Gibb (1996) of nearly 3,000 cases summarised the police interrogation process as:

> . . . banal and non-threatening.
>
> (Robertson et al., 1996)

These and similar findings found that, contrary to public opinion, there was little or no interaction between interrogator and suspect, and it was often the case that a suspect made a confession in spite of the tactics rather than because of them. It would seem that a suspect would decide whether to admit or deny an offence and was able to maintain that position irrespective of the nature of the tactics or in many cases the views of the legal adviser present (McConville and Hodgson, 1993).

Professor Baldwin effectively dispelled the 'myth' of what went on behind closed doors in the police interrogation room. Fuelled no doubt by a popular diet of police films and televised crime thrillers, the interrogation process was portrayed as a succession of tense psychological encounters where the police would often win the day after a lengthy gladiatorial combat; the reality bore no resemblance to this myth. These and other research findings led to a major review of police interrogation practice and ultimately to a structured training programme; the result of a collaboration between psychologists, lawyers, academics and police officers. The mnemonic 'PEACE' was used to identify this national training programme and took its name from the model utilised to deliver the training.[4]

The whole purpose of this new training in 'investigative interviewing' was to provide each and every police officer in the UK with a straightforward framework to obtain a credible and ethically sound interview product. Even the word interrogation was replaced by the term interviewing, as it carried with it a far less pejorative label. UK police interviews were now designed to be non-coercive and non-confrontational and there was a recognised shift in priorities away from simply attempting to elicit a confession to adopting an information gathering approach and towards that elusive goal of seeking the truth (Williamson, 1993). UK police officers were not allowed to threaten or ill-treat suspects, to lie or deceive (e.g. suggest that the suspect's fingerprints had been found in an incriminating position when they had not), or to make promises of leniency or to engage in inappropriate bartering.

Such training and practices stand in sharp contrast to what takes place in the US where officers are encouraged to lie and to deceive and to attempt a succession of manipulative tactics to elicit a confession from the detainee. Such tactics include the use of strong, psychologically oriented techniques involving isolation, confrontation and manipulation. US officers are allowed to present false and incriminating evidence. Worryingly, as the evidence from a growing DNA database is beginning to show, US officers are persisting with such tactics despite the fact that they greatly increase the risk that ordinary people are more likely to make false confessions – confess to crimes they did not commit – and that little or no regard will be paid to the psychological or other risk factors amongst the more vulnerable members of society (such as juveniles, mentally ill, those with learning disability or a tendency towards compliance and suggestibility) (Kassin and Gudjonsson, 2004).

So the picture outlined so far would tend to suggest a clear divide on national boundaries. However the majority of the UK findings, noted above, emerged from the early research in this field and related to mainly general or 'run of the mill' criminal cases – simple theft, minor assault, etc. and it is necessary to examine serious criminal cases in order to identify exactly what it is that is taking place when the stakes are raised and the police have to interview people arrested for murder, rape, robbery and other major crimes. My own research in this field, conducted with Professor Gisli Gudjonsson from the Institute of Psychiatry, examined in great detail 20 very serious UK criminal cases (Pearse, 1997; Pearse and Gudjonsson, 1999). We found that the interviewing process in these serious cases could best be described as:

> . . . intimidating, coercive and manipulative.

Or to put it another way that many of the tactics taught in US interrogation manuals had migrated to police interviews with suspects in the UK. These included tactics that amounted to browbeating – periods of relentless pressure, and manipulative and coercive tactics. As I have already pointed out, one of the key differences is that such tactics are allowed in the US and are widely used and taught there. In the UK such activity is likely to lead to the confession evidence being ruled as oppressive and therefore inadmissible in a court of law. In the 1997 sample of 20 cases there was a statistically significant finding that such tactics would be ruled inadmissible ($x^2$ p $= 0.0194$: 2-tail, Fisher exact) (Pearse, 1997).

So let us take stock of where we are and where this discussion is leading. Police tactics in the UK are now designed to be non threatening and non coercive, and this is in stark contrast to more aggressive and psychologically manipulative tactics that are permitted by the US legislature. However, despite the best intentions of the UK police training programme, in very serious criminal cases there is evidence that UK officers adopt many of the coercive and manipulative practices of their American counterparts and succeed in obtaining confessions despite the likelihood that such tactics will later be ruled inadmissible at court.

That means that whatever view one has in relation to the legality of such oppressive tactics or the ethical position that one might adopt, these tactics clearly succeed in breaking people down. I propose therefore to examine in greater detail the psychological processes that are at work in such circumstances, what is it that is actually taking place that will convince a resistant and stubborn suspect to change his not guilty position to one of admission? This understanding should in turn improve our appreciation of the totality of interrogation dynamics in the UK and the US and, importantly, those contained in James Meek's harrowing summary.

## The Reid Technique

The leading US interrogation technique is known as the 'Reid Technique' and is taken from a series of published works first appearing in 1962 with the latest edition available in 2001. It is estimated that this Chicago-based organisation has trained many thousands of law enforcement officers and its influence is often evident in the interrogation techniques employed by US military personnel. John Reid was a member of the Chicago Police Scientific Crime Detection Laboratory and his technique (also known as the 'nine steps' approach) was formulated after studying successful interrogations and de-briefing suspects after they had confessed (Inbau et al., 1986).

According to Gudjonsson (2003) the following three basic assumptions under-pin the training programme:

- A confession is required to solve many criminal investigations.
- Unless caught in the act offenders will not provide a confession unless inter-rogated over an extended period of time in private, using persuasive tech-niques involving, trickery, deceit and psychological manipulation.
- To break people down interrogators will need to employ techniques likely to be seen by the public as unethical.

(Gudjonsson, 2003 p. 11)

So for example the latest training manual includes the following observation:

> We do approve, however, of psychological tactics and techniques that may involve trickery and deceit; they are not only helpful but frequently indispen-sable in order to secure incriminating information from the guilty or to obtain investigative leads from otherwise uncooperative witnesses or informants.

(as quoted in Gudjonsson, 2003 p. 10)

The success of the nine steps technique is dependent on a thorough preparation concerning all the facts in the case and a prior 'behavioural analysis' to determine whether the suspect is being truthful or deceptive, i.e. at the outset officers are taught to distinguish between the innocent and the guilty – despite a wealth of research from across the world showing that there is little evidence to support the assertion that individuals can reliably detect the difference between truth and deception. Most people perform no better than chance at predicting deception and indeed experienced police officers actually do not do as well as less experienced officers or university students (Kassin and Gudjonsson, 2004). All that increases is the experienced officers' levels of confidence!

This rather alarming reliance on non-verbal behaviour suffuses the Reid technique and given the importance of this process I will very briefly outline the nine steps.

## STEP 1: DIRECT, POSITIVE CONFRONTATION

This confrontational approach is designed to raise or maintain high levels of anxiety and ensure that the suspect is in no doubt about the prosecution position. For example, our investigation shows that you are responsible for . . . or, we have forensic evidence that implicates you in. . . . Even though such statements may be false.

After the initial statement, the interrogator pauses to note any behavioural response whilst contemplating the next tactic.

## STEP 2: THEME DEVELOPMENT

This is a really crucial part of the process and an important distinction is made between emotional and non-emotional offenders. Any approach that minimises either the seriousness of the offence or the suspect's responsibility for it is considered appropriate for emotional offenders whose troubled conscience (shame and guilt) requires a moral excuse or easy way out. The aim is to convince him, or her, that they are a less reprehensible person and achieve an implicit, if not explicit, early, general admission of guilt.

Other themes recommended include:

- Normalising their behaviour – anyone would have done what you did.
- Minimising moral seriousness – others have committed far more shameful acts.
- Suggest a more morally acceptable reason. You didn't mean to harm anyone; you only did it because of the drink/drugs, or similar face-saving excuse.
- Sympathise with suspect by condemning others.
- Apportion some of the blame on the victim, witness or some other person.
- Appeal to suspect's pride with selective flattery.
- Point out the grave consequences and futility of denial.

For non-emotional offenders (someone who appears able to insulate themselves from the interrogation process) the authors recommend the interviewers should:

- Seek to catch the suspect lying about some incidental issue. Once this is achieved the suspect will always be faced with convincing the interrogator they are telling the truth.

- Get the suspect to place himself at the scene. If achieved early on the suspect may not fully appreciate the significance, even if the act or offence is disputed.
- Point out futility in denying involvement. Requires the interrogator to be able to convince the suspect of the weight of evidence.
- Play one co-accused against the other. Often involves a bluff of some description and therefore should be resorted to after other tactics have failed.

## STEP 3:  HANDLING DENIALS

This is an important stage. A suspect must not be allowed to achieve a psychological 'fortification' by persisting with denials. He is to be interrupted and told to listen to what the interrogator has to say. A well-known strategy often involving two officers working together, the 'friendly/unfriendly' approach, is recommended (also known as the 'sweet and sour' routine). This accentuates the difference between the two approaches, promoting the mildest tactic as more appealing to the suspect.

## STEP 4:  OVERCOMING OBJECTIONS

Unconvincing objections may be introduced by suspects to gain control over the interview as their denials weaken, especially guilty suspects. If the suspect thinks the objections are not successful, he may become withdrawn – he is now at his lowest psychological point, and the interrogator must move quickly.

## STEP 5:  PROCUREMENT AND RETENTION OF SUSPECT'S ATTENTION

The interrogator cannot allow the suspect time alone or grant a request for a cigarette for fear of losing his dominant position. By reducing the psychological distance between them (by leaning forward, touching, using the suspect's first name or acquiring good eye contact), the suspect becomes more attentive to the interrogator's suggestions.

## STEP 6:  HANDLING SUSPECT'S PASSIVE MOOD

Displaying sympathy and understanding the time is now right for the interrogator to appeal to the suspect to tell the truth. It may be necessary to remind the suspect of the additional stress he is placing on the victim or other parties by not confessing. An appeal is made to the suspect's sense of decency, honour or religion if applicable. A suspect may cry at this point or remain silent with a blank stare, in which case they are ready for the next step.

## STEP 7: PRESENTING AN ALTERNATIVE QUESTION

Here we return to a face-saving opportunity for the suspect by presenting a 'loaded' alternative question that contains an appealing or more positive side, e.g. 'Did you plan this, or was it spontaneous?' or, '. . . was the money used to take care of some bills at home, or was it used to gamble?' Such questions can also be one-sided, 'You are sorry about this, aren't you?'

The timing is important and should catch the suspect by surprise, increasing the likelihood of a confession.

## STEP 8: HAVING SUSPECT ORALLY RELATE VARIOUS DETAILS OF THE OFFENCE

Where the suspect has selected one of the alternatives in the previous step he will have made an incriminating admission. The objective is to develop this into a complete confession, including details of the offence and the motive and intentions of the suspect.

## STEP 9: CONVERTING AN ORAL CONFESSION INTO A WRITTEN CONFESSION

Given the number of people that retract their confession at court, a written version is considered stronger than an oral one. The authors argue that it is more difficult to challenge a written version with a suspect's signature on it.

The psychological principles at work in this model have been outlined by Brian Jayne, a Director at Reid Associates (Inbau et al., 1986). The model starts with the premise that people will want to avoid the consequences of their actions. They will be motivated to deceive, in order to avoid consequences that are 'real' or 'personal'. The former involves loss of freedom, the latter reduced self-esteem or loss of integrity. According to Jayne, therefore, 'Psychologically, interrogation can be thought of as the undoing of deception' (Inbau et al., 1986, p. 327). Lying increases a person's internal anxiety and, as this level of anxiety increases, so the individual invokes two main defence mechanisms, 'rationalisation' (the offender justifies his actions) or 'projection' (where he attributes blame elsewhere). The optimum scenario to achieve a confession, therefore, would be to decrease a person's perception of the (real or personal) consequences of confession and increase the (internal) anxiety associated with continued deception. This is the crux of the whole process.

The Reid model advocates the psychological manipulation of the suspect and, where necessary, exaggerating the available evidence (real or imagined) to overcome any resistance. This model has also been presented as a 'maximisation' and 'minimisation' approach (Kassin and McNall, 1991). Briefly, it identifies the suspect's weaknesses, exposes them and manipulates the suspect by either maximising the strength of evidence (for non-emotional suspects) or, for remorseful suspects, using ploys that minimise the offence or the role of the suspect in it. In the UK sample of 20 serious criminal cases mentioned earlier, I extended this dual categorisation paradigm to include the nature and context of the 'delivery' of the tactics (Pearse, 1997). As Zimbardo (1971) clearly showed we are all heavily influenced by the demand characteristics of the situation we are in and other social forces. I also introduced the concept of 'manipulation' rather than 'minimisation' as this better reflects the process that is actually taking place and the intention of those involved. I propose to use this categorisation process to help us to understand what is taking place during the much-publicised techniques at Gitmo and Abu Ghraib.[5]

In selecting Meek's short summary of tactics I am aware that I am taking at face value a newspaper report of such events. However, there have been a number of official disclosures from US government departments and authoritative reports from recognised agencies that continue to support such allegations. In particular a report in the *New Yorker* by Jane Mayer (2005) includes first hand reports from officials that have served at Gitmo and others responsible for, and subject to, interrogation training programmes.

Mayer's main premise is that a survival technique taught to US Special Forces to allow them to withstand hostile interrogation has been employed at Gitmo. The theory behind the SERE programme (Survival, Evasion, Resistance, and Escape) is that soldiers already exposed to harsh and debilitating treatment during training will be better equipped to survive if captured. Accordingly this programme seeks to maximise anxiety levels and creates an environment of uncertainty by stripping trainees of their clothes, exposing them to extremes of heat and cold, hooding them, enforcing sleep and food deprivation and then subjecting them to very harsh interrogation regimes. Indeed one former interrogator is quoted as saying that sleep deprivation techniques were commonplace and became known as 'the frequent-flyer programme', even though, according to a separate military intelligence officer most of the detainees were just dirt farmers from Afghanistan (Mayer, 2005 p. 70).

In layman's terms therefore it is important to consider the psychological impact of brute force, flagrant examples of abuse and the debilitating effect of a coercive physical environment on what is happening to a detainee and how it is affecting his thought processes and decision making ability. To take it a step further it is necessary to consider the psychological impact of individual tactics and the cumulative affect of different groups of tactics employed against a detainee. For the purpose of this chapter, I would seek to explain the many reported interrogation techniques within a slightly extended – five-category – typology, to address the idiosyncrasies of Gitmo and Abu Ghraib.

## Understanding and categorising interrogation techniques at Abu Ghraib and Guantanamo Bay

Interrogation techniques practised in a war zone or armed conflict tend to involve techniques carried out at the extremes of human behaviour, such as extreme levels of coercion and fear, and that distinction is accepted as we seek to compartmental-ise these techniques. The five categories are not intended to be mutually exclusive; it will be evident that recurring themes of religious and sexual abuse, for example, underpin a number of techniques in a number of the categories.

## Delivery and context

This is very much an overarching and ever present category that is intended to capture the wider influences at work in an interrogation environment beyond the dual categorisation model of Kassin and McNall (1991). In the narrow sense this category concerns the type of questions asked and 'how' the questions are put, i.e. the manner in which they are delivered. For example, for open, closed and leading questions, dialogue may take place in hushed or lowered tones or at the other end of the spectrum, questioning may take place in a hostile and intimidat-ing environment. For law enforcement personnel this might extend to officers using raised or aggressive tones, continually interrupting the suspect and refusing to listen to their answers, and perhaps shouting and swearing at the suspect. In the broader sense this category also includes 'where' such questioning may take place. Here, one is reminded once more, of the early press coverage of detainees at Gitmo who, shackled and clad in orange jump suits were bound to small carts and wheeled to the interrogation centre. And at Abu Ghraib where detainees have been subjected to a range of unacceptable regimes including the use of ferocious dogs as part of the 'warming up' process by the guards on behalf of the interroga-tion team.

## Maximisation

According to Kassin and McNall (1991, p. 234) maximisation represents '. . . a hard sell technique in which the interrogator tries to scare and intimidate the suspect into confessing by making false claims about evidence and exaggerating the seriousness and the magnitude of the charges'. This term has been extended to include any technique that would tend to increase a suspect's internal anxiety and any form of intimidation or challenge directed at the suspect. This will include assault and the threat of assault or continued detention. In purely descriptive terms, during a period of war or armed conflict we would expect to see an increase in the intensity of this physical and psychological regime that would effectively replace Kassin and McNall's scaring and intimidation of the suspect, with an extensive panoply of tactics designed to terrorise and place a suspect in fear for their life. Maximisation is therefore the category designed to capture the harshest of physi-cal and psychological activity.

In relation to Gitmo and Abu Ghraib this will include the shackling of detainees in irons, their 'three piece suits', forcing them to undergo interrogation whilst chained to the floor in the foetal position, and being made to stand for hours, hooded, subjected to intense heat and cold, and loud music.

## *Deprivation*

This category is in effect a sub-set of maximisation and is included because of the prevailing circumstances often peculiar to war zones and armed conflict where denial of basic human needs tend to be more common place. Included within this category will therefore be the denial of sufficient food and water, sleep and rest, suitable accommodation and toilet facilities and other basic rights specified within the Geneva Convention (1949).

Taken together these two categories are designed to capture the most basic and brutal attempts by one human being to exercise control and suborn the will of another. This may seem far removed from understanding and applying the various psychological techniques recommended by the Reid Technique but the blunt truth is likely to be that in war zones, interrogators will take short cuts, they will not have time for 'nine steps'. In the next category we will move away from trying to imagine the effect of physical brutality on a detainee, to examine more subtle tactics.

## *Manipulation*

The debilitating effect on a detainee's resolve of physical isolation, deprivation and confinement, may not, on their own be sufficient to break a person down. In the UK it was recognised by Lord Chief Justice Taylor (the most senior judge in the country), in *R. v. Paris and others* ([1993] 97 Cr. App. R. 99), that despite the presence of aggressive and intimidating interviewing tactics and the inherently coercive nature of police detention, it was the manipulative and 'insidious questioning' (page 104) that succeed in eliciting a confession. This can include reducing a detainee's perception of the crime or the consequences of his actions, but it will also include manipulating significant details, introducing themes and attacking a person's self esteem, their emotional well being or stature. Other tactics include embellishment, the manipulative use of important third parties, inducements and offers of leniency or favourable terms.

This powerful combination of psychological manoeuvres often occupies a more latent profile and tends not to grab the headlines to the same extent as the manifestly aggressive maximisation methods, but there is no doubt that undermining a detainee's perception of reality is a key feature in any interrogation regime designed to break a person down. Perhaps the most effective example of the use of manipulation that I have been exposed to recently was that practised by the Israeli Security Agency (ISA – formerly Shin Bet). In 2004 I interviewed an unsuccessful suicide bomber at an Israeli Detention Centre, located near the West Bank. So for example, according to his interrogating officer, there was no need to apply any maximisation techniques, instead he was befriended and made welcome in the traditional Arab custom.

The interrogating officer spoke excellent Arabic, immediately alleviating the problem of truncated and distorted dialogue through any third party and he went to great lengths to reassure the suspect. He then went on to manipulate the role of other parties (also detained) and also the role of influential third parties – family, village contemporaries and perhaps most important of all his religious beliefs. These, and similar manipulative tactics, elicited a full confession from this 'terrorist suicide bomber' within an hour.

### Degradation

Just as deprivation can be seen to represent a sub-category of maximisation, so this section could be subsumed within manipulation, except that the unique circumstances associated with a war zone tends to propel this specific category into the limelight. Degradation includes all those tactics that are designed to humiliate and degrade a person's self belief, a violent assault on their self esteem, and cultural or religious beliefs. What appears to have been prevalent in the Abu Ghraib prison complex is the use of simulated sexual acts, carried out by groups of naked and hooded detainees under the control of male and female guards and sometimes with fearsome guard dogs in the vicinity. Such activity clearly falls within this category.

It is hoped that by breaking down the many examples of reported techniques into five main categories the reader will more easily recognise what it is that is taking place, and be better able to appreciate the psychological impact and consequences of such tactics and the relevance of the interplay between and within all five categories.

## Conclusion

As international media coverage has highlighted an extensive array of shocking interrogation techniques practiced at Guantanamo Bay and the Abu Ghraib prison, this chapter has sought to make use of a number of psychological studies to begin to account for changes in human behaviour and in particular the corrosive influence that can be evident within hostile environments. In particular, it is always necessary to consider the omnipresent and powerful influence of the situation and how defining and regulating our own social influences can lead to a loss of social control and shape brutal and aggressive human behaviour.

It is also hoped that the presentation of a user-friendly five-layer interrogation typology will provide a better understanding of the specific psychological influences at work in these interrogations and that the combination of all these factors will undermine and suborn even the most resistant individual.

## Notes

1 However there is sufficient literature available to suggest that allegations of torture during 'conventional' police interrogation continue to be reported around the world (e.g. Forrest, 1999; Graef, 2000).
2 This requirement was brought in on 1 January 1986 by the Police and Criminal Evidence Act (PACE) 1984 and audio recording had reached all parts of the UK by 1992.
3 Vulnerable and intimidated witnesses are defined under sections 16 and 17 of the Youth Justice and Criminal Evidence Act, 1999. Police guidance from the Home Office

recommends the use of video recording facilities for these categories (e.g. child victims of sexual or violent abuse) and a major benefit of this process is that the recording can be used as the victim's evidence in chief. See Achieving Best Evidence in Criminal Proceedings: Guidance for Vulnerable or Intimidated Witnesses, Home Office 2002.
4  PEACE stands for preparation and planning, engage and explain, account, closure and evaluation.
5  Interestingly, Kassin and Gudjonsson (2004, p. 43) also provide a three level typology – custody and isolation, confrontation and minimization.

## References

Baldwin, J. (1993). Police interviewing techniques. Establishing truth or proof? *British Journal of Criminology*, **33**, 325–352.

Forrest, D.M. (1999). Examination for the late physical after effects of torture. *Journal of Clinical Forensic Medicine*, **6**, 4–13.

Geneva Convention (1949). Convention III: Relative to the Treatment of Prisoners of War.

Graef, R. (2000). An effective police officer must still be a fair cop. *The Times*, 20 January 2000. London.

Gudjonsson, G.H. (2003). *The Psychology of Interrogations and Confessions: A Handbook*. Chichester: Wiley.

Haney, C., Banks, C. and Zimbardo, P. (1973). Interpersonal dynamics in a simulated prison. *International Journal of Criminology and Penology*, **1**, 69–97.

Hinkle, L.E. (1961).The physiological state of the interrogation subject as it affects brain function. In A.D. Biderman and H. Zimmer (Eds.). *The Manipulation of Human Behaviour*, pp. 19–50. New York: Wiley.

Home Office (2002). *Achieving Best Evidence in Criminal Proceedings: Guidance for Vulnerable or Intimidated Witnesses*. London: Home Office Communications Directorate.

Inbau, F.E., Reid, J.E. and Buckley, J.P. (1986). *Criminal interrogation and confessions. 3rd edition*. Baltimore, MD: Williams and Wilkins.

Kassin, S.M. and Gudjonsson, G.H. (2004). The psychology of confessions, a review of the literature and issues. *Psychological Science in the Public Interest*, **5**, 2, American Psychological Society.

Kassin, S.M. and McNall, K (1991) Police interrogations and confessions. *Law and Human Behavior*, **15**, 233–251.

Mayer, J. (2005). The experiment. *New Yorker Magazine*, 11 & 18 July.

McConville, M. and Hodgson, J. (1993). *Custodial Legal Advice and the Right to Silence. The Royal Commission on Criminal Justice Research Study No. 16*. London: HMSO.

Meek, J. (2005). Nobody is talking. *Guardian*, 18 February.

Mikulincer, M., Babkoff, H and Caspy, T. (1989). The effects of 72 hours' sleep loss on psychological variables. *British Journal of Psychology*, **80**, 145–162.

Pearse, J. (1997). *Police Interviewing: An examination of some of the psychological, interrogative and background factors that are associated with a suspect's confession*. Unpublished doctoral thesis. University of London.

Pearse, J and Gudjonsson, G. (1999) Measuring influential police interviewing tactics: a factor analytic approach. *Legal and Criminological Psychology*, **4** (part 2), 221–238.

Robertson, G., Pearson, R. and Gibb, R. (1996) Police interviewing and the use of appropriate adults. *Journal of Forensic Psychiatry*, **7**, 297–309.

Rose, D. (2004). *Guantanamo. America's War on Human Rights*. London: Faber & Faber.

Shallice, T. (1974). The Ulster depth interrogation techniques and their relation to sensory deprivation research. *Cognition*, **1**, 385–406.

Williamson, T. (1993). From Interrogation to investigative interviewing. Strategic trends in police questioning. *Journal of Community and Applied Social Psychology*, **3**, 89–99.

Zimbardo, P. (1971). The pathology of imprisonment. *Society*, 9, 4–8.

# 11 Terrorist tactics and counter-terrorism

*Graeme Steven*[1]

## Introduction

In the age of global terrorism and high-profile attacks such as 9/11, 7/7, Mumbai, etc. there is a particular interest from business, government, military, law-enforcement, and academics in the tactics utilised by terrorist groups/cells. There are different beliefs as to why groups choose or adopt a certain strategy and specific tactics. These often focus on the resources available to the group, the acquired skill-set from a specific environment or operational theatre, or a favoured tactic based on the desired consequences or outcome (e.g. Drake, 1998; Dolnik, 2007). Often no one belief alone is true, as there are usually a multitude of factors that contribute to the use of a certain tactic, as this chapter aims to demonstrate.

Some groups have historically tended to adopt and stick to a certain tactic, almost to the extent that the tactic becomes a signature for that group, such as the use of secondary and tertiary devices in complex attacks, or the 'Barrack-Buster' Improvised Mortars developed by the Provisional Irish Republican Army (PIRA) (O'Brien, 1993). The Improvised Mortars were such a signature method/equipment that when the Revolutionary Armed Forces of Colombia (FARC) begun using them in Colombia, it highlighted the cross-training of FARC by PIRA personnel (English, 2003). More recently there is the example of suicide bombings in Iraq being a signature tactic by Sunni groups, and usually foreign fighters. A signature does not have to be a tactic, as it can be evident in the way a bomb-maker constructs a device, how a group launders money, and is potential in any action undertaken. 'Signatures' are of particular importance to practitioners and those tasked with the pursuit of terrorist groups, and the prevention, protection and preparation against terrorist activity.

The psychology of terrorist tactics, or even the increased interest in tactics, was not particularly prominent until occasions when terrorist cells *changed tactics between attacks*, thereby disrupting any 'counter' or 'anti' measures implemented by practitioners based on the expected signature method of operating of particular groups (Drake, 1998). The change in tactics made it much more difficult for the authorities to plan against the threat.

Many analysts and practitioners have been concerned by the behaviour of such unpredictable cells, in that they appear to change tactics between attacks, but without and before any obvious 'target-hardening'. Target-hardening can be proactive and/or reactive, and involves increasing the security of potential/known targets. An example of *reactive* target-hardening is the response to the Glasgow Airport attempted Suicide Vehicle Borne IED attack (SVBIED). The response included increasing armed police patrols, installing chicanes on approach roads to slow vehicles, and metal bollards around the perimeter of the building to prevent a potential SVBIED from breaching the building itself.

It is a common myth that terrorist groups or cells change tactics *only* as a result of target hardening; in fact there are numerous factors affecting the decision to change tactics between attacks, and examining these can show that many terrorist cells operate rationally and in response to their environment

Examining some of the complexities and factors that may provoke or encourage a group to choose or change certain tactics can contribute to the knowledge of the operational and practical problems in counter-terrorism as well as contributing to the academic debate on the *psychology of terrorism*:

- Psychopathology theory claims that terrorists are mad or psychopaths (suffering from a psychopathological disorder), and thus are irrational actors. Proponents of this line of thought do not take issue with the suggestion that terrorists reason logically. However, they argue that political terrorists are driven to commit acts of violence as a consequence of psychological forces . . .
- The basis of Rational Choice Theory is the notion that the decision to both become a terrorist and commit terrorist acts is influenced by factors in the environment, and that the actor is a rational one who responds and reacts to these environmental factors. This theory opposes the common misconception that 'all terrorists are mad' and looks at external as well as internal factors in trying to understand and explain such behaviour (Steven, 2004, pp.14-15).

This chapter does not intend to take sides or fuel the debate over which theory is correct or most apt, however, it does aim to argue against the misconception that terrorists are irrational and thus cannot be studied or understood. Even some psychopathologist theories state that terrorists are irrational in motivation but reason logically, such as that espoused by Post (1990). Nevertheless, many less-informed people still believe that terrorists are completely irrational and insane in both motivation and behaviour. It is sad that this counter-productive myth still exists. In terms of terrorist tactics it must be remembered that groups will often react to their environment and adapt their tactics depending on the target information presented to them, and the restrictions in which they operate. If one subscribes to the notion that *all* terrorists are insane and do not reason logically then one could be led to believe that terrorists simply choose their tactics with little or no thought or provocation to or from the environment they operate in.

The reality is that there are a number of different factors that can influence or motivate a terrorist cell to choose or change tactics, from targeting, security, different targets requiring different tactics, resources, structure, desired aims/effects, tactical life expectancy, and target hardening (Drake, 1998).

In order to demonstrate that either choice or changes in tactics are often a response to the environment, as opposed to irrational unpredictable desires, this chapter will examine and demonstrate the complexities involved in the adoption and use of terrorist tactics, the wide variety of factors that influence the decision to utilise certain tactics, the difficulty involved in changing tactics, as well as highlighting significant points relevant to counter-terrorist theorists, planners and practitioners. In order to do this, this chapter will examine the requirements and implications of a change in tactics, the targeting process in order to illustrate the factors influencing the group, as well as possible causal factors in changing tactics including tactical life-expectancy, target hardening, operational security, resources available, the decision-making process and triggers.

## Core factors

In very general terms, tactics can be affected by a broad range of factors including social, economic, geographical, political, religious, and financial ones. Some common *detailed* factors of why groups *choose* tactics will be illustrated later and throughout this chapter in response to examination of the target and environment.

There are three main requirements for a terrorist cell to change tactics between attacks; a trigger, a decision and an ability to change:

1.  A *trigger* would be any stimuli that initiates or demands the belief or recognition of a requirement to change. A trigger could be internal or external to the group.
2.  In order to change a *decision* would be required, which, structure dependent, could involve those on the ground as well as middle management and possibly leaders of the group.
3.  In order to actually change tactics, the *ability* to do so is required in terms of resources and expertise to procure the means, train in and then utilise different tactics.

The decision to change tactics or methods is usually triggered by some form of internal/external stimuli. The forms these stimuli can take are discussed in more detail in the following sections, but they can be briefly listed here as:

*   targeting
*   security,
*   resources,
*   structure,
*   desired aims/effects,
*   tactical life expectancy,
*   target hardening.

An important variable in all of these is the tactical and strategic sophistication of the group, and as part of this, their awareness of the operational capabilities and tactics of the security forces.

*Targeting*

Terrorism, insurgency, asymmetric warfare; all by nature operate by looking at particular enemy or target vulnerabilities in order to cause maximum impact. Much of this is done in reference to what they believe the targets or security forces are *expecting* and equally what they are least expecting and where or how they would thus be least well-protected.

A key factor influencing target-selection is the ability to measure and generate the perceived effectiveness of attack tactics in achieving their aim; whether that takes the form of casualties, media attention, specific goals (e.g. the assassination of a key figure), and most importantly whether they are likely to succeed or fail, and indeed how to measure 'success' (e.g. Taylor, 1988).

Different targets can lead to different tactics in order to engage the targets. For example, a high profile-figure assassination may require a stand-off attack: an attack mounted from distance due to the difficulty in getting close to the target (e.g. a sniper attack). Influential factors in terrorist tactical planning here would include anticipated crowds, if a walk or open-top drive-past is known/publicised, level of security of the close-protection teams (CPTs) or 'bodyguards' of the figure, the CPTs perceived threat of the area and their resulting security stance, whether the CPT had anti-sniper assets, potential reaction and coordination of local police and security forces and the ensuing ability of the terrorist sniper team to extract, etc.

Conversely, if a stand-off attack is not viable then some groups have been known to facilitate close-quarter attacks (CQA). An example here is that of the *Liberation Tigers of Tamil Eelam* (LTTE) – generally better known simply as the *Tamil Tigers* – who are one of the few groups to have been sophisticated enough to assassinate a state premier. They achieved this when the group killed India's Prime Minister, Rajiv Gandhi, on 21 May 1991. Gandhi was killed in dramatic fashion by a female suicide bomber while he was campaigning for the Congress Party. The LTTE had targeted the Prime Minister because he was widely seen as being responsible for the deployment of Indian troops (the Indian Peace Keeping Force or IPKF) into Sri Lanka in 1987. The Indian troops soon came into open conflict with the LTTE, and the LTTE later alleged 'war crimes' had been carried out by the IPKF (Gunaratna, 2003). As the orchestrator behind the deployment, Ghandi became a high profile target for the LTTE.

The LTTE realised a stand-off attack would be unlikely to be successful so they developed a plan for a close-quarter attack. The LTTE reportedly used informers to identify details of Gandhi's security and plans for a meeting at an election rally in Tamil Nadu. They researched and identified the security procedures and vulnerabilities and opted for a suicide-bomber to detonate amongst a welcome committee when Gandhi arrived at the location. According to Gunaratna (2003) there are different versions and rumours of the exact details of the attack. For example, there is uncertainty over whether the LTTE had infiltrated the police force to enable the female suicide-bomber to be vetted and allowed to take part in the welcome ceremony and adorn a garland around Gandhi's neck; or whether the bomber simply managed to join the three or four pre-vetted garland bearers at the last minute before the security team could react. There are also conflicting accounts over whether the bomber placed the garland round Gandhi's neck and then bent down to touch his feet as a traditional form of respect and greeting, or whether she dropped the garland shortly before Gandhi and then bent to retrieve it. The bending down was key as she wore an RDX ball-bearing suicide-vest, which was detonated by the act of bending over. Gandhi, along with 14 others, was killed in the attack.

Terrorists can be very resourceful in researching and mounting attacks. Devices can be laid into building foundations or walls if it is known a particular event will take place. An excellent example of such an approach is the attack on the 1984 Brighton Conservative Party Conference, where PIRA had hidden an IED in the hotel, resulting in the deaths of five people and 34 injured. Those killed were Anthony Berry MP, Roberta Wakeham, Eric Taylor, Muriel Maclean and Jeanne Shattock. The device had been planted several weeks earlier by Patrick Magee, who checked into the hotel under a false name (English, 2003). The PIRA had hoped that the bomb would kill Margaret Thatcher, the British Prime Minister, as well as many of her senior Cabinet colleagues. It failed in those aims, but nonetheless attracted a formidable amount of media attention for the group. In the aftermath of the attack, the PIRA famously released a statement claiming responsibility and warning the authorities: 'Today we were unlucky, but remember, we have only to be lucky once – you will have to be lucky always.'

Terrorists have used many different people in order to shake off offender-profiles, and surprise or bypass security measures. Such tactics have included the use of child-soldiers, women in traditional Islamic dress such as the Burqa who are less likely to be searched, aware as well as unaware proxy bombers, and even the elderly. For example, in December 2007 it was reported in Algeria that in a major strategic change, the Algerian arm of Al-Qaeda (AQ) appeared to be using terrorists older than 60 to carry out its attacks, after a 64-year-old suicide bomber drove a truck bomb to a target and detonated. It is believed AQ in Algeria realised that the police had learned of their earlier switch in tactics to using young people to carry out their attacks. They then realised they had to switch again in order to be able to infiltrate and engage targets so again changed their strategy and appeared to have decided to use terrorists aged in their 60s and over (Boccolini, 2007).

Terrorists have also shown an ability to factor in the responses of the security forces in how they plan attacks. This can take the form of follow-up attacks designed to hit security forces and other emergency responders as they react to a first attack. The Provisional IRA (PIRA) was particularly adept at secondary and even tertiary attacks. The classic example of such an operation was the Warrenpoint attack on 27 August 1979. The PIRA team placed two hidden bombs at the site. The first device, an 800 lb bomb, was located by the roadside and was intended to destroy a passing military patrol. The second device, again 800 lb, was hidden at a nearby gate. The IRA had judged that after the first attack more troops would be rushed to the scene and that the gate was a logical location for some of these troops to base themselves. Events went exactly as the PIRA had intended. The first bomb detonated as a military convoy passed killing six soldiers. In the aftermath, helicopters and other vehicles rushed more troops to the scene. Thirty minutes after the first bomb, the second device was detonated, killing another 12 soldiers. The total of 18 dead was the heaviest loss the British Army suffered in a single day during the conflict. A British general later said of the attack that it was 'arguably the most successful and certainly one of the best planned IRA attacks of the whole campaign' (McKittrick et al., 1999, p. 796)

The concept of multi-stage attacks has spread internationally and seen some very resourceful tactics. In theatres such as Afghanistan and Iraq there have been numerous reports of occasions where similar tactics are utilised, showing a great deal of planning. Terrorists in these regions will often record video-footage of attacks for propaganda purposes but also to study security force tactics and how to counter them. A further twist in Iraq has been the use of VBIEDs in ambulances (Multi-National Force Iraq, 2009). Such attacks have included suicide-bombers in one crowded place, followed by another suicide-bomber who would call people to gather away from the initial detonation. People would run to perceived safety and then the second bomber would detonate. Previously emplaced devices may then target responders. After several attacks of this type the security forces quickly learned to mount security cordons and prevent any vehicles from entering the area, to prevent the use of VBIEDs. The terrorists then realised that the only exception was ambulances, which people would allow to drive in to the centre of the area and everyone would flock to. The use of ambulance VBIEDs thus caused further casualties, and showed how terrorists are not only resourceful but adapt and respond to the environment.

A key variable in targeting factors is the remit of the cell and whether the particular cell is designed to undertake certain types of attacks on certain types of target, or whether they are free to select and engage targets and the best forms of attacking them. It can also be structure-dependent as some organisations have cells that research possible targets, and then pass 'target-packs' on to operational cells to minimise exposure on the ground (e.g. Drake, 1998). Furthermore, the operational 'cell' for an attack could consist of several different teams; one team to carry out reconnaissance, identify vulnerabilities and plan attack options, another team to assemble an IED, for example, another to emplace it and the third to function the device. This has the desired effect of reducing the risk to the cell members.

As one can see, there are many different types of targets, thus there are many tactics. If tactics work, then they are often adhered to – with groups adopting an 'if it's not broken don't fix it' mentality. In these circumstances, changes occur when there is an external trigger for groups to change tactics, or sometimes an internal sophisticated awareness of security forces' pursuit tactics, techniques and procedures (TTP). From this point, another, and arguably more important factor in targeting emerges; whether the target is achievable.

## *Tactical life-expectancy*

A significant factor in the decision to change tactics is the life-expectancy of the tactic. Tactical life expectancy refers to the reciprocal nature or relationship between the terrorist and counter-terrorist tactics and strategy. Terrorism and counter-terrorism are evolutionary processes. Once one side gets used to certain tactics and develops counter-measures, the other side has to innovate and develop new ones, and so on. For example, the tactic of hijacking planes was one that was increasingly used because terrorists knew there was little that could be done. It was only when target-hardening was applied to aviation security and CT teams became more proficient at assaults on such targets that the tactic became less used and bomb-placing and then stand-off attacks were used (e.g. Silke, 2001). Another example is in Northern Ireland, where security forces developed jamming measures (Electronic Counter Measures – ECM) to prevent terrorist bombs from being detonated, after which the terrorists responded by developing counter-jamming measures. The security forces then developed counter-counter-jamming measures (Geraghty, 1998). This theme is evident throughout the history of terrorism and is also evident in the conventions and political moves following such actions. Thus the relationship between terrorist and counter-terrorist seems a cyclical one whereby one continues to learn from the other. What becomes important in CT terms is to then reduce terrorists' capacity to learn, research, recruit, develop, procure, and finance themselves by making it as hard as possible for them to operate. Attacking operational as well as support networks is thus a key strategy here within a multi-dimensional, multi-level CT approach (Steven, 2004).

A further example of the symbiotic relationship between terrorist and counter-terrorist is the result of security forces' operations. In some operational theatres where numerous sophisticated explosive devices are used, there were a number of theories as to why there are occasional lulls in sophisticated device use and outbreaks of IEDs using home-made explosives (HME), in an apparent shift of tactics. One theory was that a new cell was operating, but this did not account for the lack of other sophisticated devices. Another theory was that the cell(s) had decided to switch tactics in order to outfox those pursuing them. The reality, however, is often that as a result of security forces effectively cutting off or disrupting their supply-lines, terrorist cells have to resort to using different resources and thus different tactics. As such one must remember that the actions of targets and/or security forces are both elements that can influence terrorist tactics. This is important when examining the concept and consequences of target hardening.

### Target hardening

Terrorists will often undertake a cost–benefit analysis of the means to engage the target with the pay-off. Sometimes this analysis is quite rudimentary but at other times it can be sophisticated and detailed (e.g. Silke, 2003). Thus target hardening (targets increasing their security measures) can cause a need to change targets – and consequently tactics too – on the basis that different targets will have different security and profiles thus will need different means to engage, as discussed in the section on targeting.

While target hardening can be seen as a factor affecting the use of certain terrorist tactics, there are a number of issues that are relevant to the counter-terrorist.

First, it is a common belief in the principle of crime prevention that increasing the security of a potential target may deter possible attacks and shift the focus to softer-targets (e.g. Clarke and Newman, 2006). While this is commonly true in crime it is not absolutely true in terrorism. Sometimes target hardening can have the opposite effect and make a location even more attractive as it not only denotes the perceived value attached to the location, but gives more potential for a media spectacular – especially if the location is in the public eye. Any attacks, whether 'successful' in damage or not, can serve to disproportionately raise the profile and capability of the group. The Real IRA's rocket attack (using an RPG-22 anti-tank missile) against the SIS (MI6) headquarters building in London on 20 September 2000 is a good example of this. The building was well protected and the attack itself did little damage, but because of the high profile of the target it resulted in a lot of media attention for the Real IRA. Such media coverage could be used to highlight alleged ineffectiveness on the part of the intelligence services and conversely try to demonstrate the 'organisational skill' of the Real IRA and success in evasion as they were able to procure and transport such weapons, as well as executing the attack.

The point that target-hardening, or increasing the security of a potential target, may deter possible attacks and shift focus to softer-targets is also an ethical dilemma as planners must take into account *where* they may be shifting terrorist focus to. The approach taken in the UK Government Counter-Terrorism Strategy (CONTEST) has showed an awareness that this problem exists and attempts to address it (HM Government, 2009). A key dimension to CONTEST is the argument that counter-terrorism cannot be carried out in isolation; it is a problem affecting and threatening all of society, so society as a whole should play a part in fighting it. For example, the importance of a tip-off phone call from a vigilant member of the public sighting something suspicious should never be underestimated.

It is important to note that the concept of target hardening is moving from previous notions restricted to just the physical protective security of buildings or locations. Any measures making it more difficult for terrorist groups to operate could classify as target hardening, as reflected in the wider and inclusive focus of the UK CONTEST campaign. One much publicised idea was that of ID cards for nationals as well as foreign nationals and biometric security. The UK Home Office (n.d.) believes that the identity cards will 'disrupt the use of false and multiple identities by . . . those involved in terrorist activity.' The real benefits of ID cards as a CT measure however are debatable. Some researchers have supported this type of development (e.g. Clarke and Newman, 2006) but whilst this can work well against known individuals, it does little against 'lily-whites' who have no known records or associations with terrorist groups, and a more worrying vulnerability and flaw is the ability to conduct adequate vetting and background checks on individuals who may be applying for such cards.

As target hardening can cause a *shift* in tactics one must not miss the potential for it to cause an *escalation* in tactics. As governments and societies become more aware of terrorists and their tactics, they become more resilient and thus pose more difficult targets for terrorists to research, plan and execute attacks. A side effect here is the potential for groups to then look to more extreme measures.

Groups may also change tactics due to desired outcome/effects. For example, if people believe a terrorist group always targets high-profile buildings then there is a degree of reassurance felt by those not frequenting or near such buildings. If, however, attacks appear to randomly target other areas such as smaller streets, shopping centres and everyday life such as buses and the underground as with the 7/7 London bombings, then the paranoia, fear and disruption can be as great if not greater than targeting high-profile hardened targets.

Regardless of target hardening and tactical life expectancy, many groups maintain favoured TTP and Modus Operandi (MO), and can often even be recognised by this. This brings its own disadvantages of setting patterns, being predictable and possibly compromising operational security.

### Operational security (OPSEC)

Security plays a large part in terrorist targeting and Modus Operandi (MO). While this is normally only associated with structure, whereby groups will often organise into cells so that if one is compromised the entire organisation is not, it can also affect tactics. Terrorist organisations are paranoid of infiltration, informers, as well as surveillance and monitoring of communications. For their survival, any perceived risk or compromise can often be enough to abandon operations or change tactics (Taylor, 1988).

If a group has numerous volunteers and resources, suicide operations can to an extent preserve OPSEC as there are minimal, if any, survivors to question. It is worth noting that some groups will use 'handlers' for back-up detonation if the suicide bomber does not detonate his or herself. If this tactic is abhorrent to the group's support network, or they don't have the resources, then other, more traditional attack methods would likely be used.

The first time a particular type of attack is used might limit its use in terms of surprise a second time, or preclude a second type of attack from resulting target-hardening, such as the massive increase in aviation security following 9/11. Switching tactics can thus be a defensive one in terms of preserving their own security and lifespan, as if the group continues with the same MO they know it will be easier for the authorities to track and perhaps ultimately predict them. Equally, some of the more sophisticated and security-aware groups realise that if they continually procure their equipment from the same source that will increase the risk of compromise/detection. Consequently, if a group desires to switch tactics, it must have the resources to do so.

### Resources

The resources of a group in terms of man-power, training, support-networks, logistical supply chains, financing, and even expertise are all factors in themselves in whether a group has the *ability* to switch tactics (e.g. Dolnik, 2007).

For an *organisation* to change tactics in a theatre, mass re-training or a new cell may need to be brought in for the operation. This would involve considerable communication, logistics in bringing the members in securely (when moving people across borders may necessitate use of false passports, etc), as well as the weapons or materials required for the operation, safe houses, vehicles, and significant financing and laundering, etc.

For a *cell* to change tactics in a theatre, they would require financial, logistic and supply networks to bring the materials in. Expertise, and possibly instruction and training, which itself requires instructors and a training ground, would also be required along with the time to train and adapt their targeting/execution methods. An operational lull would then be seen as the cell retrains.

For either an organisation or cell to change tactics they would need the finances and means to facilitate all of the aforementioned points as well as numerous others. As finances and resources are often hard to come by in illegal organisations, someone usually has to authorise all of the above, and decide whether it is both necessary, cost-effective, and in the interests of the organisation. A group may have the ability to switch tactics, it may even have a trigger, but ultimately a decision needs to be made and communicated to do so.

### Decision

The degree of autonomy terrorists have when it comes to decision making varies between groups. Some organisations have strategic goals and objectives and their cells have autonomy in deciding how to fulfil/achieve them, while others are extremely strict with everything being cleared through a formal chain of command. In the PIRA for example, cells (or Active Service Units as they were referred to within the organisation) had considerable autonomy in terms of selecting and carrying out local attacks. 'Spectaculars' – attacks against very high profile targets – however had to be first formally vetted and authorised by PIRA's senior commanders (English, 2003). More recently, it has been clear that Al-Qaeda's central command have very limited control and direction over the activities of some of the movement's apparent subsidiaries. The example of Al-Qaeda in Iraq, especially while that branch was under the leadership of Abu Musab Al-Zarqawi, is particularly relevant (Aaron, 2008).

Bureaucracy and means of communications bring problems here depending on whether the group utilises the internet, satellite communications, encryption technology, or couriers. All have an impact on the time taken to decide and thus the speed of the group to change, as well as varying risks of compromise, which can serve as a stimuli or trigger to change plans/tactics. The trigger would have to be recognised, initiated, communicated to the decision-maker(s) and then communicated back before actual change.

### Triggers

Various internal and external factors have been examined and discussed throughout this chapter that can serve as stimuli or triggers for a terrorist group to change tactics. Sometimes the consequences themselves of certain tactics can also be a trigger, either from resulting responses in new legislation or even negative public reaction.

Terrorism is inextricably linked to the media. Margaret Thatcher once stated that 'Terrorists crave publicity: it gives them purpose, spreads their message, and is their "oxygen" for survival' (Steven, 2004, pp. 117-118). As the terrorist seeks to influence the public, conversely the public reaction can also influence the terrorist. The reaction to certain tactics can have a massive impact on the support for terrorist groups. For example, the Omagh bombing in 1998 which resulted in the deaths of 31 men, women and children had a profoundly negative impact on the terrorist group responsible: the Real IRA. In the aftermath of the bombing, angry public protests took place outside the homes and workplaces of known or suspected members and the organization was forced to declare a ceasefire (English, 2003).

In sum, triggers can thus be internal or external, and can even emerge as a consequence of the use of particular tactics themselves.

## Conclusion

There are a multitude of factors that contribute to why terrorist groups choose or adopt a certain strategy and specific tactics. This chapter focused mainly on why terrorist groups *change* tactics, as it better demonstrates the rational response and considerations associated with tactics. A secondary motivation was the current interest in the alleged unpredictability of terrorist cells that seemingly change tactics between attacks for no apparent reason. As illustrated, it is in fact difficult for groups to suddenly switch tactics as there are three *main* requirements for a terrorist cell to actually change tactics; a trigger, a decision and the willingness/ability to change.

The chapter has focused mainly on what factors cause groups to change tactics to illustrate that terrorists act rationally and in response to their environment as opposed to being insane unpredictable entities or individuals. If one subscribes to the notion that terrorists are insane and do not reason logically then one could be led to believe that terrorists simply choose their tactics with little or no thought to the environment they operate in. The evidence in terms of how terrorists actually operate, however, simply does not support such a view.

In contrast, it is clear that it is very misleading to view terrorists as irrational actors, and holding to such a view can only hinder work that is aimed at preventing and protecting against terrorist attacks, and pursuing terrorists engaged in campaigns of violence. Some of the complexities and factors that may provoke or encourage a group to choose or change certain tactics were examined in this chapter to help show the potential value and contribution to the knowledge of the operational and practical problems in counter-terrorism.

Effective counter-terrorism requires the ability to study and learn from attacks, to improve incident management, as well as having pre-emptive capabilities, and planning, and implementing CT approaches that are inclusive, multi-level and multi-dimensional. If society can understand the factors affecting the use and change of terrorist tactics, it will be a significant step in contributing to counter-terrorism and disrupting terrorist operational and support planning and activity.

## Note

1 Parts of this chapter are based on an earlier article by the author: Steven, G., 'The Tactical Terrorist', INTERSEC, Vol. 19, Issue 7, July/August 2009.

## References

Aaron, D. (2008). *In Their Own Words: Voices of Jihad*. Santa Monica: Rand.
Boccolini, H. (2007). Algeria: Al-Qaeda uses elderly terrorists in change of tactics. Available at http://www.adnkronos.com/AKI/English/Security/?id=1.0.1665340094, accessed 27 September 2009.
Clarke, R. and Newman, G. (2006). *Outsmarting the Terrorists*. London: Praeger Security International.
Dolnik, A. (2007). *Understanding Terrorist Innovation*. Abingdon: Routledge.
Drake, C.J.M. (1998). *Terrorist Target Selection*. New York: St Martins Press.
English, R. (2003). *Armed Struggle: A History of the IRA*. London: Macmillan.
Geraghty, T. (1998). *The Irish War: the hidden conflict between the IRA and British Intelligence*. London: HarperCollins.
Gunaratna, R. (2003). Personal communication.
HM Government (2009). *The United Kingdom's Strategy for Countering International Terrorism*. Norwich: TSO.
Home Office (n.d.). Why we need identity cards. At http://www.homeoffice.gov.uk/passports-and-immigration/id-cards/why-we-need-id-cards/, accessed 27 September 2009.
McKittrick, D., Kelters, S., Feeney, B. and Thornton, C. (1999). *Lost Lives*. London: Mainstream Publishing.
Multi-National Force Iraq (2009). Terrorist tactics. At http://www.mnf-iraq.com/index.php?option=com_content&task=view&id=727&Itemid=44, accessed on 27 September 2009.
O'Brien, B. (1993). *The Long War: The IRA and Sinn Fein*. O'Brien Press: Dublin.
Post, J. (1990). Terrorist psychologic: terrorist behavior as a product of psychological forces. In Walter Reich, (ed.), *Origins of Terrorism: Psychologies, ideologies, theologies, states of mind*, pp. 25–42. Washington: Woodrow Wilson Center Press.
Silke, A. (2001). When sums go bad: mathematical models and hostage situations. *Terrorism and Political Violence*, 13/2, pp. 49–66.
Silke, A. (2003) Beyond horror: terrorist atrocity and the search for understanding – the case of the Shankill bombing. *Studies in Conflict and Terrorism*, 26/1, pp. 37–60.
Steven, G. (2004). *Counter-Terrorism*. Santa Barbara: ABC-CLIO.
Steven, G. (2009). The Tactical Terrorist. *INTERSEC*, Vol. 19, Issue 7, July/August.
Taylor, M. (1988). *The Terrorist*. London: Brassey's.

# 12 Deterring terrorism?

## Target-hardening, surveillance and the prevention of terrorism

*Peter Fussey*

## Introduction

During recent history, two of the most significant forces reshaping the built environment have been the threats of crime and terrorism. More specifically, physically constricting the opportunities for these activities and reducing their impact should they occur (for example, erecting bollards to mitigate the risk of vehicle-borne improvised explosive devices (VBIEDs)) has now become a key part of architects' and urban planners' work. This approach, dubbed 'resilient design' by some (see Coaffee et al., 2008), may be located in a wider shift where societies increasingly replace the threat of natural or environmental calamities with the risks of man-made threats (Beck, 1999).

This chapter draws especially from the recent experiences of mainland Britain and, in particular, London. What is also significant here is a burgeoning process whereby strategies aimed at targeting more 'conventional' forms of criminal conduct are being transferred onto the prevention of terrorism. This raises questions over the points of similarity and divergence between these two phenomena, particularly in relation to their decision-making processes and, ultimately generates debates over the likely efficacy of the strategies that attempt to influence them.

While such overlaps between the 'criminal' and the 'terrorist' spheres have been scrutinised before in studies of policing (Walker, 2000) and of jurisprudence (Hillyard, 1993), this interchange has received relatively little academic attention regarding the strategies that shape our urban environments. When such analyses have been undertaken (e.g. Clarke and Newman, 2006), they largely assume a fairly straightforward application of crime prevention strategies to counter-terrorism and arguably overstate the similarities of these activities. In an attempt to redress this imbalance, this chapter argues that significant space exists for debate to assess the likely effectiveness and relative capabilities of strategies designed to address these two forms of action. In doing so, key themes are explored over four main areas of discussion. First, the instrumental drivers influencing these processes are briefly studied to assess some of the reasons for the form in which they take. Following this is an anatomical examination of the central components of the anti-terrorism strategies deployed into Britain's public spaces. Particularly prominent features are identified here as (symbiotic) target-hardening and surveillance-based techniques; both of which are buttressed through an increased commitment to technology-based solutions. Given its prominence in current and projected counter-terrorism approaches, the role of surveillance is examined in further detail in part three. The final area of discussion draws from a range of criminological sources to reconsider the impact, applicability and potential for ancillary consequences of such strategies.

## Part I. Demands for greater protection

One notable driver behind the expansion of situational and surveillance-based approaches is the demand for enhanced protection. Particularly strong are those demands voiced from commercial and public domains. Regarding the former, Marcuse (2004) shows how, in response to the proliferation of terrorist attacks against economic targets, anti-terrorist provisions are becoming *the* major feature of new and developing financial spaces. Indeed, this perhaps owes something to the corollary of terrorist threats in financial centres beyond damage to individuals and property to incorporate sustained damage to the reputation of an area, spiralling insurance premiums and extended obligations under the Health and Safety at Work Act.

Public opinion also appears to support such measures. Although opposition has been articulated in a number of fora (see, for example, a recent European Court of Human Rights ruling restricting the UK's DNA database (see BBC, 2009), an Information Commissioner's Office report warning of a 'surveillance society' (Information Commissioner's Office, 2006) and campaigns by the media (see, for example, *Guardian*, 2009) and third sector agencies (for example, Joseph Rowntree Foundation, 2009) on the threat of surveillance to civil liberties), a long history of studies highlight that public opinion generally backs the enhancement of such provisions despite any misgivings or attendant inconvenience they may cause. Clearly, things have changed since (former Home Secretary) Michael Howard raised concerns over the potential disruption caused by the landmark fortification of the City of London's so-called 'ring of steel' during 1993. A study by the *Guardian* (2002a) newspaper shortly after September 11, for example, indicates that 72 per cent of the UK population would swap 'privacy' for 'security' (also see Richards, this volume). Straddling both themes of public and private demands for protection, a more recent survey by ICM market research into the impact of public fears over terrorism upon consumer activity highlights how 80 per cent of the public desire greater CCTV coverage as protection from terrorism, the highest of all potential measures assessed (ICM, 2004).

Despite such seemingly strong backing, caution is still advisable when ascribing public support to various forms of control. For example, a study into CCTV acceptability in Scotland demonstrates how methodological inconsistencies concerning the structuring of interview questions can lead to wild variations in estimates of public assent. Here, measures of public support for the cameras varied from a seemingly unequivocal 91 per cent to a more modest and less conclusive

56 per cent, depending on whether questions over CCTV acceptability were first prefaced by questions on rising crime or civil liberties (Ditton, 1998).

Nevertheless, demand for tangible anti-terrorist measures have become translated into a number of practical strategies. Of key importance here is the argument that many current strategies to tackle terrorism in the public domain are often continuations of existing approaches aimed at reducing crime and the fear of crime (*inter alia* Davis, 1998; Lyon, 2004). This is a crucial point, and one that creates a space for criminological reflection on the efficacy of utilising such strategies to control terrorism. Moreover, what is also notable about this blurring of the prevention of 'conventional' crime and terrorism is the centrality of two processes: target-hardening and enhanced surveillance provision. Each of these is now discussed in turn.

## Part II: Components of public space counter-terrorism strategies

### *Target-hardening*

Drawing on notions of situational crime prevention, rational choice and routine activity theory (e.g. Felson, 1988; Cullen and Agnew, 1988; Clarke, 1980), target-hardening approaches have been increasingly employed to prevent terrorism. Typically, these involve measures seeking to influence offenders' decision-making processes by reducing the attractiveness of targets whilst increasing the likelihood of apprehension and thus elevating the chances that a perpetrator will fail to act on their intentions.

In servicing this commitment towards target-hardening throughout the UK, security advice on reducing the risks of terrorist victimisation is distributed to the public and private sectors via the National Counter-Terrorism and Security Office (NaCTSO), originally part of MI5's National Security Advice Centre (NSAC) and now funded by the Association of Chief Police Officers (ACPO). This office coordinates networks of police Counter-Terrorism Security Advisors (CTSAs) who disseminate practical advice on avoiding victimisation. At the time of writing, one of NaCTSO's most significant initiatives is 'Project Argus', a programme aimed at training those working in crowded spaces to prevent and prepare for potential terrorist attacks. Such initiatives are complemented with government guidance on protecting pubic spaces such as stadia, shopping centres, tourist attractions and commercial areas. Central to this security advice are recommendations to deploy a range of physical measures to counter terrorism. For example, flying glass has long been recognised as the principle means of terrorist-related injury. To mitigate this, NaCTSO recommends fitting splinter-proof glass into new developments or to retro-fit anti-shatter film or blast curtains to existing glazing. Interventions like these are designed to minimise the impact of a terrorist attack should one occur.

Other interventions are designed to influence and interrupt the decision-making processes of potential terrorists. Such measures generally attempt to affect perpetrators' perceptions of the opportunities for action, their chances of success or the likely impact of their attack. For example, to reduce the likelihood of VBIEDs, one of the most common terrorist tactics in urban environments, NaCTSO advocates the use of well-lit barriers or bollards, traffic calming measures (to prevent high-speed attacks), strict regulation on the use of underground parking facilities (as exploited by Ramzi Yousef in the 1993 World Trade Center bombing), access and parking restrictions and, ideally, keeping non-essential vehicles at least 30 metres from buildings. Other physical preventative measures advocated include defining and securing the boundary between public and private areas of buildings, introducing strong locks and bolts and, importantly (for this chapter), the introduction and monitoring of CCTV as a means of deterring, raising alarms and assisting in post-event investigation (adapted from NaCTSO, 2006, 2007, 2008). Indeed, this deployment of surveillance technologies can be cited as an integral feature of practical, target-hardening situational anti-terrorist measures.

## *The centrality of surveillance*

Deploying surveillance strategies to prevent and detect terrorist activity is a sizable and varied endeavour (see, for example, Ball and Webster, 2004). Surveillance practices can generally be grouped within two broad categories: that of directed surveillance (upon individuals or particular characteristics of individuals) and of more non-directive open-street surveillance practices. Regarding the former, Lyon (2003) identifies how established commercial forms of surveillance are increasingly utilised in the service of terrorism prevention. Such practices are now routine and have enabled the posthumous gathering of information on Mohammed Atta, the July 7 bombers and others into a coherent picture of their respective movements, for example. Although potential for overlap between these two forms of surveillance exists, it is in the second sense that surveillance strategies are increasingly (although not exclusively) an intrinsic feature of situational prevention.[1]

Although such surveillance may take 'informal' and 'low-tech' forms, such as increasing pedestrian flows or enhancing sight-lines by removing obstacles such as hedges and the adoption of more open-plan architectural techniques, open-street electronic surveillance (particularly CCTV cameras) is increasingly relied upon and considered a key tool in tackling terrorism. This is further facilitated by the much-quoted statistic that the UK has more public CCTV cameras than any other post-industrialised nation (see Graham et al., 1996),[2] with particular concentrations in London, where even 10 years ago, individuals could expect to be filmed by, on average, around 300 cameras a day (Norris and Armstrong, 1999). Significantly, the proliferation of CCTV in the UK contrasts sharply with other EU countries, such as Denmark (Wiecek and Sætnan, 2002) (where they are banned from many public spaces), Belgium (Information Commissioner's Office, 2006) and Germany (Töpfer, 2006) (where they are opposed by mainstream politicians), and France (Germain, 2007) and Poland (Waszkiewicz, 2007) (which also encounter public opposition).

The employment of CCTV in this respect underscores the trend for co-opting existing crime control strategies into efforts to prevent terrorism. Perhaps nowhere is this more clearly demonstrated than in the capture of the neo-nazi nail-bomber David Copeland in 1999. Over a period of three weeks, Copeland carried out three bomb attacks in London killing three people and injuring scores more. London's existing surveillance infrastructure allowed the Metropolitan Police to acquire 26,000 hours of CCTV footage. Analysis of this footage eventually led to the positive identification and arrest of Copeland (Metropolitan Police, 2005). Another more recent example of this convergence of crime and terrorist prevention through CCTV is the Metropolitan Police's 'Operation Rainbow', which they describe as:

> . . . the longest running operation in police history. The primary purpose of the operation is to assist in the detection and apprehension of any terrorists working within the London area.
>
> (Metropolitan Police, undated)

The cornerstone of this project concerns the 'construction and maintenance of a database of CCTV locations' (Ibid.), to generate the potential for uninterrupted information flows across the capital. However, perhaps the clearest example of the convergence and predominance of such target-hardening and CCTV surveillance practices in tackling terrorism can be seen from the expanded security cordon around the City of London.

### London calling: the city as exemplar

In an authoritative study, Coaffee (2003) documents the development of the so-called 'ring of steel' encircling important locations within the financial district of London's 'square mile'. Following the bombing by the Provisional IRA of Baltic exchange in St. Mary's Axe 1992, and the 1993 Bishopsgate bomb, a process of increasing physical and technological demarcation and separation of the City of London from the wider urban environment began (Power, 2001 cited in Coaffee, 2004). This began by monitoring and restricting access to the eastern part of the city. Whilst these target-hardening measures have substantially altered the urban landscape of the area, according to the local constabulary, it is camera surveillance (and contingency planning) that has formed the most important feature of the anti-terrorist strategy in the area (City of London Police, 1994 cited in Walker and McGuiness, 2003). This is demonstrated by the first restrictive measures in the area, which involved the installation of two cameras at each entry and exit point – one for each vehicle's number plate and one for the driver (Coaffee, 2004). This also occurred during a period of rapid and enthusiastic CCTV expansion across Britain in a period that has since been described as 'an era of uptake' (Webster, 2004). This electronic monitoring was enhanced during 1995 via the introduction of automatic number plate recognition (ANPR) systems. With this, surveillance cameras had the ability to match vehicle number plates with the identity of drivers, both to verify identity and also to raise alarms over any irregularities. Here we have the first of many automated 'filters' to focus the human agent's attention onto particular events.

The next significant expansion occurred during 1996 with the addition of over a thousand cameras and a substantial upgrading of existing camera provisions, now enabling operators to monitor suspects across the City (Coaffee, 2004). During this time, the City of London became the most intensely monitored space in the UK (ibid.), and thus, in likelihood, Europe. Of additional interest is the fact that much of this expansion occurred during a time of reduced threat owing to the PIRA ceasefire prior to the Docklands bombing in February 1996. Hence, important questions are raised concerning the drivers behind this expansion and their relationship to objective measurements of risk (for discussion on the political, social and cultural drivers of CCTV expansion see Fussey, 2004). Today, the 'ring of steel' remains one of the most surveilled spaces in the UK with well over 15,000 cameras watching the 'square mile' in the heart of the City (Coaffee, 2003) and new initiatives being launched to bring about even greater integration of the monitoring systems.

So far, the discussion has traced the role and convergence of situational target-hardening and technological surveillance in countering terrorism in Britain's public spaces. However, this relationship is not static. Recently, the technological component of this preventative package has experienced particular development. This chapter will now examine some of these developments and their application to the counter-terrorism context before reconsidering issues concerning their applicability and effectiveness.

## Part III. Averting terrorism through technological innovation – Surveillance 2.0

This growing emphasis on electronic surveillance demonstrates how situational approaches are increasingly orientated around technological innovation. Before examining this trend in greater detail, however, it is important not to overstate the novelty of using technology to tackle crime and terrorism. In the US, for example, many current forms of technologically assisted policing have developed from responses to the 1960s riots via the 'war on drugs' of the 1990s (Nunn, 2003). CCTV has also featured on London's streets since the 1960s (Williams, 2003). Because of these extended histories, many past lessons have resonance today.

Nevertheless, there are two different, and particularly striking, features about current forms of technological policing. First is the convergence of military and civil forms –technologies are developed to fulfil both purposes at the outset, rather than transferring from military to civilian applications over time – what Haggerty and Ericson (2001) call 'dual use' formats. This marks a significant departure from more established viewpoints arguing that technological mechanisms of civil control have military genealogies (Dandeker, 1990); clearly the distinction between the two spheres is collapsing. Such technologically enhanced security provisions have manifested in a number of new strategies in the UK. Although new technological counter-terrorism approaches have traditionally been first 'tested' in Northern Ireland – such as helicopter monitoring, night vision, sophisticated phone taps and automatic vehicle tracking systems (Matassa and Newburn, 2003), increasingly, they are now rolled out first on London's streets. Typically, these new technological approaches are increasingly automated, relying on computer systems to scan and filter, and hence reduce the volume of images that require human attention.

The second point concerns the shift from technology as a supplement to policing towards its occupation of a more centralised role.[3] Although we have seen that many current responses to terrorism have drawn from existing approaches to tackle crime and disorder, 9/11 unquestionably accelerated the trend towards more technological policing and security strategies. This is reflected in the elevated value of security commodities. In the US, for example, a US consultancy, Security Stock Watch, portfolios an index of 100 security industry stocks (primarily comprising of companies specialising in technological security). Between 2003 and 2008, it comprehensively outperformed both the standard and technology-focused Dow Jones and NASDAQ indices (Security Stock Watch, 2008). In the aftermath of 9/11, the Security Stock Watch index doubled between 2003 and 2006 and, three years ago was worth over US $400bn (Information Commissioner's Office, 2006). However, it is important to recognise that this 'acceleration' is not a paradigm change, merely an intensification of existing trends. Indeed, the current growth of the security industry can be traced back to the early 1980s (Marcuse, 2004) and was one of the fastest growing industries in the world for many years before September 11, 2001 (see, for example, Beck and Willis, 1995).

Together, many of the technologies deployed to tackle terrorism in public spaces develop conventional camera systems to incorporate automated functions and processes (for example, via the use of software), whilst others, such as those involving biometric verification, require the development of new hardware *and* processes. However, what many of these strategies share is an attempt to automatically organise and 'filter' information depending on its potential significance in terms of threat. Together, many of these strategies can be conceptualised as a new form of technological surveillance – 'second generation CCTV' – where cameras actively identify and inform operators of phenomena worthy of attention rather than passively receive events. Some of the more notable example strategies are briefly described below.

### *Automatic Number Plate Recognition (ANPR)*

Perhaps the oldest form is the increased use of automatic number plate recognition (ANPR) technology to scan number plates and identify individuals entering particular spaces. Though its most widespread function in the UK today is in identifying vehicles that require payment of London's Congestion Charge, this represents a 'function creep' from its origins in policing the City of London following the PIRA bombings of 1992 and 1993 (as already discussed). A recent manifestation of this technology has been its incorporation into police vehicles and installation in many public streets (it is widely deployed across many London boroughs, with Hackney providing a notable example) and is thus now more ubiquitous in its application. Whilst proponents point to its utility in tracking suspects and identifying stolen vehicles (Wells, 2007), some critics have argued it has irrevocably changed socio-legal notions of reasonable suspicion (Nunn, 2003).

### Intelligent Pedestrian Surveillance (IPS)

Another surveillance device evolved from conventional CCTV camera systems is the development of IPS systems. Adopting a similar filtering function as ANPR, IPS works by digitally comparing a picture of an empty space with the received image. In doing so, IPS is thus designed to automatically spot (and hence overcome frail human attention spans) 'suspicious' discrepancies – such as individuals loitering suspiciously or dubious packages – between the two images (*New Scientist*, 2003). Hence, in addition to drawing operators' attention to irregular phenomenon, this approach is also intended to overcome the difficulties of exponential increases in image data that accompany enhancements to surveillance infrastructures. Although ultimately intended for use in identifying suspicious packages and individuals at airports (as operational in Iceland), IPS was introduced into London's public spaces during July 2003 as part of a 12-month trial at Liverpool Street and Mile End London Underground stations.[4]

### Facial recognition surveillance

Another, more controversial, advancement on existing camera surveillance systems is the development of facial recognition CCTV (FRCCTV) technology. Developed in the early 1990s and deployed during the same decade, this technology works by converting facial characteristics into numerical values. For example seemingly unchangeable facial characteristics, such as the distance between eyes or that between the nose and lips, are measured and committed to a database. The intention is then to spot potential criminals or terrorists by comparing suspects with a previously obtained list of numerical values.

Increasingly, facial recognition technology is deployed into environments where high densities of people congregate. In particular, this has led to its application in policing major sporting events and in more controlled environments. Regarding the former, sporting events offer particular attractions for deployment. For example, these cameras were famously deployed at the 2001 Superbowl final in Tampa, Florida where it was claimed that 19 petty criminals were detected amongst a crowd of 100,000 people (Lyon, 2003, also see below). In the UK, a prototype version was trialled at Manchester City's former Maine Road stadium during the mid-1990s (Davies, 1996). In more controlled spaces, facial recognition technology is increasingly used to monitor airports and has been introduced across Canada, Iceland and into Boston's Logan Airport (Lyon, 2004). With regard to more open public spaces, this type of surveillance was pioneered in the (east) London Borough of Newham during the 1990s, where around 300 cameras were equipped with the technology largely in response to perceived PIRA threats (*Guardian*, 2002b).

## Part IV. Reconsidering target-hardening and surveillance-based approaches and counter-terrorism

Although the above discussion has established target-hardening and surveillance approaches as central features of anti-terrorism strategies, their deployment does not necessarily denote their success. This chapter now seeks to consider a number of key debates concerning the use of such practices for the prevention of terrorism and, in doing so, is organised over seven areas of analysis. These are:

1. displacement;
2. 'rational actor' models;
3. pre- and post-event effectiveness;
4. maintaining effectiveness;
5. the impact of expanding surveillance networks;
6. the social environment of technology; and,
7. a reassessment of these strategies.

Running throughout these discussions, are two key arguments. The first considers whether traditional crime prevention techniques can be easily extended into the prevention of terrorist violence and assesses the potential for additional and perhaps unintentional outcomes. The second urges a reorientation of debates over social-technological counter-terrorism measures to recognise that both the social environment and the role of human agency are instrumental to the efficacy of such strategies.

### *Displacement*

A common theme in evaluations of target-hardening and surveillance-based crime control strategies is the issue of displacement. In brief, the displacement of offences can take a number of forms, including the commission of a criminal act in another location (spatial displacement), at different times (temporal displacement) and undertaking other, less detectable, forms of offending behaviour (tactical displacement) (Felson and Clarke, 1998). We will now consider how displacement issues have been analysed in reference to anti-terrorism provisions before considering how displacement issues may affect the growing trends of employing 'conventional' crime control tools highlighted earlier.

Although only a limited amount of research addresses this theme, during the late 1980s and early 1990s a body of work developed with the aim of assessing the actual and potential displacement effects of a range of anti-terrorist strategies (Cauley and Im, 1988; Enders and Sandler, 1993). For example, by adopting a range of statistical modelling techniques cross-referenced with coded data sets from the International Terrorism: Attributes of Terrorist Events (ITERATE) database (comprising publicly available materials documented in global press reports), the impact of target-hardening strategies in airports and embassies were evaluated whilst simultaneously assessing the displacement of terrorist activity against predicted future trends.

Amongst other findings, this research found that while the global proliferation of metal detectors at airports (introduced during January 1973) led to a significant reduction in skyjackings, terrorist activity was entirely tactically displaced into other forms of hostage attacks and assassinations (Cauley and Im, 1988).

Applying the same methodological apparatus to the evaluation of other strategies, another study assessed the effectiveness of embassy fortification following three cycles of target-hardening and investment (during 1976, following the 1979 siege of the US Embassy in Tehran, and an additional $US 2.4Bn investment between 1986 and 1991) (Enders and Sandler, 1993). Again, whilst attacks against the 'hardened-target' (US embassies) were identified as substantially reduced,[5] high levels of tactical displacement were once more apparent. Here, however, terrorist activity was substituted into the assassinations of individuals once they had left secured locations (Enders and Sandler, 1993). Based on these assertions – and an acceptance of rational-choice descriptors of human action – Enders and Sandler argue that whilst hostage activities may possibly entail one of the most resource-intensive and intricate forms of terrorist activity, by making more logistically simple activities – such as bombing – more difficult, terrorists are likely to revert to other, formerly more complex, tactics.

However, whilst these conclusions seem reasonable enough, there are a number of potential limitations. For example, one problem that afflicts all databases grounded in media reports of terrorism is that the reporting of terrorist activity necessarily changes over time. Hence, media accounts of terrorism are not necessarily comparable over extended periods because of changes in the way in which terrorism is reported and considered as a newsworthy event.

In addition to the tactical substitution of terrorist activity, commentators have recently stressed the likelihood of its spatial displacement, such as the targeting of 'softer' targets following the fortification of urban spaces. For example, during the 1996 Olympics, Eric Rudolph planted his pipe bomb in the less secured and public Centennial Park rather than the more fortified Olympic site. In the UK, some have argued that in 1996 PIRA decided to bomb London's Docklands because of the difficulty of ensuring operational success within the increasingly fortified 'ring of steel' surrounding the square mile (Coaffee, 2003).

Another issue surrounding displacement, which also illuminates differences between criminal and terrorist action, is that of target attractiveness. One rare point of (near) consensus within the literature on terrorism is the role that symbolism plays in target selection processes. This can be attributed to the various intended audiences of terrorist attacks that supersede actual and potential victims to include diverse audiences such as domestic constituencies, patrons or even rival groups (Bloom, 2005). In sum, this introduces a dynamic to terrorist action that is likely to be absent in more materialistically-oriented criminality and stresses the importance of a target's 'symbolism' within terrorist decision-making, and when considering any potential displacement effects. Fundamental questions are thus raised over whether strategies that may display efficacy in tackling conventional criminality can easily translate into the effective prevention of terrorism.

Overall, this raises two important implications for the protection of public spaces. First, that symbolism may impact on the attractiveness of certain targets (potentially including fortified ones).[6] Secondly, the relationship of these varying constituencies to a terrorist groups' ideology exerts an important influence on the selection of targets.

## Preventing terrorism and the 'rational actor' thesis

In addition to questioning the transferability of strategies, debates over displacement also cast doubt on the value of situational and rational choice theories in explaining and averting terrorism. This is not to say that perpetrators of terrorist violence are in some way 'not rational',[7] but that rational cost–benefit calculations may be a limited framework for explaining action in such circumstances. Indeed, the suitability of concepts of 'rational choice' as descriptors of criminal behaviour has long been debated in many critical schools of criminological theory. For example, adding to the volumes of research contesting the impact of 'deterrence' upon crime reduction (Cavadino and Dignan, 2001), there is evidence to suggest that, at best, increasing the certainty of apprehension and severity of punishment has only a small to moderate impact on criminal behaviour (Akers, 1990). At the very least, this may suggest the importance of re-orienting this cost–benefit calculus to incorporate issues of reduced pay-offs and post-event benefit to the terrorist. Moreover, what is also clear is that purely deterrent-based measures are not sufficient on their own, thus underlining the importance of the social context in which strategies are implemented.

Another issue here concerns the danger that, in this sense, rational actor models may mask over the diverse methods and motivations that underpin different forms of terrorist activity. This is clearly articulated by the shifting security priorities and changing threats since September 11, including the ebbing and resurgence of violent Irish Republicanism; the emergence (as an acknowledged threat) – and continual evolution – of violent jihadi extremism and the persistence of single-issue groups. The constantly changing nature of terrorist threats generates debate both over the flexibility of existing preventative measures and, also, the applicability of models of terrorist action (e.g. how well will tactics designed with the PIRA in mind work with regard to jihadi extremists?).

Whilst such discussions may paint a pessimistic picture of the possibilities of preventing terrorist attacks through target-hardening and surveillance measures, there is clear value in debating and acknowledging their potential limitations. In particular, this may develop greater awareness of unanticipated effects of specific strategies. As Enders and Sandler (1993: 843) note, this is not a minor consideration:

> the unintended consequences of an antiterrorism policy may be far more costly than intended consequences, and must be anticipated.

Aside from such 'costly' negative effects, analysis of unintended impacts of strategies may reveal other wide ranging outcomes. One such example could be the incidence of any reverse displacement effects, what Ronald Clarke (1997) describes as a 'diffusion of benefit'. Alternatively, such critiques enable a consideration of any prospects of effectiveness that may be augmented, particularly those involving changes to the social environment into which they are introduced. A key aim of the remainder of this chapter is therefore to consider the strengths, weaknesses and potential ancillary repercussions of applying strategies to prevent terrorism.

## Pre- and post-event effectiveness

As seen earlier, much of the situational provision for tackling terrorism is designed to disrupt activity prior to its commission, largely by manipulating environments to influence the choices available to the perpetrator (Felson, 1998). Whilst this may be true for measures that manipulate the urban environment and attempt to apply an 'architecture of control', analysis of the central feature of these target-hardening approaches – open street camera surveillance – in the prevention of terrorism presents a different story. Notwithstanding debate in the area, many studies of CCTV's effectiveness against conventional crime cite a pre-event deterrent effect (Tilley, 1998). When applied to terrorism, however, this emphasis generally shifts to post-event efficacy (Fussey, 2007a). Moreover, this post-event effectiveness is also likely to vary depending on a range of circumstances, including the type of terrorist activity and the configurations of the groups involved. This point can be demonstrated through reference to the role of CCTV in two separate bombing campaigns in London prior to the July 2005 attacks.

As mentioned earlier, one of the most evocative uses of CCTV for counter-terrorism purposes has been the identification and apprehension of nail bomber David Copeland. Here, despite a number of technical complications (such as outdated equipment, worn tapes and poor image quality) the Metropolitan Police managed to get an image of the prime suspect from CCTV footage. In a demonstration of the value of human intelligence in the supplementation of technological strategies, a breakthrough in the investigation came from a taxi driver's call to the Anti Terrorist Hotline stating that he had taken a fare from Waterloo station to the Brick Lane area of London. This indicated to police that the suspect probably lived in southern England (Metropolitan Police, 2005). This was followed by a positive identification of Copeland from one of his colleagues, responding to the broadcasted CCTV images.

Although CCTV had a vital impact in securing the capture of Copeland, and undoubtedly preventing further attacks, it is important not to cite this as sole justification that CCTV will always work in such circumstances. In particular, there were arguably features of the Copeland bombings which enhanced the potential for successful CCTV intervention. Primarily, Copeland's activities entailed a continuing campaign occurring over a relatively short period accompanied by high levels of media coverage and attendant public awareness. In addition, Copeland was acting alone without the support and assistance of an organised group which increased the likelihood of his identification given the nature of the attacks.

Whilst this episode undeniably constitutes a success story for CCTV, it is also important to note that it has been less successful in tackling other terrorist activity. For example, the 'Real IRA' (RIRA) bombing campaign of mainland Britain between 2000 and 2001 generated scores of CCTV images subsequently broadcasted by the global media. With regard to the last of the three RIRA bombs, in Ealing, both the suspect and explosion were caught on camera. What is notable about these events are first, the Police lamentation that the public gave a 'disappointing response' to a number of high profile appeals for information based on media images the CCTV footage (BBC, 2001a) and, also, the Deputy Assistant Commissioner of Anti-Terrorism Branch's view that 'I would not expect anyone to name the bomber from what we see here . . . that is not the breakthrough that we are looking for' (BBC, 2001b). In fact, three suspects were later convicted of the bombings in 2003, but this was only after they were eventually uncovered through a Customs and Excise investigation into a fuel tax fraud (*Guardian*, 2003).

More recent attacks have demonstrated the nature of CCTV's role in counter-terrorism more clearly. For example, in the aftermath of violent jihadi extremist attacks on London between 2005-2007, CCTV proved very useful in helping police to reconstruct the sequence of events leading up to the actual or failed attacks. Whilst this remains a clearly valuable application, these differing examples indicate the post-event utility of CCTV strategies in countering terrorism which, ultimately, represents a very different function to its perceived deterrence applications. Indeed, none of the above attacks were at all deterred by the presence of CCTV. This connects with key debates within the surveillance literature regarding the role of CCTV as a deterrent or detector. Although claims are made for both, these are clearly different applications and equal ability in both tasks is unlikely. Of further significance is the central role of human engagement to fulfil any potential CCTV may have; an increasing important feature once emphasis is shifted from pre-event deterrence to post-event investigation. Thus despite the many claims that cite technological efficacy in countering terrorism, unless situated within effective intelligence settings or infrastructures that allow adequate analysis, interpretation and response to the captured images, on their own, these provisions can be argued to be insufficient.

## Expanding the networks of surveillance

One of the key issues associated with enhanced surveillance provision is the capability to deal with the expansion in systems and data. A greater volume of data necessarily brings about changes to working practices and the ability to identify and manage visual events whilst also generating a range of additional implications. In the first instance, the tendency of CCTV operators to make actuarial classifications to 'filter-out' suspicious behaviour (Norris and Armstrong, 1999). As consequence, some groups may find themselves catalogued within samples of suspicion and hence 'over-policed'. The consequence of this may be twofold. In the first instance, the prospects of community co-operation may be diminished, thus replicating errors made in the 'war on drugs' whereby entire communities became suspected and marginalised (Tonry, 1995 cited in Lyons, 2002). Additionally, such practices may contribute towards levels of exclusion that stimulate and legitimise the conditions of grievance underpinning terrorist activity.

On a more prosaic level, widening surveillance networks requires a serious increase in their maintenance infrastructures. Put simply, the greater the numbers of cameras, the more maintenance resources are required to service them to maintain their prospects of effectiveness. Although funding maintenance clearly carries less political capital than new installations, the value of expanded surveillance networks is limited if they cannot be kept working. This point is perhaps best illustrated through reports that the surveillance cameras on the number 30 bus in Tavistock Square, destroyed in the July 7th bombings, had not been working for months. Such issues are particularly germane to recent calls for blanket surveillance coverage of the London Underground network.

The scale of the UK's surveillance infrastructure means that this post-hoc utility generates additional operational considerations. Expanded surveillance networks lead to an increase in data which in turns makes analysing this data a more difficult and demanding task. Indeed, the scale of such tasks can be clearly seen from the post-July 7th investigation. To take an example from just one of the 32 London Boroughs, Hackney; following the bombings the Metropolitan Police's Anti Terrorism Branch (SO13) requested *all* CCTV footage from that area for the hours between midnight and 1 pm. According to the deputy CCTV manager, this translated into 22,015 hours of footage, equivalent to around 56,000 CDs of data (Wells, 2007). As such, increasing surveillance capacities does not necessarily render the system more efficient.

## Technology and its social environment

In addition to these practical issues associated with the implementation of anti-terrorism strategies, this chapter argues that the social environment into which strategies are deployed is a crucial factor governing their success. Remaining on the theme of technological surveillance, this is particularly an issue for the generation of intelligence.

Although the benefits of CCTV in tackling terrorism may lie primarily in post-event analysis, one way in which the value of CCTV could be enhanced in pre-event preventions could be in its intelligence-gathering capacity. Indeed, strong intelligence has long-since been recognised as the most effective means of tackling terrorism (Bamford, 2004) and is occupies a particularly important role in tackling the challenges posed by its more nebulous and transnational forms. However, despite claims to the contrary, the most recent research into the use CCTV for intelligence gathering purposes suggests its operation is limited in this respect. This is not to suggest that CCTV occupies no intelligence-gathering role, but that its current capabilities are restricted by a number of environmental and situational circumstances. Notably, these refer to training issues and discordant occupational cultures. One comprehensive study into CCTV operation and policing, for example, notes that intelligence functions are constrained through a prohibitive separation of tasks between the police and CCTV operators (Goold,

2004). Operators rarely used cameras for intelligence-gathering purposes and, in any case, they were generally excluded from police intelligence briefings. Indeed, this point regarding organisational turf-rivalries and the difficulties of integration over institutional boundaries is by no means a new one with regard to intelligence industries (Herman, 2003) and an issue likely to be a growing concern as the volume of data rises with the expansion of surveillance provisions.[8]

Such issues connect with debates over what level of significance is attributed to collected data. The visibility of information is one element of a more important process involving its categorisation and decisions over its value. Indeed, a poignant reminder of the importance of human scrutiny is the (partial) operation of the Computer Assisted Passenger Pre-Screening (CAPPS) system in Washington on September 11th. Here, three of the American Airlines Flight 77 hijackers were identified as requiring additional security scrutiny, including Hani Hanjour, the suspected pilot of the aircraft that was flown into the Pentagon. The consequence of this selection was the retention of their checked bags from the plane until their boarding was confirmed (National Commission on Terrorist Attacks, 2004). Thus, it is clearly one thing to have information and another to have prior-knowledge of its significance. Moreover, decisions over significance are further affected by operational considerations over temporal and fiscal resources as evinced by the security services' decision-making processes surrounding their awareness of Mohammed Siddique Khan prior to July 7th, 2005 (Intelligence and Security Committee, 2009).

As such, the effectiveness of counter-terrorism strategies are dependent on their operational contexts. This again stresses the importance of human engagement, the social environments in which these strategies are deployed and the problems of asocial preventative measures. Whilst there is a drive to deploy ever-more sophisticated hardware to tackle terrorism, the key issue of how these strategies are applied in the real world is perhaps a more pressing issue. The limitations of these strategies also suggests that the technological determinism which has become an increasing feature of civil libertarian, practitioner and academic commentaries of electronic surveillance should be revisited.

## Technological filtering and the prevention of terrorism revisited

As the opening sections of this chapter identified, in a move to tackle these problems of identifying what is 'suspicious' amongst growing volumes of data detailing ordinary daily activity and hence bolster pre-event analysis, a number of technological and automated strategies are being introduced. Aside from discussion over the cultural currency of technology (Deleuze 1995), surveillance (McGrath, 2004) and of visual representations in general (Heidegger, 1977), these developments have stimulated intense debate over their relative merits and societal impact amongst practitioners, academics and civil libertarians alike.

This use of increasingly automated technology to tackle terrorism raises two further points of analysis. The first is that many such commentaries overstate its potential. This applies equally to claims of successful technological solutions in tackling terrorism and to presumptions that such strategies represent a threat to civil liberties because of their ability. Secondly, from a practical perspective, such measures can generate a range of unintended consequences which can actually make the task of preventing terrorism more difficult and resource intensive.

Both of these points are demonstrated by an examination of the effectiveness of FRCCTV. In brief, like open-street CCTV surveillance, one of the key problems concerning facial recognition surveillance is the scarcity of evaluations that are either methodologically sound or undertaken by independent researchers. Of the few evaluations that can be deemed independent and methodologically robust (of which the occasional Facial Recognition Vendor Tests sponsored by the US department of Defense (FRVT, 2000; see Phillips et al., 2003) are examples), the evidence suggests that FRCCTV is of extremely limited value in practice.

Indeed, even amongst the best performing systems, variations in lighting and the time lapse between the matching of individuals to their inputted image led to severe deterioration of the technology's capabilities. Systems are limited by the angle of the facial position in relation to the camera – for example, a 15 degree angle led to a drastic drop in effectiveness whilst facing the camera obliquely at more that 45 degrees rendered the cameras virtually useless (FRVT, 2000). Other difficulties include the deterioration of FRCCTV effectiveness over time (because automated systems cannot necessarily compensate for ageing effectively). Further, as the databases involved increase in size (for example, when systems have more images to compare), the accuracy of the assessments drops off with an ever increasing number of potential matches being highlighted (Introna and Wood, 2004). Added to this, FRCCTV cameras are notorious for triggering false alarms, with current estimates citing an average of around 250 false 'recognitions' for every correct one (*The Register*, 2001). In particular, this high level of 'false positives' may badly compromise the original automated filtering intention and, conversely, result in an even more resource-intensive strategy (as each potentially significant 'false positive' has to be followed up).

These limitations severely undermine the effectiveness of these systems in real-world environments. Early claims of success have often proved unfounded on closer inspection. For example, the aforementioned claims that Tampa's FRCCTV system flagged 19 'criminals' was ultimately proved to be untrue following a freedom of information request by the American Civil Liberties Union (ACLU, 2003) which found that a number of the 19 were actually false positives (ACLU, 2003). A subsequent failed FRCCTV pilot in Tampa's Ybor City district and its abandonment by the US Immigration and Naturalisation service led to the technology being rejected during the 2002 Salt Lake City Winter Olympics security planning. Such events contrast sharply with FRCCTV manufacturer's claims that 9/11 could have been prevented had their products been deployed (Gates, 2006) and demonstrates the limitations of technological 'solutions' to terrorism.

Compounding this is the impact of increased levels of scrutiny upon innocent people, which may ultimately undermine levels of legitimacy of enforcement agents. Finally, presenting an inflated picture of a strategy's capabilities, whilst intended to maximise a deterrent effect, may undermine more effective, low-tech and informal 'human surveillance' by inducing complacency. The combination of this with an ineffective strategy may lead to enhanced risk of victimisation.

## Conclusions

Overall, this chapter has sought to identify and re-examine two key processes shaping the deployment of counter-terrorism strategies in public spaces. These are the increasing role for technological surveillance and the policy of taking measures designed to tackle conventional crime and applying them now to avert terrorist attacks.

Regarding the former, a central argument presented here concerns the importance of the human actor and the social context in technologically driven counter-terrorism strategies. In addition to recognising that, at best, these technologies are likely only to be successful when combined with other strategies, it is important that their ability in tackling terrorism is not overstated. This is particularly true when considering the most significant current forms of terrorist threat. Indeed, whilst a number of commentators have suggested that none of the recent biometric provisions would have prevented the 9/11 attacks (Wood et al., 2004), the same may be said for most major terrorist attacks in the West since then including the March 11th 2004 bombings in Madrid and for the London attacks of July, 2005.

Also apparent from this debate are clear sets of issues concerning the grafting of strategies designed to tackle crime onto terrorist prevention. Often, many crime prevention strategies are based on models that reduce human decision-making to a mix of motivation and opportunity and assume perpetrators engage in largely objective and value-free strategic and operational choices. Whilst these explanations may be found wanting in their explanations of criminality (Katz, 1988; Fussey, 2008), the infusion of values, ideology and perceived grievance that informs many politically violent actions (Horgan, 2005; Silke, 2008) can be argued to limit their application further.

Cultivating greater awareness over the limitations (in addition to abilities) of these models, explanations and strategies is clearly valuable. Research has shown how many crime-control strategies are deployed into public-space without any serious consideration of the problem, largely owing to managerial and political pressures for tangible action and, in some cases, may end up useless or unused (Fussey, 2007b). Given the severity of terrorist activity it is thus important to adopt a nuanced approach which takes into consideration the nature of the threat, the likely impact and potential for any unintended consequences.

In addition to crime control strategies being applied to counter-terrorism, a counter process may also be observed whereby terrorism aversion strategies revert to more conventional crime control functions. For example, CCTV operators monitoring London's 'ring of steel' have yet to catch *anyone* involved in terrorist activities but have been successful in tackling more 'ordinary' forms of crime. Indeed, during 1998, the area's ANPR CCTV system elicited 340 arrests and tracked 359 stolen vehicles whereas in 2001/2 a further 12,000 offences were detected using the CCTV system (Graham and Marvin, 2001 cited in Coaffee,

2004). Here, a dual process can be observed surrounding the blurring of terrorism with other, very different, forms of crime. More than a semantic issue, this cross-over of crime prevention and counter-terrorism raises fundamental questions regarding the applicability, effectiveness, legitimisation, accountability and drivers behind such strategies.

## Notes

1 Camera surveillance has now also become a central feature of new architectural projects and has become synonymous with notions of redevelopment and regeneration (Fussey, 2007).
2 However, Britain's dubious accolade of being the planet's most intensely observed nation is probably out of date. In likelihood, China's mega-event driven developments (including the 2008 Beijing Olympics, Shanghai's 2010 World Expo and Guangzhou's hosting of the 2010 Asian Games) have been accompanied by the deployment of hundreds of thousands of networked cameras both within these epicentres of tourism and beyond (including the nationwide 'Safe Cities' programme which aims to establish CCTV in 600 cities).
3 Some critics of surveillance expansion since September 11th argue that technology is normally seen as a first resort when tackling terrorism (see Lyon, 2004).
4 The (human mediated) fallibility of CCTV in Underground stations was underlined at Mile End station during September 2002, when Stephen Soans-Wade loitered in the station for hours before murdering an innocent commuter by pushing him under an oncoming train, all of which was later viewed on CCTV.
5 Although it is important to note that this research was undertaken some years before the 1998 bombings of US embassies in East Africa.
6 Whilst this may appear to contrast with the earlier discussion about displacement, the point here is that although various crime prevention strategies may affect terrorism, it may affect this form of transgression in entirely different ways to more traditional forms of criminality. Presented here are some of the various ways behaviour may be affected.
7 In the sense that 'irrational' motivations or other singular causalities – such as psychopathology – are the sole instrumental drivers of terrorist behaviour. Horgan (2005) provides a more detailed analysis on the complex psychological issues surrounding terrorism.
8 Although it is also important to note that a number of mechanisms have now been introduced within the UK intelligence community to overcome such institutional boundaries. These include the development of the Joint Terrorism Analysis Centre (JTAC). See Bamford, 2004 op. cit. for a comprehensive overview of these provisions.

## References

ACLU (2003) *Q & A on Face-Recognition*, available from http://www.aclu.org/privacy/spying/14875res20030902.html, accessed 30 June, 2009.
Akers, R. (1990) Rational choice, deterrence, and social learning theory in criminology: The path not taken, in *Journal of Criminal Law and Criminology*, 81, 653–676.
Ball, K. and Webster, F. (eds.) (2004) *The Intensification of Surveillance: crime terrorism and warfare in the information era*, London: Pluto.
Bamford, B. (2004). The United Kingdom's 'war against terrorism'. *Terrorism and Political Violence*, 16 (4), 737–756.
BBC (2001a) *'Poor' Response to Bomb CCTV*, 7 August 2001, available from http://news.bbc.co.uk/1/hi/uk/1477304.stm, last accessed 30 June 2009.

BBC (2001b) *Bomb Suspect Caught on CCTV*, 6 August 2001, available from http://news.bbc.co.uk/1/hi/uk/1476489.stm, last accessed on 30 June 2009.

BBC (2009) *DNA Database 'Breach of Rights'*, available from http://news.bbc.co.uk/1/hi/uk/7764069.stm last accessed 20 June 2009.

Beck, A., and Willis, A. (1995) *Crime and Security: managing the risk to safe shopping*, Leicester: Perpetuity Press.

Beck, U. (1999) *World Risk Society*, Malden: Polity Press.

Bloom, M. (2005) *Dying to Kill: The allure of suicide terror*, New York: Columbia University Press.

Cauley, J. and Im, E. (1988) Intervention policy analysis of skyjackings and other terrorist incidents, in *American Economic Review*, 78 (2) pp. 27–31.

Cavadino, M. and Dignan, J. (2001) *The Penal System: An introduction*, London: Sage.

Clarke, R. (1980) Situational crime prevention: theory and practice, in *British Journal of Criminology*, 20 (2) pp. 136–147.

Clarke, R. (1997) *Situational Crime Prevention: successful case studies*, New York: Harrow and Heston.

Clarke, R. and Newman, G. (2006) *Outsmarting the Terrorists*, Westport CT: Praeger Security International.

Coaffee, J. (2003). *Terrorism, Risk and the City: The making of a contemporary urban landscape*, Aldershot, UK: Ashgate.

Coaffee, J. (2004) Recasting the 'ring of steel': Designing out terrorism in the city of London. In S. Graham (Ed.), *Cities, War and Terrorism: Towards an urban geopolitics* (pp. 276–296), Oxford, UK: Blackwell.

Coaffee, J., Moore, C., Fletcher, D. and Bosher, L. (2008) Resilient design for community safety and terror-resistant cities, in *Proceedings of the Institute of Civil Engineers*, June, pp. 103–110.

Cullen, F. and Agnew, R. (1988) *Criminological Theory: Past to Present*, Los Angeles: Roxbury Publishing.

Dandeker, C. (1990) *Surveillance, Power and Modernity. Bureaucracy and discipline from 1700 to the present day*, Cambridge: Polity Press.

Davies, S. (1996) *Big Brother*, London: Pan.

Davis, M. (1998) *The Ecology of Fear: Los Angeles and the Imagination of Disaster*, New York: Metropolitan Books.

Deleuze, G. (1995) *Negotiations 1972–1990*, New York: Columbia University Press.

Ditton, J. (1998) public support for town centre CCTV schemes: Myth or reality? in C. Norris, J. Moran and G. Armstrong (eds.) *Surveillance, Closed Circuit Television and Social Control*, Aldershot: Ashgate.

Enders, W. and Sandler, T. (1993) The effectiveness of anti-terrorism policies: vector–autoregression–intervention analysis, in *American Political Science Review*, 87 (4) pp. 829–844.

Felson, M. (1988) *Crime and Everyday Life*, London; Sage.

Felson, M., and Clarke, R. (1998) *Opportunity Makes the Thief: Practical Theory for Crime Prevention*. Police Research Series Paper 98, London: Home Office Research, Development and Statistics Directorate.

FRVT (2000) *Facial Recognition Vendor Test 2000* available from http://www.frvt.org/FRVT2000/default.htm, last accessed 30 June 2009.

Fussey, P. (2004) New Labour and New Surveillance: Theoretical and political ramifications of CCTV implementation in the UK , in *Surveillance and Society* 2 (2/3) pp. 251–269.

Fussey, P. (2007a) Observing Potentiality in the Global City: Surveillance and Counter-terrorism in London, in *International Criminal Justice Review*, 17 (3), 171–192.

Fussey, P. (2007b) An interrupted transmission? Processes of CCTV implementation and the impact of human agency, in *Surveillance and Society*, vol. 4 (3), 229–256.

Fussey, P. (2008) Beyond deterrence: Critically exploring the relationship between CCTV and terrorists' target selection, presented at the *InVisibilities: The Politics, Practice and Experience of Surveillance in Everyday Life* conference, Sheffield University, 3 April.

Gates, K. (2006) Identifying the 9/11 'Faces of Terror': the promise and problem of facial recognition technology, in *Cultural Studies*, 20 (4–5), 417–441.

Germain, S. (2007) The rise of CCTV in France: an analysis of a municipal experimentation, paper given at the *European Society of Criminology Conference*, Bologna, Italy, 28 September.

Goold, B. (2004) *CCTV and Policing Public Area Surveillance and Police Practices in Britain*, Oxford: Oxford University Press.

Graham, S., Brooks, J. and Heery, D. (1996) Towns on the television: Closed circuit TV in British towns and cities, in *Local Government Studies*, 22 (3), 3–27.

*Guardian* (2002a) *Big Brother*, available from http://image.guardian.co.uk/sys-files/Guardian/documents/2002/09/06/privacy3.pdf, last accessed 30 June 2009.

*Guardian* (2002b) Robo Cop, 13 June 2002, available from http://www.guardian.co.uk/g2/story/0,3604,736312,00.html, last accessed 30 June 2009.

*Guardian* (2003) Three convicted over Real IRA bombing campaign, 8 April 2003, available from http://www.guardian.co.uk/terrorism/story/0,12780,932362,00.html, last accessed on 30 June, 2009.

*Guardian* (2009) *Liberty Central*, available from http://www.guardian.co.uk/commentisfree/libertycentral, last accessed 20 June 2009.

Haggerty, K. and Ericson, R. (2001) The military technostructures of policing, in P. Kraska (ed.) *Militarizing the American Criminal Justice System: The Changing Roles of the Armed Forces and the Police*, Boston: Northeastern University Press.

Heidegger, M. (1977) *The Question Concerning Technology and Other Essays*, New York: Harper Torchbooks.

Herman, H. (2003) Counter-Terrorism, Information Technology and Intelligence Change, in *Intelligence and National Security*, 18 (4), 40–58.

Hillyard, P. (1993) *Suspect Community: People's Experience of the Prevention of Terrorism Acts in Britain*, London: Pluto.

Horgan, J. (2005) *The Psychology of Terrorism*, London: Frank Cass.

ICM (2004) *Terrorism Survey*, available from http://www.icmresearch.co.uk/pdfs/2004_april_retail_week_terrorism.pdf, last accessed 30 June 2009.

Information Commissioner's Office (2006) *A Report on the Surveillance Society*, available from http://www.ico.gov.uk/upload/documents/library/data_protection/practical_application/surveillance_society_full_report_2006.pdf, last accessed 30 June 2009.

Intelligence and Security Committee (2009) *Could 7/7 Have Been Prevented? Review of the Intelligence on the London Terrorist Attacks on 7 July 2005*, London: HMSO.

Introna, L. D. and Wood, D. (2004) Picturing algorithmic surveillance: The politics of facial recognition systems, in *Surveillance and Society*, 2 (2/3), 177–198.

Joseph Rowntree Foundation (2009) *Database State*, York: Joseph Rowntree Reform Trust, Ltd.

Katz, J., (1988) *The Seductions of Crime: Moral and Sensual Attractions in Doing Evil*, New York: Basic Books.

Lyon, D. (2003) *Surveillance after September 11th*, London: Blackwell.

Lyon, D. (2004) Technology vs 'terrorism', in S. Graham (ed.), *Cities, War and Terrorism*, Oxford: Blackwell, 297–311.

Lyons, W. (2002) Partnerships, information and public safety: community policing in a time of terror, in *Policing: an International Journal of Police Strategies and Management*, 25(3), 530–542.

Marcuse, P. (2004) The 'War on Terrorism' and life in cities after September 11, 2001, in S. Graham (ed.) *Cities, War and Terrorism*, Oxford: Blackwell, 263–275.

Matassa, M. and Newburn, T. (2003) Policing and terrorism, in T. Newburn (ed.) *The Handbook of Policing*, Cullompton: Willan.

McGrath, J. (2004) *Loving Big Brother: Performance, privacy and surveillance space*, London: Routledge.

Metropolitan Police (2005) *Operation Marathon: The Investigation*, available from http://www.met.police.uk/news/stories/copeland/thehunt.htm, last accessed on 1 August 2007.

Metropolitan Police (undated) *Operation Rainbow*, available from http://www.met.police.uk/barnet/anti_terrorism.htm, last accessed 30 June, 2009.

NaCTSO (2006) *Counter Terrorism Protective Security Advice for Stadia and Arenas*, online guidance available from http://www.nactso.gov.uk/documents/Stadia%20and%20Arenas.pdf, last accessed 20 June 2009.

NaCTSO (2007) *Counter Terrorism Protective Security Advice for Visitor Attractions*, online guidance available from http://www.nactso.gov.uk/documents/Visitor%20Attractions%202009.pdf last accessed 20 June 2009.

NaCTSO (2008) *Counter Terrorism Protective Security Advice for Commercial Centres*, online guidance available from http://www.nactso.gov.uk/documents/Commercial%20Centres%202009.pdf, last accessed 20 June 2009.

National Commission on Terrorist Attacks (2004) *The 9/11 Commission Report: The Full Final Report of the National Commission on Terrorist Attacks Upon the United States*, New York: W.W. Norton.

*New Scientist* (2003) *Your Every Move Will be Analysed*, issue 2403, 12 July.

Norris, C. and Armstrong, G. (1999) *The Maximum Surveillance Society*, Oxford: Berg.

Nunn, S. (2003) Seeking tools for the war on terror: a critical assessment of emerging technologies in law enforcement, in *Policing: an International Journal of Police Strategies and Management*, 26 (3) 454–472.

Phillips, P., P. Grother, R. Micheals, D.M. Blackburn, E. Tabassi and J.M. Bone (2003), *Face Recognition Vendor Test 2002: Overview and Summary* available from http://www.frvt.org/DLs/FRVT_2002_Overview_and_Summary.pdf, last accessed 30 June 2009.

*Register, The* (2001) Face recognition useless for crowds, available from http://www.theregister.co.uk/2001/09/27/face_recognition_useless_for_crowd, last accessed 30 June 2009.

Security Stock Watch (2008) *100 Index Monthly Chart – April 2008*, available from http://www.securitystockwatch.com/InvestmentGuides/Index_Chart_2008_03.html, last accessed 30 June 2009.

Silke, A. (2008). Holy Warriors: Exploring the psychological processes of Jihadi radicalisation. *European Journal of Criminology*, 5/1, pp.99–123.

Tilley, N. (1998) Evaluating the effectiveness of CCTV schemes, in C. Norris, J. Moran and G. Armstrong (eds.) (1998) *Surveillance, Closed Circuit Television and Social Control*, Aldershot: Ashgate, pp. 139–175.

Töpfer, E. (2006) Unleashed: The FIFA World Cup 2006 as a catalyst for the expansion of public area CCTV in Germany, paper presented at Policing Crowds – Privatising Security conference, Berlin, 25–26 June.

Walker, C. (2000) Briefing on the Terrorism Act 2000, in *Terrorism and Political Violence*, 12 (2), 1–36.

Walker, C. and McGuiness, M. (2003) Commercial risk, political violence and policing the city of London, in A. Crawford (ed.) *Crime and Insecurity: The Governance of Safety in Europe*, Cullompton: Willan.

Waszkiewicz, P. (2007) The effectiveness of CCTV (the case of Warsaw), paper given at the European Society of Criminology Conference, Bologna, Italy 28 September.

Webster, W. (2004) The evolving diffusion, regulation and governance of closed circuit television in the UK, in *Surveillance and Society*, 2 (2/3), 230–250.

Wells, A. (2007) The July 2005 bombings, paper given at the *Local; Government Agency 2007 CCTV Conference: The Development of a National Strategy, Innovative Systems, Effectiveness and Standards*, Local Government House, London, 4 July.

Wiecek, C. and Sætnan, A. (2002) Restrictive? Permissive? The contradictory framing of video surveillance in Norway and Denmark, Working paper no. 4 from *Urban Eye: On the Threshold to Urban Panopticon? Analysing the Employment of CCTV in European Cities and Assessing its Social and Political Impacts European Commission Project*. Available from http://www.urbaneye.net/results/ue_wp4.pdf, last accessed 30 June 2009.

Williams, C. (2003) Police surveillance and the emergence of CCTV in the 1960s in *Crime Prevention and Community Safety*, 5 (3), 27–38.

Wood, D., Konvitz, E., and Ball, K. (2004) The constant state of emergency: Surveillance after 9/11, in K. Ball and F. Webster (eds.), *The Intensification of Surveillance: Crime, Terror and Warfare in the Information Era*.

# 13 Countering the psychological impact of terrorism

## Challenges for homeland security

*Anthony Richards*

## Introduction

Most definitions of terrorism describe the phenomenon as intending to have a psychological impact beyond the immediate victims of a terrorist attack. Terrorism is intended to terrorise and is designed to communicate a message to a wider population. It is the duty of democratic governments, therefore, not just to protect their citizens from the physical threat posed by terrorism but also to protect them from its psychological effects and so it is important that governments should adopt a counter-psychological approach as part of a robust strategy against terrorism. The following chapter will argue that in the current international context, where the US and the UK are culpable to at least some degree for the increased terrorist threat, a key challenge for homeland security is to reduce the impact of terrorism at home. Above all it must make sure that domestic measures do not exacerbate the threat in the same way that some international responses have.

This chapter focuses primarily on the UK situation though many of the observations and insights will have relevance for other countries – especially in the West. The chapter will draw on the results of a number of polls taken since 9/11, which generally confirm previous research that there is a disproportionate fear of becoming a victim of a terrorist attack. The chapter will also consider whether or not the government, through the language of national security and public protection, has contributed to this heightened state of fear. One theme from surveys and polls of the British public conducted since 9/11 appears to be constant – a public desire for much harsher measures in response to terrorism at home, while polls of British Muslims show an increasing fear of being unfairly targeted. Nevertheless, the chapter ultimately argues that, however tempting it may be to court the majority view in a democracy, such an approach risks polarisation and an increase in the terrorist threat. Finally, these issues raise questions as to what is meant by 'counter-terrorism' and, indeed, who and what it is for.

## Components of a psychological response to terrorism

There are many elements that can be included in a 'counter-psychological' response to terrorism. One of these is adequate preparation for the treatment of those who may have been directly and psychologically affected by being in close proximity to a terrorist attack (Meredith et al., 2007; Institute of Medicine, 2003). A US RAND report noted, for example, the value of community-oriented responses in managing the psychological consequences of such an event (Tanielian and Stein, 2006). A London Assembly report into the July 2007 bombings of the London transport system found that 'the most striking failing in the response . . . was the lack of planning to care for people who survived and were traumatised by the attacks' (London Assembly, 2006, p. 120). It stated that 'procedures tend to focus too much on incidents, rather than on individuals, and on processes rather than people' (p. 124). The report noted the lack of survivor reception areas despite the estimated 3,000 people who are said to have suffered from post-traumatic stress, along with a further 3,000 who were directly affected. The UK Health Protection Agency (2006) found from follow up questionnaires that were completed by 158 survivors that, apart from hearing difficulties, survivors were suffering from psychological effects and that 80% had experienced 'emotional upset'. Addressing this particular aspect of a psychological response should remain a priority for governments.

Another key component of a psychological response to terrorism is to counter the propaganda of terrorist networks like Al-Qaeda. Alex Schmid (2005), the former head of the UN Office of Drugs and Crime, has observed:

> The fact that an act of terrorism is more than an act of violence, that it is first and foremost an act of violence-induced communication, makes the public affairs and propaganda dimension of both terrorism and counter-terrorism crucial. Nevertheless, psychological operations in the fight against terrorism are receiving often only minor consideration. In my view, this is the single biggest shortcoming in strategies against terrorist violence.
>
> (p. 230)

The battle for 'hearts and minds' has increasingly (and perhaps belatedly) been seen as of paramount importance in undermining the support for extremism. There is a real need to challenge more effectively the ideology of Al-Qaeda and not to undertake activity that can be exploited in support of its narrative – a narrative that is so vital as a binding influence for what is largely a decentralised and global terrorist threat. The British government, in its latest approach towards countering international terrorism (CONTEST II), has acknowledged the importance of this propaganda dimension by including a section on 'counter-terrorism communications'. It outlines the purpose of the new Research, Information and Communications Unit (formed in June 2007), which includes 'exposing the weaknesses of violent extremist ideologies and brands' and 'supporting credible alternatives to violent extremism using communications' (HM Government, 2009, p. 153). In particular, its role is to challenge and disrupt the narrative of Al-Qaeda.

While the battle for 'hearts and minds' is arguably the most important element of an effective counter-terrorist strategy the main (though not unrelated) focus of this chapter is the psychological impact of both terrorism and counter-terrorism on the broader British public (i.e. beyond the immediate victims and those directly affected). One challenge for any democratic government faced with a terrorist threat is to ameliorate the public anxiety caused by terrorism and not to exacerbate its impact. One theme that emerges from a number of polls carried out in the UK since September 11, 2001 is that the majority appears to be in favour of harsher responses to terrorism. The minority community of Muslims, however, seem to feel that such measures risk targeting them as a community. In a democratic society where political parties are accountable to the electorate this raises the dangerous possibility of a government courting the majority (through the language of national security and public protection) at the expense of minority views, risking polarisation and arguably therefore an increased risk of terrorism – the opposite of what counter-terrorism is presumably supposed to achieve.

## The international context

Before such a discussion can begin on the psychological impact of counter-terrorism at home, however, it is important to acknowledge the underpinning global context, particularly the Iraq war and the 'Global War on Terror', and their impact on domestic security within the UK. The Director General of the UK's Security Service warned in November 2007 that there were at least 2,000 people who were a 'direct threat to national security and public safety, because of their support for terrorism' (Evans, 2007). A BBC/ICM Poll in February 2003 of 1,003 respondents found that 87% thought that Britain's support for America's war against terrorism made it more likely that Britain would be a target for terrorists (ICM, 2003), while a Populus poll of 1,506 (conducted in July 2005, shortly after the London terrorist attacks) found that 64% believed that Britain's involvement in the war in Iraq increased the risk of terrorist attacks such as those of 7/7 (Populus, 2005b).

The point on the impact of the international realm is really driven home when one explores the recruitment strategies of Al-Qaeda. The messages that are being disseminated are not covert or secret. The enormous scope for the dissemination of Al-Qaeda's doctrine and propaganda that the Internet and the mass media have provided has meant that its strategies for motivating others to join its jihad are transparent, public and accessible. In the propaganda videos and audios of Al-Qaeda ideologues and suicide bombers the approach is clear – it is precisely the foreign policies of the US and the UK (including the Iraq war) that the organisation focuses on as the means to boost recruitment internationally and to carry out attacks in the UK and elsewhere.[1]

As the author has noted previously:

> . . . it is precisely the decentralised and disparate nature of the Al-Qaeda network, often with the absence of any formal structure, that makes its ideology and narrative so important as a binding influence. This is particularly the case for those relatively autonomous groups or cells who are not part of a terrorist organisation per se but see themselves as part of bin Laden's 'global jihad'.
>
> (Richards, 2007, p. 34)

As noted by Schmid (2005), the key, therefore, to reducing this terrorist threat is to deconstruct this 'gel' by undermining the ideology, narrative and justification that Al-Qaeda projects. Yet, in some ways the United States has actually helped to sustain it and Bin Laden's own propaganda platform, as well as helping the terrorist leader to present himself and the network that he inspires as the new global adversary. The US, for example, has framed the conflict in precisely the same way that Al-Qaeda has: as a bi-polar one, using the parallel rhetoric of 'you are either with us or against us', helping to elevate Al-Qaeda as the global adversary in a bi-polar struggle that it is not. Secondly, the term 'global war on terror' again implies a bi-polar struggle that fits neatly into Al-Qaeda's narration, enabling its leader to portray a conflict of global proportions (Schmid, 2005).

In summary, one cannot isolate the psychological impact of terrorism and counter-terrorism at the international level from the national, especially as it is a threat that we have been 'at war' against. The US approach, its 'global war on terror' and its presentation of Al-Qaeda as its global adversary has been used to justify what are arguably draconian anti-terrorist measures not just within the United States but also within the UK, with Prime Minister Blair asserting that 'the rules of the game are changing' (Blair, 2005). The political impulse of Downing Street to stand shoulder to shoulder with Washington has not only exposed the UK to greater terrorist threat but has therefore in turn underpinned domestic measures that might not otherwise have been countenanced. One therefore has to question the extent to which the British government has itself been culpable in helping to generate an increase in both the physical and psychological impact of terrorism at home. Indeed, a Times Populus poll in September 2006 found that 73% believed that

> the British govt's foreign policy – especially its support for the invasion of Iraq and refusal to demand an immediate ceasefire by Israel in the recent war against Hezbollah in Lebanon – has significantly increased the risk of terrorist attacks on Britain.
>
> (Populus, 2006b)

It also found that 62% of the 1,504 surveyed believed that 'in order to reduce the risk of future terrorist attacks on Britain the Government should change its foreign policy, in particular by distancing itself from America, being more critical of Israel and declaring a timetable for withdrawing from Iraq'.

## The British experience

The British are, of course, no strangers to the threat of terrorism, having suffered in recent times from Irish related terrorism for the best part of three decades. The contemporary terrorist threat, however, is of an entirely different nature to that presented by the Irish Republican Army. Indeed, there are particular features of the current threat that give an added dimension to its psychological impact. For the first time suicide terrorism has been used as a tactic in the United Kingdom – and it is a method that arguably has a greater psychological impact than other acts of terrorism. Firstly, the suicide bomber is the perfect targeting device where he or she is able to detonate his or her device at the exact time and place of their choosing. Thus, as studies have shown (e.g. Merari, 2005; Hoffman, 2005; Pedahzur, 2005), it is a more lethal method that is able to reap maximum casualties. Secondly, the fact that individuals are willing, and indeed even eager, to sacrifice themselves in the act is even more shocking and seemingly even more inexplicable than those acts where terrorists are able to escape. It sends a very different message – that the perpetrators are so determined to commit themselves to their cause that they are willing to embrace certain death by blowing themselves up in the process.

Another feature of contemporary terrorism that enhances its psychological impact is that it aims to cause mass casualties. Brian Jenkins (1975, p. 15) wrote that 'Terrorists want a lot of people watching . . . not a lot of people dead'. But now it appears that terrorists (in the form of Al-Qaeda) want a lot of people dead too. From a British perspective the psychological impact of terrorism is enhanced by the assessment that that there are large numbers of British nationals within the UK that are willing to perpetrate or facilitate mass casualty attacks.

## Measuring public anxiety

Notwithstanding the July 7 attacks and the threat facing the UK, public fear of terrorism appears to be disproportionately high compared to the risk of actually becoming a victim of a terrorist attack. In April 2009 the UK's Mental Health Foundation (2009, p. 4) produced a report entitled 'In the Face of Fear' and argued that 'the psychological factors that affect our attitudes and behaviour are largely omitted from public debate.' The Foundation commissioned a survey of 2,246 British adults between 5 and 8 January 2009 with a focus 'both on people's personal experience of fear and anxiety, and their perceptions of fear and anxiety in the wider world' (p. 21). The survey found that 77% of those polled thought that people 'in general are more frightened and anxious than they used to be (only 3% disagree)', and that 60% of these cited fear of terrorism as a factor while 60% of them say it's because the world has become a more dangerous place.[2] Seventy-seven per cent of all those polled said 'that the world has become a more frightening place in the last ten years (only 7% disagree).' The report cites the view that 'fearful language (words like 'epidemic', 'plague', 'terror', 'crisis' or 'syndrome') are often employed by advocacy groups and this may be leading to a greater sense of anxiety.

Further back, in August 2007, YouGov conducted an online poll (again commissioned by the Mental Health Foundation) of 2,012 British adults that found that terrorism was people's greatest fear (70%), followed by immigration issues (58%), climate change (38%) and natural disasters (23%) (Mental Health Foundation, 2007). Another survey conducted in June 2006 found that one in five British citizens cited terrorism as among their top two concerns in life while the British public was ranked third globally for being most concerned about terrorism (Nielson, 2006).

According to yet another YouGov poll in 2006 the public's views on the like-lihood of further terrorist attacks seem to be clear – asked whether or not they thought the UK would suffer another major terrorist attack in the following 12 months 34% said very likely and 52% said fairly likely. A figure of 79% said that we were not winning the war against terrorism, and 73% believed that the West is in a global war against Islamic terrorists who threaten our way of life, and only 6% expected the conflict against Islamic terrorists to last five years or less. Eighty-eight per cent believed that the risk of a major terrorist attack would either remain at the current level (as at 2006) (28%), would get worse (38%), or would get much worse (22%) (YouGov, 2006a).

One tangible indication of the anxiety caused by terrorism are changes of behaviour amongst members of the public as a result of the perceived terrorist threat. For example, a Harris poll, in drawing a comparison between the US and the UK in 2004 – and while stating that large majorities in both countries did not change their behaviour – argued that even small percentages represent significant numbers of people. The survey found that as a result of fears about terrorism:

- 11% in the U.S. and 10% in G.B. say they are avoiding travelling by air 'a lot'.
- 7% in both countries say they are avoiding big sporting or other events 'a lot'.
- 5% in the U.S. and 3% in G.B. say they are travelling 'a lot' less.
- 5% in U.S. and 6% in G.B. say they are avoiding visiting big cities 'a lot' (Taylor, 2004).

The belief that public fear of terrorism is disproportionately high to the actual risk of becoming a victim of a terrorist attack is not new. Hoffman (1998) cited a US RAND survey in the 1980s that found that, while 14% of those polled thought that they would be the victim of a terrorist hijacking or plane bombing, the odds of being a victim of hijacking were in fact 1 in a 100,000; and in 1989 an American was just as likely to be killed by a dog as by a terrorist attack – 'yet nearly a third of those surveyed that year stated that they would refuse the opportunity to travel abroad because of the threat of terrorism' (p. 149). In the aftermath of the protracted hostage crisis following the TWA847 hijacking in June 1985, and the bombing of another TWA flight bound for Athens from Rome in April 1986, 80% of Americans had apparently cancelled plans to travel abroad 'despite the fact that the fears generated by the threat of terrorism were grossly divergent from the real risk' (Hoffman, 1998, p. 150).

A YouGov/Daily Telegraph survey polling 1,757 British adults in August 2006 found that 42% were either a lot more nervous or a little more nervous about flying following the reported plot to blow up transatlantic passenger aircraft (YouGov, 2006b). An earlier poll, carried out by ICM in 2004 (of 1,001 British adults) posed the question: has the threat of terrorism made you change how you feel about doing any of the following (figures in brackets represent the percentage of affirmatives): travelling on public transport (16%), going to very crowded areas (16%), going to busy town centres (14%), going to out of town shopping centres (11%), none of these (75%). The same poll (i.e. a year before the July bombings) found that 20% were more scared about travelling on public transport than the year before (72% said that they felt no different) (ICM, 2004b). A Populus survey of 1,005 British adults conducted in the immediate aftermath of the July 2005 bombings, however, found that 21% would 'change any plans or normal routines when it comes to things like travel, holidays or trips to central London as a result of Thursday's [July 7th 2005] terrorist attack on Britain' (Populus, 2005a).

In summary, it seems reasonable to argue that terrorism generates a disproportionate sense of fear (when compared with the actual risks), and this can prompt changes in behaviour from large numbers of people. The concern is that, especially in the post-9/11 and 7/7 environment, this sense of fear has and might be exploited for political gain by parties competing with each other to present themselves as the public's protectors against this 'new evil', at the expense of more appropriate responses (i.e. those that are informed by honest appraisals as to what actually causes terrorism in the first place in its varying contexts). This was arguably no better exemplified than when both main party leaders in the US 2004 presidential election obliged bin Laden's attempt to intervene in the poll by responding to his taped message in an endeavour to present themselves as 'tough on terrorism', whatever a more *effective* response might be.

## The British response

Notwithstanding the impact of the international environment on domestic security (and the counter-productive nature of some elements of the 'war on terror') the onus is on the British government to ameliorate the effects, both physical and psychological, of terrorism. The UK has carried out a series of measures through its CONTEST (and more subsequently, CONTEST II) strategy based on the 'four Ps' (Prevent, Pursue, Protect and Prepare) (HM Government, 2006). It is, however, difficult to know what counter-terrorism measures reassure the general public and which ones cause greater anxiety. For example, do emergency response exercises (and subsequent media coverage of them) cause greater anxiety or do they ameliorate the psychological effects of terrorism by assuring the public that various terrorist incident scenarios are being prepared for? Likewise are reports of the mass procuring of decontamination units for the Fire and Rescue Service alarming or reassuring?

Some counter-terrorism measures have been less controversial than others. The creation of the Joint Terrorism Analysis Centre (JTAC) and the expansion of MI5 (including the establishment of regional offices) have seemed logical developments given the scale of the threat and the findings from the House of Commons Intelligence and Security Committee that resource limitations were a factor behind the decision not to prioritise attention on two of the July 7 bombers, although they were known to the Security Service (Intelligence and Security Committee, 2006). The wholesale (and long overdue) review of the UK's emergency response arrangements through the Civil Contingencies legislation seems to have been widely accepted as necessary (though this was set in motion before 9/11 in response to the foot and mouth crisis, fuel protests and flooding).

One dilemma is the extent and nature of public information that should be disseminated to the general public about both the terrorist threat and what the government is doing about it. It does seem eminently sensible to generate greater public awareness in relation to the nature of the terrorist threat (as, for example, the UK government has done through its very public introduction of threat levels[3]), to encourage greater public vigilance and to equip the public with the knowledge as to what to do in the event of a major terrorist attack. This development of a *culture of awareness* would be of benefit if and when it does come to another major terrorist event because, as the National Steering Committee on Warning and Informing the Public (2003, p. 4) has argued, people 'are better able to accept . . . risk if they understand the protective action they should take in the event of an emergency'. Part of a public education strategy should emphasise that, despite the seemingly all-pervasive media coverage of terrorist related events and responses, statistically it is actually very unlikely that one will be a victim of a terrorist attack. As the Mental Health Foundation (2009, p. 37) report argued, 'If we realise that the degree to which we experience fear is not always in proportion to the apparent threats that trigger it, we increase our potential for reacting appropriately.'

Public information should therefore be at least partly concerned with educating the population about the real nature of the risk and should never be a political (or indeed an alarmist) exercise in order to justify harsher measures, and this leads us to one of the more controversial areas of UK counter-terrorism strategy – legislation. Measures such as extended detention without trial, the use of control orders and, indeed, the offence of the 'glorification' of terrorism have all sparked controversy with human rights organisations and others who argue that civil liberties are being eroded in the name of combating terrorism. So fraught have the debates been and so eager has the government been to stave off defeat in the House of Commons that (perhaps inevitably) highly charged rhetoric has been used to support harsher measures.

Through the language of national security and public protection, Prime Minister Gordon Brown speaking in March 2008 proclaimed that 'the nature of the threats and risk we face have, in recent decades, changed beyond recognition and confound all the old assumptions about national defence and international security.'[4] He spoke of the threat of 'great insecurities', leading some to suggest that 'politics has internalised the culture of fear . . . British politics is dominated by debates about the fear of terror, the fear of food, the fear of asylum seekers, the fear of antisocial behaviour, fears over children, fear about health, fear for the environment, fear for our pensions . . .' (Mental Health Foundation, 2009, p. 30).

The Mental Heath report suggested that 'Governments should take account of the harmful effects of fear induced by the policies they make and promote. Perhaps most importantly they should stop unnecessarily using the language of fear as an instrument to promote their own policies and approaches' (Mental Health Foundation, 2009, p. 11). The report goes on to argue:

we daily see and hear patterns of catastrophic thinking in public debate . . . There is a tendency for events to be covered in politics, media and general culture in ways that give prominence to the most calamitous scenarios . . . 'Catastrophising' is a well-known thought process that has been identified by psychologists as one of the triggers for common mental health problems such as anxiety and depression.

(p. 29)

It has been argued that ameliorating the psychological impact of terrorism should be an important part of a rigorous counter-terrorism strategy – yet any temptation to engage in the 'politics of fear' would have the opposite effect. This is most certainly not to diminish the reality of the threat that MI5 has warned of but it is about finding a sense of proportion. In fact, a former Director General of the organisation was herself reported as arguing (in February 2009) that the British government was exploiting the fear of terrorism in order to introduce legislation that restricted civil liberties (BBC News Online, 2009a). In summary, therefore, it appears that if democratic states are not careful there can develop a self-rein-forcing dynamic between the public's disproportionate fear of terrorism and the politics of fear. The danger is that this can lead to draconian and ill-advised coun-ter-terrorism policies.

## Public attitudes towards responding to terrorism

The Mental Health Foundation (2009) report noted above makes the important point that 'our fear response is often an inadequate guide to risk'. Perhaps this helps to account for one attitude that has been fairly constant in recent polls. In general there appears to be strong public support for tougher responses against terrorism. In a YouGov/Spectator survey of 1,696 British adults 64% said that they felt safer with stricter airport security while 55% agreed that passenger pro-filing (selecting passengers based on their background or appearance) should be introduced and 69% agreed with the view that it should be possible to detain terror suspects who have not been charged with any offence for up to 90 days (YouGov, 2006a). In the aftermath of the July 2005 bombings a Populus poll of 1,005 British adults found that 86% agreed with giving the police new powers to arrest people they suspected of planning terrorist attacks, while 70% agreed with giving police increased powers to stop and search people on the street (Populus, 2005a). Another Populus poll of 1,003 British adults found that 73% agreed with the statement that 'government should put combating terrorism ahead of concerns for civil liberties, and give police whatever powers they need' (Populus, 2007).

Even before the July 2005 attacks an ICM Terrorism survey (in 2004) of 510 respondents found support for the following: indefinite detention of foreign ter-rorist suspects (62%), indefinite detention of British terrorist suspects (63%), indefinite detention of those associating with terrorist suspects (58%), for bring-ing in the death penalty for terrorist offences that kill people (59%), police powers to stop and search anyone at any time (69%), for detaining all immigrants and asylum seekers until they can be assessed as potential terrorist threats (66%). There was also support for making it easier to get a conviction in cases involving terrorism by changing the rules in court so that someone can be convicted on the balance of probabilities rather than beyond all reasonable doubt (49% support, while 45% disagreed, and 6% didn't know/refused to respond). Of the 510 polled 68% were Christian, 22% had no religious affiliation and 3% were Muslim (ICM, 2004c).

Other surveys include a YouGov (2006c) poll of 1,173 electors in Greater London in August and September 2006. Of those surveyed, 62% supported extending the detention limit to 90 days for those suspected of having committed terrorist offences, while 69% of respondents supported extending the limit to 42 days in a YouGov *Daily Telegraph* poll taken in June 2008 (just before a House of Commons vote on the Counter-Terrorism Bill that included proposals to increase the limit from 28 to 42 days).[5] Another poll found public support for extra security measures in shops: more CCTV cameras (80%), extra security guards (66%), and routine bag searches (50%). Of the 1,001 respondents 2% were Muslim, while 62% were Christian, and 25% had no religious affiliation (ICM, 2004b).

The desire for tough responses is not just limited to firmer legislative measures but can also apply to military retaliations against terrorist acts. Andrew Silke (2003) has noted the high level of domestic public support for such retaliations in the United States, such as the strike against Libya in 1986 and against an apparent Al-Qaeda related target in 1998 (both of these received a 77% approval rating of those polled). In Israel of those polled 92% 'supported the assassination of terrorist leaders [and] 75% supported the bombing of terrorist bases (even if it jeopardised civilian life)' (Silke, 2003, p. 225). This is despite the fact that, as Silke argues using a number of examples, military reprisals for acts of terrorism are ultimately counter-productive. Yet, he notes that there appears to be a human and psychological desire for revenge and retribution: 'human psychology is inclined to support and tolerate such hard-line approaches even if the policies only exacerbate and prolong the conflict'.

While military retaliations may exacerbate the problem of terrorism, overly harsh legislative measures risk undermining the very values that we are seeking to protect from terrorists, echoing Louise Richardson's sentiments, who was quoted as saying 'I still see the threats and risk to our future as something we will do to ourselves, not something anyone else will do to us' (Howie and Pykett, 2009), while Conor Gearty remarks:

> The very mention of something being a counter-terrorism measure makes people more willing to contemplate the giving up of their freedoms. It is as though society is in the process of forgetting why past generations thought these freedoms to be so very important.
>
> (National Centre for Social Research, 2007, p. 13)

There does, therefore, seem to be a danger of a further self-reinforcing dynamic – a public impulse for harsher counter-terrorism measures and a government inclination to appear tough on terrorism. Whether or not the government has contributed to such public attitudes, connecting with the public mood in this way is not necessarily the most effective way to counter terrorism – indeed, it can be dangerous and polarizing. In any case it appears that a large proportion of the British public remain to be convinced if a Populus (2007) survey of 1,003 British adults (noted above) is anything to go by. It found that 60% agreed with the statement that 'Gordon Brown's proposed new counter-terrorism measures are more about looking tough on terrorism than making Britain safer' (only 29% disagreed), while 51% thought that 'new laws will not make any difference to the level of terrorist threat Britain faces'.

It is understandable that polls that aim to be representative of the population as a whole should include just a small percentage of Muslim respondents. Surveys of Muslims alone, however, project a very different attitude to those expressed above. In March 2004 an ICM poll found that 82% of 500 Muslim respondents said that they didn't believe the US government when it said it wanted to create an independent sovereign democratic state in Iraq and a worrying 68% disagreed with the views of Bush and Blair that the war against terrorism was not a war against Islam (ICM, 2004a). But 73% still said that AQ attacks against the United States were unjustified (though 13% said they were justified), while only 18% said that they thought that anti-terrorism laws were used fairly against the Muslim community (with 64% saying that they are used unfairly). A Times Populus survey in July 2006 found that 74% of the Muslims polled believed that Muslims were treated with suspicion by their fellow citizens while 79% agreed with the view that Muslims had experienced more abuse and hostility since the London bombings of July 2005 (Populus, 2006a). The survey also found that 47% disagreed with the view that Britain's anti-terror laws were being applied fairly to the Muslim population (compared to 34% of Muslims who agreed). A BBC poll carried out in June 2009 of 500 Muslims aged over 16 found that 'almost a third of respondents said they thought the police, government and British society were anti-Muslim' (BBC News Online, 2009b).

## Conclusion: Implications for 'counter-terrorism'?

The above discussion has implications for what we mean by counter-terrorism. What are the motivations behind counter-terrorism and whom does counter-terrorism serve? One might be forgiven for assuming that counter-terrorism is about reducing the threat from terrorism and to that end the British government has brought forward a very comprehensive strategy under the pursue, prevent, protect and prepare strands. Counter-terrorism is now very much a holistic term that covers almost every aspect of homeland security, ranging from pursuing terrorists abroad to equipping the Fire and Rescue Service with additional decontamination units. Yet, there are other motivations for counter-terrorism that may not be primarily concerned with reducing the threat. One of these could be to satisfy public demand or perceived public demand and to be seen to be 'doing something'. Democracies, where governments and leaders are accountable to the public, and where elections are held regularly, are highly sensitive to public opinion. But, while there may be public demand for a 'tough' response towards terrorism this does not necessarily equate to an *effective* response.

'Counter-terrorism' can serve many interests – it can be abused by states in pursuit of broader strategic objectives abroad or by those wishing to suppress minorities. It can serve the interests of big business who lobby politicians to secure lucrative contracts for the provision of ever more advanced technological solutions in the face of the terrorist threat. But discussion of these issues is beyond the remit of this chapter. As the above has indicated, counter-terrorism can also be a political tool to enhance the government's popularity in the eyes of the public. This chapter has focused on one particular area that could prove counter-productive in the government's counter-psychological response to terrorism: the relationship in a democracy between the public in general believing that harsher measures are necessary and a government that presents itself as the solution to these fears. This could ultimately prove counter-productive in reducing the terrorist threat as the very community that the government needs to engage with could feel further marginalized. Reassuring the majority at the expense of further alienating a minority is not a recipe for reducing terrorism.

## Notes

1 It is, of course, difficult to assess the degree that these international 'causes' of Muslim 'suffering' are seen as genuine grievances rather than used as propaganda in a broader ideological struggle. The fundamental point, however, is that issues in the international realm have been being exploited in order to perpetrate attacks in the UK. Nor is it suggested that the US and the UK should refrain from making foreign policy decisions that would offend Al-Qaeda or indeed that they should automatically shirk from any action that would enhance the latter's propaganda and recruitment potential.
2 Other factors cited include the economic situation (63% of the 77%), loss of solidarity and community (61%), impact of the media (60%), risk of crime (59%), loss of certainty and security (54%), increase in availability of information about threats to safety (54%).
3 The five threat levels are: critical, severe, substantial, moderate, low (see Home Office website at: http://www.homeoffice.gov.uk/counter-terrorism/current-threat-level/, accessed 25 June 2009)
4 Gordon Brown, House of Commons Hansard debate, 19 March 2008, available at: http://www.publications.parliament.uk/pa/cm200708/cmhansrd/cm080319/debtext/ 80319-0004.htm (accessed 25 June 2009).
5 See: http://www.telegraph.co.uk/news/uknews/2107480/42-day-terror-detention-British-public-overwhelmingly-in-favour--poll-shows.html (accessed 22 June 2009). An ICM poll also found support for the 42-day detention limit (see: http://www.guardian.co.uk/ politics/2008/jun/08/terrorism.uksecurity, accessed 22 June 2009)

## References

BBC News Online (2009a). Ministers 'using fear of terror'. http://news.bbc.co.uk/1/hi/ uk/7893890.stm.
BBC News Online (2009b). UK Muslims split on Taliban fight. At http://news.bbc.co.uk/1/ hi/uk/8119273.stm.

Blair, T. (2005). PM's press conference, 5 August, available at: http://www.number10.gov. uk/Page8041.

Evans, J. (2007). Intelligence, counter-terrorism and trust. Transcript of speech available at: http://www.mi5.gov.uk/output/intelligence-counter-terrorism-and-trust.html.

Health Protection Agency (2006). London bombings – key long-term health issues announced. http://www.hpa.org.uk/webw/HPAweb&HPAwebStandard/HPAweb_C/119 5733738561?p=1158945066097.

HM Government (2006). *Countering International Terrorism: The United Kingdom's Strategy*. London: HMSO.

HM Government (2009). *Pursue Prevent Protect Prepare, The United Kingdom's Strategy for Countering International Terrorism*. London: HMSO.

Hoffman, B. (1998). *Inside Terrorism*. Cassell.

Hoffman, B. (2005). The logic of suicide terrorism. In Russell Howard et al, *Homeland Security and Terrorism*, the McGraw-Hill homeland security series.

Howie, M. and Pykett, E. (2009). History will show war on terror was huge mistake says university chief. *Scotsman*, 20 March 2009. http://news.scotsman.com/afghanistan/ History-will-show-war-on.5092219.jp.

ICM (2003). Terrorism Poll. http://www.icmresearch.co.uk/pdfs/2003_february_bbc_ Radio_five_live_terrorism_poll.pdf#search="terrorism.

ICM (2004a). *Guardian* survey. At http://www.icmresearch.co.uk/pdfs/2004_march_ guardian_muslims_poll.pdf#search="march2004".

ICM (2004b). Retail week Terrorism Survey. http://www.icmresearch.co.uk/pdfs/2004_ april_retail_week_terrorism.pdf#search="terrorism".

ICM (2004c). BBC Terrorism Survey. http://www.icmresearch.co.uk/pdfs/2004_may_ bbc_terrorism_poll.pdf#search="terrorism".

Institute of Medicine (2003). *Preparing for the Psychological Consequences of Terrorism, A Public Health Strategy*. Washington, D.C.: National Academies Press.

Intelligence and Security Committee (2006). *Report into the London Terrorist Attacks on 7 July 2005*, http://www.cabinetoffice.gov.uk/media/cabinetoffice/corp/assets/ publications/reports/intelligence/isc_7july_report.pdf.

Jenkins, B. (1975). International terrorism: A new mode of conflict. In David Carlton and Carlo Schaerf (eds.), *International Terrorism and World Security*. London: Croom Helm.

London Assembly (2006). *Report of the 7 July Review Committee*. London: Greater London Authority.

Mental Health Foundation (2007). Terrorism people's greatest fear, 8 October 2007, available at: http://www.mhf.org.uk/information/news/?entryid17=50602&q=0%C2% ACfear%C2%AC (accessed 17 April 2009).

Mental Health Foundation (2009). In the face of fear. http://www.mentalhealth.org.uk/ publications/?entryid5=71551&char=I (accessed 17 April 2009).

Merari, A. (2005). Social, organizational and psychological factors in suicide terrorism. In Tore Bjørgo (ed.), *Root Causes of Terrorism*, Routledge.

Meredith, L., Eisenman, D., Tanielian, T., Taylor, S. and Basurto-Davila, R. (2007). *Preparing Hospitals and Clinics for the Psychological Consequences of a Terrorist Incident or Other Public Health Emergency*. Los Angeles: RAND.

National Centre for Social Research (2007). Press Release: A price worth paying: Changing public attitudes to civil liberties under the threat of terrorism, at http://www.natcen.ac.uk/ natcen/pages/news_and_media_docs/BSA_%20press_release_jan07.pdf.

National Steering Committee on Warning and Informing the Public (2003). *Third Report*. At www.nscwip.info/thirdreport.htm.

Nielsen (2006). Survey: Terrorism never far from Britons' minds. http://uk.nielsen.com/news/pr20060814.shtml.

Pedahzur, A. (2005). *Suicide Terrorism*. London: Polity Press.

Populus (2005a). Terrorism, 10 July 2005. http://www.populus.co.uk/the-times-terrorism-100705.html.

Populus (2005b). Political attitudes, 24 July 2005, available at: http://www.populus.co.uk/poll-search.php?category=4&page=11.

Populus (2006a). Times survey, Muslim 7/7 Poll, July 2006 http://www.populuslimited.com/the-times-itv-news-muslim-77-poll-050706.html.

Populus (2006b). Political Attitudes, 3 September, available at: http://www.populus.co.uk/the-times-political-attitudes-030906.html.

Populus (2007). Counter-terrorism measures, 26 July 2007. http://www.populus.co.uk/the-daily-politics-counter-terrorism-measures-260707.html.

Richards, A. (2007). Myth breaker. *Intersec*, September.

Schmid, A. (2005). Prevention of terrorism. In Tore Bjørgo (ed.), *Root Causes of Terrorism*. Routledge.

Silke, A. (2003). Retaliating against terrorism. In Andrew Silke (ed.), *Terrorists, Victims and Society* (pp. 93–108). Chichester: Wiley.

Tanielian, T. and Stein, B. (2006). Understanding and preparing for the psychological consequences of terrorism. In D. Kamien (Ed.), *McGraw-Hill Homeland Security Handbook* (pp. 689–701). McGraw-Hill.

Taylor, H. (2004). Similar levels of fear of terrorism in USA and Great Britain. http://www.harrisinteractive.com/harris_poll/index.asp?PID=437 (accessed 17 April 2009).

YouGov (2006a). *Spectator* poll results. http://www.yougov.co.uk/extranets/ygarchives/content/pdf/SpectatorPollResults.pdf.

YouGov (2006b). *Daily Telegraph* survey. http://www.yougov.co.uk/extranets/ygarchives/content/pdf/TEL060101014_1.pdf.

YouGov (2006c). Survey. http://www.yougov.com/archives/pdf/results060903terrorism.pdf.

# Index

Made in the USA
Monee, IL
14 January 2021

57677196R00122